Sebald's Bachelors
Queer Resistance and the Unconforming Life

LEGENDA

LEGENDA, founded in 1995 by the European Humanities Research Centre of the University of Oxford, is now a joint imprint of the Modern Humanities Research Association and Maney Publishing. Titles range from medieval texts to contemporary cinema and form a widely comparative view of the modern humanities, including works on Arabic, Catalan, English, French, German, Greek, Italian, Portuguese, Russian, Spanish, and Yiddish literature. An Editorial Board of distinguished academic specialists works in collaboration with leading scholarly bodies such as the Society for French Studies and the British Comparative Literature Association.

MHRA

The Modern Humanities Research Association (MHRA) encourages and promotes advanced study and research in the field of the modern humanities, especially modern European languages and literature, including English, and also cinema. It also aims to break down the barriers between scholars working in different disciplines and to maintain the unity of humanistic scholarship in the face of increasing specialization. The Association fulfils this purpose primarily through the publication of journals, bibliographies, monographs and other aids to research.

Maney Publishing is one of the few remaining independent British academic publishers. Founded in 1900 the company has offices both in the UK, in Leeds and London, and in North America, in Philadelphia. Since 1945 Maney Publishing has worked closely with learned societies, their editors, authors, and members, in publishing academic books and journals to the highest traditional standards of materials and production.

GERMANIC LITERATURES

Germanic Literatures includes monographs and essay collections on literature originally written not only in German, but also in Dutch and the Scandinavian languages. Within the German-speaking area, it seeks also to publish studies of other national literatures such as those of Austria and Switzerland. The chronological scope of the series extends from the early Middle Ages down to the present day.

Managing Editor
Dr Graham Nelson, 41 Wellington Square, Oxford OX1 2JF, UK
www.legendabooks.com

Sebald's Bachelors

Queer Resistance and the Unconforming Life

HELEN FINCH

LEGENDA

Germanic Literatures 2
Modern Humanities Research Association and Maney Publishing
2013

Published by the
Modern Humanities Research Association and Maney Publishing
1 Carlton House Terrace
London SW1Y 5AF
United Kingdom

LEGENDA is an imprint of the
Modern Humanities Research Association and Maney Publishing

Maney Publishing is the trading name of W. S. Maney & Son Ltd,
whose registered office is at Suite 1C, Joseph's Well, Hanover Walk, Leeds LS3 1AB

ISBN 978-1-907975-90-5

First published 2013

Printed in Great Britain

Cover: 875 Design

Copy-Editor: Nigel Hope

CONTENTS

FOR MARY

ACKNOWLEDGEMENTS

This book has been many years in the making, and many wise and generous scholars and friends contributed to it. It has its origins in my PhD thesis, undertaken at Trinity College, Dublin, and I would like to thank both the Irish Research Council for the Humanities and Social Sciences (now Irish Research Council) for their generous financial support, and my PhD supervisors, Jürgen Barkhoff and Moray McGowan, for their guidance over five years.

Thanks are also due to the DAAD, which funded ten months' postgraduate research in Berlin, and to the British Academy for a Small Research Grant held in 2008, which funded an archival trip to Marbach to help research this work.

My colleagues in Leeds have provided encouragement, support, and advice in the long thinking and writing process since 2007, particularly Frank Finlay, Richard Hibbitt, Chris Homewood, Ingrid Sharp, and Stuart Taberner. Thanks are also due to the students of the final-year module 'W. G. Sebald: The Politics of Literature' (Leeds 2011–12), whose lively discussions and sensitive responses to Sebald's work and my ideas helped shape this book in its final stages.

I am lucky to be able to draw on the knowledge and kindness of friends from Ireland to the US and beyond, who are not only excellent scholars and critics but also sources of conversation, sympathy, and love. Thanks always to, among many others, Barry McCrea, Caitríona Ní Dhúill, Jason Edwards, and Lynn Wolff.

My thanks go particularly to Anne Fuchs, for her careful and critical reading, and to Graham Nelson and Ritchie Robertson at Legenda.

Without the love and support of my parents, and the home full of books, music, and wit where I grew up, I would never have come to write this book. Thank you so much.

This book is dedicated to Mary Macfarlane. Her love, generosity, insight, and critique have been with me since the book's inception, and are woven deeply into its fabric.

H.F., Leeds, February 2013

ABBREVIATIONS

The following abbreviations are used throughout for references to Sebald's primary works:

A *Austerlitz* (Frankfurt am Main: Fischer, 2003)

Ae *Austerlitz*, trans. by Anthea Bell (London: Penguin, 2002)

AN *After Nature*, trans. by Michael Hamburger (London: Penguin, 2003)

BU *Die Beschreibung des Unglücks: Zur österreichischen Literatur von Stifter bis Handke* (Frankfurt am Main: Fischer Taschenbuch Verlag, 1994). All translations mine

CS *Campo Santo*, ed. by Sven Meyer (Munich: Carl Hanser, 2003)

CSe *Campo Santo*, ed. by Sven Meyer, trans. by Anthea Bell (London: Penguin, 2006)

DA *Die Ausgewanderten: Vier lange Erzählungen* (Frankfurt am Main: Fischer, 2002)

Döblin *Der Mythus der Zerstörung im Werk Döblins* (Stuttgart: Ernst Klett, 1980). All translations mine

E *The Emigrants*, trans. by Michael Hulse (London: Harvill, 1996)

NdN *Nach der Natur: Ein Elementargedicht* (Frankfurt am Main: Fischer, 1989)

RS *Die Ringe des Saturn: Eine englische Wallfahrt* (Frankfurt am Main: Fischer, 1997)

RSe *The Rings of Saturn*, trans. by Michael Hulse (London: Harvill, 1998)

SG *Schwindel. Gefühle.* (Frankfurt am Main: Fischer, 1994)

Sternheim *Carl Sternheim: Kritiker und Opfer der Wilhelminischen Ära* (Stuttgart: Kohlhammer, 1969). All translations mine

UH *Unheimliche Heimat* (Frankfurt am Main: Fischer, 1995). All translations mine

V *Vertigo*, trans. by Michel Hulse (London: Harvill, 1999)

INTRODUCTION

Naegeli's Bones

Dr Henry Selwyn

We meet the first emigrant in *Die Ausgewanderten* [*The Emigrants*], Dr Henry Selwyn, living with his wife Hedi in exile in Norfolk. Selwyn is one of Sebald's congenial melancholics, whose life has taken a wrong turn somewhere. Talking about his increasing estrangement from his wife Hedi, he tells the narrator:

> Genau weiß ich es immer noch nicht, was uns auseinandergebracht hat, das Geld oder das schließlich doch entdeckte Geheimnis meiner Abstammung oder einfach das Wenigerwerden der Liebe.
>
> [I still don't know for sure what made us drift apart, the money or revealing the secret of my origins, or simply the decline of love.] (*DA*, 35; *E*, 21)]

Selwyn's pitiful account of his marriage brings together two key concerns of Sebald's literary project: memory and, as I will argue in this book, the no less crucial question of love, 'a madness most discreet', as Michael Hulse, echoing *Romeo and Juliet*, names it in his English translation of *Schwindel. Gefühle.* [*Vertigo*]. The first item in Selwyn's attempt at explaining his alienation from his wife, money, serves as an allegory for the destructive powers of modern capitalism, which Sebald's entire oeuvre explores and critiques. The glancing reference to 'the secret of my origins' obliquely names Selwyn's Jewish origins, and thereby invokes the Holocaust, whose shadow hangs over the entire novel. In this, as in many other ways, the short narrative of Henry Selwyn is emblematic for Sebald's literary methodology. Selwyn's descent into isolation and eventual suicide is punctuated by a series of motifs that are classically Sebaldian: solitary withdrawal into a ruinous landscape, a lost or repressed Jewish childhood in Europe, a history of emigration, a feeling of closeness to plants and animals, the involuntary return of memory, chronic melancholy, and isolation. The brief history contains in it traces of the aesthetic and political themes that have also been identified as central to Sebald's work: an overarching critique of modernity, the erasure of Jewish identities, the shadow of the Holocaust, and the narrator's latent revulsion from German culture. In keeping with this revulsion, in the German version of the text, a startlingly ugly sideboard is said to be correctly described as *altdeutsch*, or 'old German' (DA, 15). The story of Henry Selwyn also enlists the celebrated Sebaldian techniques of intermediality, indirection, archive, dialectical style, intertextuality, and baroque allegory.

So what of the final item in Selwyn's doleful list of causes, the death of love? Is its slow death, its decline, merely one more item in the inventory of destruction catalogued throughout Sebald's work? Or does love serve as a profoundly important and often-overlooked counter-force to the natural history of destruction? The history of Dr Henry Selwyn is also paradigmatically Sebaldian in its conflict between Thanatos and Eros, the Freudian death and sex drives. In the rich secondary literature on Sebald, it is melancholy Thanatos that is generally held to win out, both within Sebald's texts and also in terms of the amount of critical attention devoted to the themes of melancholy, death, and destruction. Richard Sheppard, in a personal and biographical essay on Sebald, writes that Sebald's works are throughout his writing life increasingly marked by the victory of Thanatos over Eros, possibly because of Sebald's erroneous conflation of the two drives. Sexuality, Sheppard writes, is at best morally suspect in Sebald's works, and more usually is linked to death.[1] Similarly, Brad Prager suggests that erotic fulfilment, in *Schwindel. Gefühle.*, is 'coupled with a search for subjective dissolution', and that the connection between Eros and Thanatos reveals the idea 'that death lies behind all erotic desire'.[2]

Yet the narrative of Dr Henry Selwyn also contains another moment of love, one that is also akin to a moment of resistance. If Selwyn is alienated from his wife, his biography contains a grand moment of passion for Johannes Naegeli, a mountaineer who is taken from him by the First World War. 'Er hatte sich nie in seinem Leben, weder zuvor noch später, derart wohl gefühlt wie damals in der Gesellschaft dieses Mannes' [Never in his life, neither before nor later, did he feel as good as he did then, in the company of that man] (*DA*, 24; *E*, 14). Selwyn's youthful affection for Naegeli is directly opposed to his less successful heterosexual relationship. Whereas Hedi has grown ever stranger to him over the years, Naegeli appears to him, even after death, 'jedesmal, wenn er auftaucht in meinen Gedanken, vertrauter [...] obschon ich ihn in Wirklichkeit seit jenem Abschied in Meiringen nicht ein einziges Mal mehr gesehen habe' [closer whenever he comes to my mind, despite the fact that I never saw him again after that farewell in Meiringen] (*DA*, 24; *E*, 15). Not only is this affection hidden from the world, it is largely hidden from critics. For instance, Claudia Öhlschläger comments on this sentiment in passing, assuming that the 'taboo' of homophilia is one more social affliction that adds to Selwyn's alienation and inner exile.[3] Öhlschläger thus elides the discussion of Selwyn's 'homophilia' into a more general discussion of alienation, the return of memory, and the intermedial character of the text. Naegeli's death on the mountains, and the subsequent return of his body in the glacier seventy-two years later, is simply taken to be a paradigmatic representation of the effects of trauma and repression central to *Die Ausgewanderten*, and the narrator's chance discovery of the story in a local newspaper is regarded as one more example of the key Sebaldian techniques of *mémoire involuntaire* and intermediality.[4] The queer element in Selwyn's narrative is buried beneath a landslide of downward-tugging melancholy, just as Naegeli's body is hidden in the glacier for seventy-two years. Yet, at the end of the story, Naegeli returns. The work of this book is to demonstrate that the return of Naegeli, who disappeared at the beginning of Sebald's calamitous short twentieth century, in 1914, is of profound significance to Sebald's literary project. If his work is predominantly concerned with destruction and the death of love, doomed homosexual love is not just one more of the classic tropes of melancholy modernism with which Sebald's profoundly scholarly texts are decked out. Rather, Naegeli's return points towards the fundamental importance of homosexuality, as well as queerness, for the entire text and, beyond this, for the significance of Sebald's contribution to the debates surrounding the politics of literature in the latter half of the twentieth century.

Let us free Naegeli from the glacier where he has been buried, and allow his remains to speak. In the first place, Naegeli is associated with the Alpine sublime, which links him to those moments of levitation and transcendence that, as Ben Hutchinson points out, provide the dialectical counterpart to the downward tug of melancholy in Sebald's work and form a mechanism to escape the heaviness of history.[5] Levitation and lightness are powerful redemptive forces in Sebald's poetics; in an essay on Peter Handke, Sebald suggests that the sense of levitation achieved in Handke's writing helps the reader 'den Verlockungen der Schwermut standzuhalten [to withstand the temptations of melancholy].[6] In keeping with this power of levitation and sublime height, a moment when Dr Henry Selwyn shows the Sebaldian narrator slides of the Lasithi plateau suspends the mood of melancholy in the narrative and bathes the viewers in a merciful light. The 'poetics of suspension' associated with Naegeli, which are seen paradigmatically in the slide show, link to a queer Eros rather than to an inexorable Thanatos or saturnine melancholy.[7] Eshel's argument, that Sebald's poetics throughout his work suspend 'notions of chronology, succession, chronology and closure', links Sebald to a rich line of queer theories that celebrate precisely the refusal of linear, determinate narratives in favour of a suspended, transgressive, or even retrogressive poetics.[8] I address these theories in more detail below; suffice it to say here that Naegeli's atemporal suspension in ice and subsequent return disrupts the forward-moving arc of tragedy described by Selwyn in his progress from Jewish immigrant to deracinated careerist to isolated melancholic. Selwyn's career, as he narrates it to his attentive interlocutor, resembles a traditional linear plot, typical of the naturalistic novels that Sebald frequently decried in interviews.[9] This linear narrative is radically disrupted, firstly by the fragmented, intermedial, and dialectical nature of Sebald's poetics, but secondly, through the irruption of Naegeli's bones. In what follows, I will be teasing out the queer implications in Sebald's work of this poetics of transgression, return, and disorientation. Naegeli stands for a Sebaldian model of queer Eros: uncanny, spectral, overshadowed by melancholy, but nonetheless containing within it both utopian potential and the potential for resistance. This queer Eros gathers up within it moments of homosexuality (Selwyn's love for Naegeli), homosociality (the all-male gathering viewing the slides), and brotherhood (which is of most importance in Sebald's critical writing, as we will see), imbuing them with an immanent political power.

In the second place, Naegeli appears at a crucial point in Selwyn's youth, when he has crossed the border between Jewish and Gentile, 'und änderte in einer Art zweiter Konfirmation meinen Vornamen Hersch zu Henry und meinen Familiennamen Seweryn zu Selwyn' [and in a kind of second confirmation [...] changed my first name Hersch into Henry, and my surname Seweryn to Selwyn] (DA, 33; E, 20).

The queer encounter takes place on a racial borderline, at the moment of assimilation, or reorientation towards a Gentile self-presentation. Selwyn has performed
precisely that step away from the ghetto to bourgeois society that Sebald
pathologizes in his essay on nineteenth-century ghetto narrative, 'Westwärts —
Ostwärts: Aporien deutscher Ghettogeschichten' [Westwards — Eastwards. Aporias
of German Ghetto Narratives] (*UH*, 40–64). In itself, then, this repression of Jewish
identity is enough to make of Selwyn a haunted man. The appearance of Naegeli
adds a queer twist to the already uncanny story. When discussing Dr Henry Selwyn
in an interview, Sebald uses a telling phrase: 'The first time I thought, *this is not a
straight English gentleman*, was at a Christmas party they gave'.[10] Sebald is ostensibly
here referring to Selwyn's disguised Jewish identity. Yet the phrase 'not a straight
English gentleman' points towards a conflation of Jewish and queer masculinities.
Suggestively, Maya Barzilai has written about the way in which Sebald constructs
'the Jewish man as uncanny and possibly homosexual'.[11] She here draws on an
established cultural trope which opposes the uncanny queer Jew to the heterosexual
and *de facto* German Gentile. If, in the nineteenth century, German manhood was
constructed as Gentile, heterosexual, and national, it required a 'countertype', which
was constructed as Jewish, queer, pathological, and cosmopolitan.[12] Matti Bunzl has
shown that modern anti-Semitism and homophobia thus arose concurrently and
mutually defined each other as the 'constitutive outsides of respectable Germanness'
in the nineteenth century, as they did in other European cultures.[13] In symptomatic
accounts of the relationship between Jewishness and queerness in modernity, the
uncanny and unassimilable Jew is opposed to the heterosexual Gentile, who has
successfully resolved an Oedipal complex to take his place in the family and in
society as a reproductive male. The narrator's suspicion that Selwyn is 'not a straight
English gentleman' points to a failure in Selwyn's mimicry of heterosexual Gentile
manhood. The return of Naegeli thus disrupts the narrative of Selwyn's assimilation
to Western European heterosexuality, as it holds within it both a reminder of both
Selwyn's Jewish origins and the queer love of his youth.

Moreover, it is not Selwyn who discovers the newspaper article about the return
of Naegeli, as he has already shot himself by the end of 'Dr Henry Selwyn'. Instead,
the Sebaldian narrator discovers the article while he is on a train in the Alps. High
up in the sublime Alpine landscape, he enters a strange intimacy with Selwyn's lost
lover; it is to him that the revenant returns. Is this, then, an ethically questionable
German appropriation of Jewish loss, a harmonizing happy ending? Mary Cosgrove,
in her analysis of intimacy and sentimental affect between narrator and subject of
narration in the similar scene at the end of *Austerlitz*, argues that it is not, or not
entirely. Both 'Dr Henry Selwyn' and *Austerlitz* end with the narrator parting from
his Jewish interlocutor, returning to a site significant for his biography, and reading
a document which contains traces of the emotional life of the Jewish protagonist.
Such moments should not be read as entirely melodramatic or exemplifying a
naïve identification of narrator with protagonist, critiques that have sometimes
been levelled at Sebald.[14] Rather, as the narrator acts as a 'guardian angel' to his
characters, such moments of empathy can develop in the reader the emotion that
is necessary for the development of ethical memory.[15] Here, as in *Austerlitz,* there

seems to be a distinctly queer element to this repeated intimacy between Gentile narrator and Jewish protagonist. Certainly, the narrator of 'Dr Henry Selwyn' states that he is married to a woman, Clara, but the emotionally charged moments in the story are without exception homosocial. The narrator enters the story with Clara, but leaves it in the spectral company of men, a transition from bourgeois household formation to an imaginary affiliation with the queer dead. If, as Stuart Taberner has suggested, *Die Ausgewanderten* mourns a German–Jewish symbiosis, I argue that Sebald's fictional texts, from *Nach der Natur* [*After Nature*] to *Austerlitz,* repeatedly reinstate this symbiosis in queer form.[16] Despite the potential for ethical memory enabled by this queer affiliation, it also runs the risk of a sentimental and recuperative trope. Both Sebald's narrators and his German characters become repeatedly embroiled in queer loves that reach across the boundary of the ghetto and sometimes, as in the case of Dr Selwyn, across the boundary of death.

At this point, as Naegeli's return opens up a broad range of political and psychoanalytical implications of the theme of queer German–Jewish love. The return also approaches the question of poetics, for it is my contention that the aesthetics, as well as the thematics, of Sebald's work are most definitely queer. Indeed, poetics cannot be separated from thematics in Sebald's prose. Theodor W. Adorno argues that the key to any artwork must lie in its technique, and Öhlschläger and Hutchinson concern themselves with the stylistics rather than the thematics of Sebald's work, considering thematics a less productive and near-illegitimate line of enquiry.[17] If we are to take seriously the supremacy of poetics and stylistics over thematics, we must ask to what extent Sebald can be said not only to marshal queer themes and queer characters throughout his prose, but also to approach a queer poetics. To put the question differently, does his work incidentally contain biographies of homosexual men, or is it inherently queer? Is a queer aesthetic inherent to his style and poetic order? In attempting to approach what might be meant by the 'Sebaldian queer', it is useful to note that although at times the term 'postmodern' has been used to describe Sebald's prose, in its temporal preoccupations, intertexts, and poetics it is also profoundly modernist. As such, it also enters into the concerns around gender identity and desire that are key to the modernist literary project. Just as the works of the canonical modernists Eliot, Joyce, and Proust are shaped by the late nineteenth-century turmoil surrounding gender identities, and take on the modern challenge to normative understandings of manhood and paternal authority, Sebald's texts continue to work through this challenge.[18] We have already seen that his project concerns itself with the modern moment of Jewish assimilation to Western European culture; it is also concerned with the overarching problems of modernity and its institutions.[19] Anxieties surrounding sexuality are, as we have seen, inherent to modernity, and for J. J. Long, Sebald's modernist concern with sexuality is inherently bound up in a Foucauldian model of discipline, and of the production of sexual knowledge by techniques of power. Homosexual themes in Sebald's work appear at the 'intersection of the categorization of peripheral sexualities and the confessional *mise-en-discours* of sexuality that proliferated during the nineteenth century'.[20] The tragic portrayals of homosexuals in Sebald's work, particularly Roger Casement and Ambros Adelwarth, demonstrate the hegemonic practices of power in modernity, according to this reading. In this reading, homosexuality is one among many sexual phenomena of modernity that is produced and subsequently persecuted by such practices of power.

If we are to attend to the claim that queer sexuality and its problematization of heterosexual modernity lie at the heart of the literary project, however, it becomes clear that homosexuality is as much a concern of form as it is one of subject matter — or subjection, as Long suggests — in Sebald's prose. This reading of Sebald suggests that the structural features of his prose are in themselves inherently queer. In particular, Sebald's recursive and vertiginous prose, saturated in the ironic techniques of post-realism, would seem to have an affinity with poetic elements often associated with queer modernism.[21] Gary Schmidt suggests that 'if one focusses on the [...] richness of detail that speaks for itself and resists summarization and categorization, Sebald's post-Holocaust aesthetic might be thought queer'.[22] In modernist texts, queer sexuality and queer textuality interpellate and structure each other reciprocally, as modernism departs from the linear, heterosexual family plots of the bourgeois nineteenth-century novel. Thus, for instance, Barry McCrea states that homosexuality in Proust and Joyce is conventionally associated with 'indeterminacy, the deferral of closure, the undermining of overarching structures and master narratives'.[23] Such characteristics are fundamental to the structures of Sebald's prose, with its digressive sentence structure, backwards-looking narrative gaze, and associative rather than linear textual structure. Sebald's refusal of narrative authority also queerly undermines the sovereign gaze of the writing subject; his constant recourse to intertextuality undermines any directly deictic form of reference. In keeping with his rejection of patriarchal systems of dominance, Sebald rejects any authoritative 'master narrative' under the control of a single narrative viewpoint in favour of a periscopic style, in which narratives are nested within narratives, and authority is distributed and undermined. His associative works refuse the coherence of the marriage plot and mimetic characters that drive the bourgeois novel. Equally, his extended sentence structures (parataxis) refuse any straightforward progression, instead slowing down and baffling narrative direction, focusing on minor details and taking metaphysical turns that leave the reader disoriented and dizzy. Further, while his prose is often elegiac and leans on the baroque style of Thomas Browne, an all-pervading irony is present even in Sebald's most harrowing or metaphysical turns of phrase, and his prose often teeters on the edge between pathos and bathos in a mode not dissimilar to camp. 'Ich begann meine Geschichte nochmals von vorn, und sogar mir selbst schien sie jetzt unglaubwürdig' [When I told my story all over again, it no longer sounded plausible, even to me] (*SG*, 125; *V*, 110), says the narrator at one point. Redoubling and duplicitous, as well as backwards-looking and disoriented, by his own admission Sebald's narratives are queer.

As these multivalent aspects of Sebald's prose suggest, queer poetics, modernist or not, need not necessarily be associated with melancholy. I began this introduction by talking about the return of Naegeli as a moment of queer hope. Such a positive usage of the term 'queer' has much in common with Eve Kosofsky Sedgwick's conception of queerness as something both troubling and productive: 'a continuing moment, movement, motive-recurrent, eddying, *troublant*'. 'Queer' is a word etymologically related to the German *quer*, used to denote indirection, stubbornness, or obliqueness.[24] Queerness is further associated not only with sexual desire for a gendered opposite, but with literary and political resistance to regimes of the normal, which makes strange supposed social givens.[25] Given this more transgressive and optimistic way of approaching queerness, this book contends that thwarted male homosexuality is not just one more melancholy moment in Sebald's metaphysics of destruction, nor is queerness just one more feature of Sebald's celebrated prose style but that, rather, a troubling queerness lies at the heart of Sebald's work. Here, my argument crosses with that of Eric Santner, who states: 'The natural history of modern life — and this is, as I have tried to show, Sebald's singular topic — is always a history of sexuality'.[26] For Santner, sexuality, be that queer sexuality or reproductive heterosexuality, is fundamental to the subjection of the human, or its *creaturely life*: a dimension of human being where its animal nature is disordered, thanks to its exposure to a traumatic dimension of political power in modernity.[27] Thus, Sebald's discussions of sexuality are for Santner a series of painful points where the stigmata of oppression can be read on the creaturely body. Yet Santner further shows that homosexuality, when analysed in textual detail, is a very queer topic in Sebald's prose, moving between moments of melancholy, paranoia, and political resistance, not easily assimilated to any one mode of analysis. Building on this suggestion, I suggest that the unruly body of Naegeli represents a peculiarly Sebaldian moment of hope that queer love can resist the structures of societal repression and of gender normativity. Queer love can be a counter-force to the baleful power of the sovereign that binds us in the natural history of destruction. Naegeli's return functions as a spectral sign that Dr Henry Selwyn's twin subjection to the structures of bourgeois heterosexuality and Gentile assimilation is not accomplished in totality. Naegeli's bones are not just a metaphor for the return of memory as *mémoire involuntaire*, but they are also a remnant, both physical and spectral, of a surplus that is unassimilable to the natural history of destruction. On the level of prose, of textual structure, and of metaphysical underpinnings, queerness disrupts and subverts both the overweening melancholy in Sebald's work and the structures of bourgeois literature and of bourgeois society that form the order which Sebald's writing attempts to resist.

The 'Sebaldian Queer': Theoretical Approaches

By letting Naegeli's bones speak, I make a claim not only for the centrality of queerness to Sebald's poetic project, but also for its status as a mode of resistance to oppressive structures. This book delineates a disruptive, at times utopian, at times joyful concept of the 'Sebaldian queer'. In defining this concept, I am indebted to several theorists, all of whom develop models of queer theory, queer writing, and queer reading that depart from pervasive models of homosexuality in modernity as melancholy, backwards, and tragic. Very broadly speaking, my reading of Sebald is allied with theorists, chief among them Sara Ahmed, Gilles Deleuze and Félix Guattari, and Michael D. Snediker, whose versions of queer identity and queer textuality express transgression and immanence, rather than with negative or melancholy views of homosexuality, such as those of Lee Edelman and Judith Butler. Building on Snedicker's suggestion, I argue against reading into Sebald the categories of 'melancholy, self-shattering, shame, the death drive' that have become categories to conjure with in queer theory.[28] Rather, I claim that the Sebaldian queer, although inflected and constrained by melancholy, contains the possibility of an immanent, ethical, and critical optimism.

The key role that I assign to textual homosexuality in a poetics of resistance draws on the work of Deleuze and Guattari, in particular their *Kafka: Towards a Minor Literature*, which Sebald knew well, as well as their *Anti-Oedipus*.[29] Their theories have several key features that are essential for my reading of the Sebaldian queer. Firstly, they reject unitary Oedipal structures of the self in favour of a 'schizo-analysis' that describes how the subject becomes a hybrid, shifting between animal and machine.[30] As we have seen in the case of Dr Henry Selwyn, repressive Oedipal structures govern the allied regimes of male heterosexuality, society, and psychoanalysis in modernity. Deleuze and Guattari's 'schizo-analysis' deviates from these neurotic Oedipal structures, which they view as necessarily linked to societal mechanisms of oppression. 'A schizophrenic out for a walk is a better model than a neurotic lying on the analyst's couch', they argue in *Anti-Oedipus*, and by 'better', they mean more revolutionary.[31] In place of the Oedipal triangles that corral desire and reduce it to the sphere of the family, they describe a schizophrenic 'universe of productive and reproductive desiring-machines' that are linked with each other, with society, and with history.[32] Deleuze and Guattari's radical vision of politics and textuality has fruitful potential for queer theory, as the two theorists emphasize the revolutionary potential of 'becoming', and of 'becoming-queer', in the place of mainstream Freudian pathologies of homosexuality, which constantly search for a disordered origin of homosexuality within the patriarchal family.[33] For them, queer desire is instead associated with the margins of society, and with a becoming-minoritarian; their focus on the prefix 'becoming' indicates that queer desire (like schizophrenic desire) is fixated not on the past, but rather on immanence and potential.[34] Instead of Oedipal subjection to patriarchal structures of the self, they argue for a system of desire that overflows the boundaries of the human, rather shifting state to become both machine and animal. Here, we might think of Dr Henry Selwyn's affinity for the natural world, and his intimate compassion for the abused horses Herschel, Humphrey, and Hippolytus; 'Herschel' echoes Selwyn's original name 'Hersch', suggesting a link between them (*DA*, 11; *E*, 6). The immanent and revolutionary potential of the Deleuzo-Guattarian alliance between the marginalized and queer desire is, I argue, fundamental to the Sebaldian queer.

Deleuze and Guattari's work on Kafka's literature provides a further guide as to how we might read the revolutionary queer potential in Sebald's work. In *Kafka: Toward a Minor Literature*, they diagnose Kafka's as a 'minor literature' on a 'line of flight' away from the subjection imposed by bourgeois society's Oedipal structures. Kafka's works constantly move away from the Oedipal family towards the borders, away towards far geographical locations. Sebald's work, too, I argue, sets off on lines of flight away from a paternal inheritance of German bourgeois culture, and over the border to far-flung places, such as the Lasithi plateau in Selwyn's slide show, or up into the Alps where Selwyn and Naegeli find emotional bliss. Like Deleuze and Guattari's Kafka, Sebald is a potential 'escape artist', and the 'line of flight' in his work is connected to queer desire.[35] Because Sebald's work seeks to move away from Oedipal structures, the figure of the bachelor, who refuses to become an Oedipal patriarch, is crucial for Sebald, as it is for Kafka. Deleuze and Guattari draw out the sexual-political significance of Kafka's bachelor, which they term a 'bachelor-machine', because it is plugged into the vast array of desiring machines that Oedipus seeks to structure and dominate. The bachelor-machine refuses Oedipus; hence non-reproductive sexuality is crucial to the bachelor-machine, particularly incest and homosexual desire. The same, I argue, is true of Sebald's bachelors as they pursue their 'lines of flight'.[36] Deleuze and Guattari oppose the bachelor's liberating 'schizo-incest' to neurotic Oedipal incest that focuses on the mother, a 'single signifier' that holds everything within the family.[37] Kafka's schizo-incest, instead, focuses on the figure of the sister rather than the mother, and represents 'a line of escape instead of a circular reproduction'.[38] A further key figure along the line of flight is the singular series of the artist, 'manifestly homosexual, who possesses the power of the continuous and which overflows all the segments and sweeps up all the connections'.[39] Although the queer artist does not appear in 'Dr Henry Selwyn', throughout Sebald's critical and literary work, Sebald pursues affinities with congenial bachelor-artists who are indeed often homosexual, as we will see in future chapters. The 'bachelor-machine' is, for Deleuze and Guattari, an essential component in Kafka's minoritarian flight from oppressive social structures. 'With no family, no conjugality, the bachelor is all the more social, social-dangerous, social-traitor, a collective in himself'.[40] Analogous queer alliances and anti-hierarchical strategies pursued by Sebald's bachelors represent a danger to the repressive order of society.

Nonetheless, to claim that Sebald's texts contain queer revolutionary potential is not to say that Sebald's bachelors complete their escape; like Henry Selwyn, few manage to escape the devastating effects of loss and historical calamity, or, in Deleuzoguattarian terms, to escape the 'blocks' placed by family and the law. However, the rhizomatic character of Sebald's texts — their non-linear, open-ended, fragmentary quality — means that, like Kafka's texts, they are 'burrows', that is, they occupy an immanent space that can be entered at any point. In this sense, like Naegeli's bones, the queer revolutionary potential of Sebald's bachelors is preserved in the texts and can be accessed through any point. Thus, they can be read as 'queer archives', to use Judith Halberstam's terminology: repositories of queer resistance and queer history that can be activated by the compassionate reader.[41] Moreover, as Snediker shows, poetic writing functions as a queer archive of its own beyond queer theory, experimenting with affect, immanence, and alliance, delineating queer forms of love, friendship, and family beyond erotics.[42] This emphasis on alliance and queer love brings us back to Deleuze and Guattari's description of the rhizomatic text's opposition to arboreal hierarchies: 'the tree is filiation but the rhizome is alliance'. Sebald's texts, like Sebald's bachelors, form queer alliances with forgotten texts, overlooked writers, historically marginalized peoples, instead of the bourgeois novel's disciplined adherence to lineage, patriarchy, and patrimony. The

Sebaldian queer tests the possibility of alliances and solidarity beyond Oedipus. 'Oedipus', in Deleuze and Guattari's sense, can describe not merely a normative psychoanalytical complex, but an entire system of law and oppression governing society in modernity. The Oedipus complex, in Freud's account, is the rebellion of son against father, preparatory to the son's successful integration into bourgeois society, but in Deleuze and Guattari, its power of domination goes far further into the social sphere.

If we applied Sebald's own biographical mode of criticism, an Oedipal rebellion of son against father, and a refusal to complete the Oedipal process, could be viewed at work in Sebald's own poetics. Sebald may be viewed as a paradigmatic member of the 1968 generation who was locked in a lifelong unresolved Oedipal contest with his National Socialist father and his father's generation.[43] For some Sebald critics, among them Mary Cosgrove, Anne Fuchs, Graham Jackman, and Peter Morgan, Sebald's poetic project is largely conditioned by his generational rebellion against the perpetrator generation of his father, and his sense of generational mission that moves from any attempts at active *Vergangenheitsbewältigung* [coming to terms with the past] to a 'left-wing melancholy'.[44] Inherent, then, in Sebald's generational understanding of German history is a critique of that destructive historical progress, repressive law, and familial reproduction that are figured by the Oedipus complex. Rather than resolving the Oedipal conflict and taking on the normative and reproductive inheritance of German masculine identity, Sebald's melancholic literature turns away and backwards from this paternal inheritance, on the level of sentence structure, plot, and indeed also in terms of the biographical elements that inform his texts. Instead of taking on the inheritance of his father, Sebald turns backwards to his grandfather's generation in his search for alliances. Thus, Mark M. Anderson reads the fictional relationship between Selwyn and Naegeli as a direct reflection of Sebald's warm relationship to his maternal grandfather Josef Egelhofer, a relationship which represented 'a link through his grandfather to the nineteenth century'. In turn, Anderson directly opposes this relationship, at once close and nostalgic, to Sebald's distant relationship to his disciplinarian soldier father, who had fought for the Nazis on the Eastern Front. Anderson goes on to ask 'whether Sebald's narrators, who often find themselves deeply (though non-erotically) attached to much older men, do not in some way reflect his early attachment to Josef Egelhofer'.[45] Anderson's argument seems to be that Sebald's poetics move backwards in time away from contemporary Germany, overshadowed by his father, to an 'imaginary homeland' close to the literature of the nineteenth century and to the Alps, and represented by the idealized figure of his grandfather. Even as Anderson points towards Sebald's imaginary flight away from his paternal inheritance and back to his maternal grandfather, he disavows any possible erotic content to this refusal to resolve the Oedipus complex. Instead, he links this complex to Sebald's creation of an 'imaginary homeland'; but this homeland, I argue, is reached via the queer line of flight in Sebald's work. The rejection of Oedipus is an essential aspect of the Sebaldian queer.

It should by now be clear that although melancholy and queerness lie close together in Sebald's poetics, the 'Sebaldian queer' contains a utopian moment distinct from melancholy's power to resist dominance. Here, my formulation of the Sebaldian queer draws on Deleuze and Guattari's distinction between 'Oedipal homosexuality' and Kafka's 'homosexuality of doubles, of brothers or of bureaucrats'.[46] Such doppelgangers and brotherly allies also recur as figures of melancholy and temptation throughout Sebald's work, and this distinction provides a productive way to draw out their revolutionary potential, which is distinct from melancholy. Whereas, Deleuze and Guattari argue, critics are quick to attribute Oedipal homosexuality to modernist writers, and to diagnose 'a mother fixation, a dominant depressive nature and a sadomasochistic guilt' as a result, Deleuze and Guattari argue instead for a schizoid, less Saturnine, anoedipal, and inclusive queerness with revolutionary potential.[47] The melancholy models of homosexuality that Deleuze and Guattari dismiss derive from Freud, who claims that as homosexuality is the product of an arrested Oedipus complex, it is connected to incompleteness and loss. In 'Massenpsychologie und Ich-Analyse' [Group Psychology and the Analysis of the Ego], Freud argues that the genesis of male homosexuality comes when a young man is excessively fixated on his mother during the Oedipal phase; in this pathology, the young man introjects the object instead of leaving it to complete his heterosexual development. Freud argues that melancholy is another example of this introjection.[48] Butler has developed this negative and backwards-looking account of queer identity further. For Butler, Freud's account of subject formation involves a gender formation that forbids desire for the homosexual object. Successful gender formation is necessarily heterosexual, because of the social taboo against homosexuality; in same-sex gender identification, the lost homosexual object must be grieved, but it is introjected, preserved as part of the ego and hence occasions melancholia.[49] Freudian-inflected understandings of melancholy homosexuality have influenced the few queer readings of Sebald that currently exist. Thus, both Santner and Katja Garloff diagnose a melancholy of gender in Sebald's texts that is close to Butler's, which describes a queer subject who is immobile and in pain.[50] Drawing on Butler's reading of Derrida, which suggests that a Freudian introjection can also be a respectful incorporation that does not absorb the other, Garloff suggests that the use of Kafka as a figure on loan in *Schwindel. Gefühle.* is 'a fantasy of incorporation that preserves the other's alterity'.[51] However, Garloff, like Anderson, immediately disavows explicitly queer content to her gender analysis, arguing instead that homoeroticism expresses Sebald's melancholy attachment to the racially Jewish other in the wake of the Holocaust. She points towards the 'stiff' or 'immobilized' body of the Sebaldian queer as a sign of gender melancholy.[52] Indeed, melancholy is rightly celebrated by Sebald scholars as an active form of resistance to the oppressive structures of capitalism and modernity.[53] Sebald's queer bachelors — Dr Henry Selwyn and his literary brothers — are certainly often melancholics, but their queerness is not merely a product or symptom of their melancholia. Instead, queerness plays an independent role within Sebald's overall poetics of resistance, by performing an immanent critique and enabling an escape of its own beyond the backward-looking critique associated with melancholia. In Deleuze and Guattari's anti-psychoanalysis, what Freud codes as a failure to complete the Oedipus complex and Butler views as a melancholy of gender becomes instead the revolutionary and joyful 'line of escape' that Kafka takes on his literary path, as he puts together his bachelor-machine. This queer 'line of flight' in Sebald's work disrupts not only the Oedipal structures of patriarchal societies, but also the overwhelming sadness of Sebald's prose, opening up moments of humour, camp, and love. Crucially, the line of escape is neither backward-looking (melancholy) nor future-oriented (messianic), but immanent.

Despite Sebald's affiliation for the minority culture of the rural Alps, Sebald's poetic project does not encompass the full revolutionary ambitions of Kafka's machine of minoritarian expression. Instead of the messianic hope of another possible community, the queer hopes in Sebald's work seem turned away from any possible futurity. Here, Sebald's project in part foreshadows that of queer theorist Edelman, with its resolute rejection of futurity as itself a bourgeois heteronormative concept. Edelman outlines his project in *No Future* as 'the impossible project of a queer oppositionality that would oppose itself to the structural determinants of politics as such'.[54] For Edelman, the rejection of reproductive futurity — of a belief in the sacredness of children and in the hope of the future — would also mean the refusal of those oppressive structures of identity, of history as linear narrative, which Sebald's work also unpicks and destabilizes. Edelman's project aims to afford 'an access to the *jouissance* that at once defines and negates us', a Lacanian concept which hardly seems compatible with melancholy, but whose promise of sexual and subjective fulfilment erupts at several points in Sebald's more homoerotic texts.[55] Edelman, however, turns his face against that very compassion that marks one of the manifestations of the Sebaldian queer, and his polemical ethics demands a sustained anti-social negativity on the part of queer subjects, a negativity that is far from Sebald's compassionate ethics.[56] Nonetheless, Edelman's determinedly anti-reproductive project provides a useful way to situate in queer theory Sebald's repeated constellation of a bachelor who turns away from marriage to the company of books, to *Wahlverwandtschaften* [elective affinities] with dead writers, and sometimes to the company of a boon male friend or lover. Such queer turning away carries with it a political charge, over and above pathological melancholy.

To ally the 'Sebaldian queer' with political immanence and with pleasure is not to deny that Dr Henry Selwyn's story is freighted with melancholy, for it surely is. We are warned as much when Selwyn shows his ancient hunting gun, declaring 'daß einen allein ihr Rückschlag schon ums Leben bringen könne' [that the recoil alone was enough to kill one] (*DA*, 20; *E*, 11). This moment of prolepsis, prefiguring Selwyn's suicide, contains within it a deathly recoil, or backwards turn. Such backwards turns, so typical of Sebald's prose, are read by Heather Love as inherently queer tropes, as she reads them as allegories of queer historical experience. The backwards turn can also reveal the signs of queer destruction, 'like Lot's wife turning to look at the destruction of Sodom & Gomorrah'.[57] But the queer turn need not be a melancholy return in Sebald's work. John Zilcosky's crucial insight is of key importance to my entire argument here, that 'Sebald suggests that homosexuality might offer a way out of a system of eternal heterosexual return', that is, of heterosexual return to the calamitous path of history and to past catastrophes.[58] While Zilcosky argues that 'neither the narrator nor Kafka ever makes the decisive step toward this (dis)orientation', I build on this vital distinction to argue that the queer textuality of Sebald's prose itself contains moments of liberating disorient- ation, rather than describing a linear arc of return.[59] Here, Sara Ahmed's work on queer phenomenology is also useful in thinking through the orientation of Sebald's queer figures. The crooked inclination or indirect gaze is privileged throughout Sebald's work, from the slantwise gaze of the painter Grünewald in *Nach der Natur*, to the painfully inclined neck of the young Max Aurach in *Die Ausgewanderten*. Ahmed reads this turn away from the straight as inherent to queer existence, and generates a queer phenomenology that accounts for the way in which queer bodies are oriented in space and society. Following in part from Butler, but taking a more optimistic direction, she argues that part of subjection — subject formation — is a turning that results from social interpellation, and that the queer subject, turning as it does in a different direction, has frequently been coded as deviant or an aberra- tion.[60] Ahmed's phenomenology moves away from pathological and psychoanalytical accounts of homosexuality, and provides a more positive way to read Sebald's deviants, who turn away from normative family structures and in unruly directions.

To think about 'orientation' is also to note a more troubling aspect of the Sebaldian queer. While Garloff suggests that Sebald's homophile German–Jewish relations are an ethical response to the post-Holocaust condition, at times, particularly in the tale of 'Ambros Adelwarth', queer orientation is close to queer Orientalism. While the Sebaldian queer creates moments of resistance, playfulness, and suspension in his texts, it can also play with modernist clichés that associate male homosexuality with decay, inversion, paedophilia, and Orientalism. Sometimes, German characters experience a homoerotic longing or love for Jewish characters; sometimes, this turns into a sentimentality that blurs the line between victim and perpetrator, oppressor and subaltern. Further, we must recall that Selwyn's passion for Naegeli is allied to his 'death of love' for his wife, Hedi. The Sebaldian queer is most resolutely masculine, an ideal that entirely excludes feminine or genderqueer possibilities; women are reduced to the roles of spectral mother, marginalized wife or fiancée, or depersonalized oracle, rarely if ever accorded a sexuality of their own. At the same time as the Sebaldian queer turns away from heterosexuality, it also denies the more radical possibilities of an equivalent lesbian, transgendered, or non-gendered queer redemption. Despite his text's allegiances with the marginalized, from colonized peoples to tormented animals and the trees destroyed by the great storm of 1987, Sebald accords almost no revolutionary power to feminism. In taking account of these grave ethical troubles in the 'Sebaldian queer', which reproduce some of the most persistent oppressions of modernity, it is no wonder that, while the Sebaldian narrator may yearn for a male friend or lover, he may instead become the victim of an uncanny haunting or persecution, represented by the sinister figure of the doppelganger. The idealized male–male bond becomes here transformed into an eerie haunting and doubling of the self that shows that the fractures of the bourgeois self are condemned to replicate the painful fissures that run through history.

The Sebaldian queer, while containing its own moment of ethical resistance, is thus also troubled both by its own reliance on misogynist and Orientalist tropes, and subject to the painful logic of history. While I have argued that it is distinct from melancholy in his works, it also shares an oppositional moment with it, just as, although it offers an immanent resistance to history beyond the backward turn or the reproductive logic of futurity, it nonetheless is also affected by the natural history of destruction. It is therefore linked to Sebald's redemptive historiography, which shares Benjamin's vision of the task of the historical materialist, whose mission it is to fan the sparks of hope in the past. Tracing this mission in Sebald's writing, R. J. A. Kilbourn sees a purgatorial death as the ultimate telos of Sebald's messianic project 'of exile, wandering and waiting'; a Thanatic logic that is linked to the 'death of love' mourned by Selwyn.[61] This apparent victory of Thanatos over Eros saddens some critics, such as Sheppard, who suggests that Sebald's fixation on Thanatos may have indirectly contributed to his early death, or Daniel Medin, who argues that Sebald's essay on Kafka's *Das Schloß* wilfully excludes Eros from its relentlessly Thanatic reading.[62] More sceptically, Anne Fuchs early suggested that such melancholy might be suspiciously close to a self-regarding pose, and, because of its constant recourse to metaphysics, contains a politically questionable ahistoricity.[63] Most critics instead admire the pervasive melancholy of Sebald's texts, viewing Sebald's gloom as an ethical response to the catastrophes of modernity. This celebration of Sebaldian melancholy is grounded in the programmatic statement in the introduction to *Die Beschreibung des Unglücks* [The Description of Calamity], that 'Die Beschreibung des Unglücks schließt in sich die Möglichkeit seiner Über-windung ein' [the description of calamity includes within it the possibility of overcoming it] (*BU*, 3). Thus, Sebald's anatomy of melancholy carries within it, if not a utopian impulse, at least a moment of hope that the pervading epistemological discourses of capitalism can be overturned by means of melancholic resistance. Furthermore, Öhlschläger argues that for Sebald melancholy is a condition that allows reflection on imminent catastrophe, enabling a form of resistance that has nothing to do with a death wish.[64] This book shows that the Sebaldian queer offers a parallel and at times complementary moment of resistance to that offered by melancholy. Although sexuality and death are at times intimately linked, Sebald's poetics also tend towards a hope for an immanent space of brotherhood or homo-sexual love, beyond death, and beyond personal guilt. Redemption, in Sebald, is not merely the promise to recover history in the light of a perfect future, as Adorno demands, or to brush history against the grain, in a Benjaminian sense. It is also the search for an immanent *Heimat* beyond the borders of the German nation, often one in letters, and for a homosexual or homosocial and brotherly love that disrupts the linear reproduction and Oedipal structures of the bourgeois family. The queer textuality of his works is often its own immanent space of resistance not only to Oedipus, but to the tyranny of meaning itself.

Chapter Outline

This volume both provides a queer reading of Sebald's work, and also gives an account of queer moments and movements within it. In Chapter 1, I trace the development of Sebald's critique of the bourgeois family and bourgeois sexuality in his earlier academic work, showing how Sebald's early and mid-career literary criticism constantly linked the themes of sexual deviance and of Jewish assimilation with an overarching critique of the dominant structures of normative German society. The young Sebald's stinging attacks on Alfred Döblin and Carl Sternheim can be read as the foundation stones for a critique of the way that German bourgeois society reproduced itself via its literature, thereby also propagating the germs of fascism. In Chapter 2, I analyse the motif of the bachelor in Sebald's work, most particularly *Die Ringe des Saturn* [*The Rings of Saturn*], but also *Nach der Natur*, as part of a literary line of flight, mobilizing Deleuze and Guattari's theories on Kafka to show how figures such as Edward FitzGerald and Algernon Swinburne attempt to construct an alternative literary order, congenial to Sebald's own, where brotherhood and elective affinities take priority over familial reproduction. Chapter 3 shows how Sebald links queerness to the history of colonialism, the practice of Orientalism, and also to political resistance against colonial oppression. I also demonstrate how such resistance nonetheless becomes embroiled in Orientalist clichés. Chapter 4 analyses perhaps the queerest of Sebald's texts, *Schwindel. Gefühle.*, where the Sebaldian narrator's longing for Kafka appears as an uncanny desire to reverse history and raise the dead. This is what Kilbourn calls Sebald's 'unique contribution to an erotic-salvific model predicated on a specific relation between a narrative subject and an *other* as embodiment of the promise — or hope — of redemption'.[65] Pursuing a close affinity with the non-German other and the dead is no straightforward mechanism of redemption, however, and the Sebaldian narrator remains caught between queer desire and subjective dissolution in a playful text whose very queerness refuses interpretation. In conclusion, I look briefly at *Austerlitz* and again at *Nach der Natur* and *Schwindel. Gefühle.* to demonstrate how the lure of incest can at times not spur the bachelor further on a line of flight, as Deleuze and Guattari claim, but rather relentlessly return him to the normative sphere of the German family. This brief outline of my project will also show its limits. It is not my intention to claim that queer sexuality is to be found in every moment of Sebald's writing, and thus I do not attempt a queer reading of every text Sebald wrote; his magnum opus *Austerlitz* is analysed only very briefly, only two of the wings of the triptych of *Nach der Natur* form part of the study, his short poetry is not considered at all, and not all of Sebald's critical essays prove relevant to my argument. My study does not concern itself, except fleetingly, with the Holocaust and its representation in Sebald's literature, nor does it attempt a fresh model of the two great Sebaldian themes of memory and melancholy.

Finally, it should also be said that this study confines itself to Sebald's literature only, and makes few claims about his biography and none about his personal orientations. A bewitching image reproduced on page 70 of *Wandernde Schatten*, the catalogue of a Sebald exhibition held in Marbach in 2008, shows a full-face portrait of Sebald printed in the magazine of the *Süddeutsche Zeitung*.[66] On the facing page, Sebald has lain a portrait of Omar Sharif from a perfume advertisement, taken in almost exactly the same format, at the same size and with the same blue filter, such that when the magazine is open, the two male faces — each mustachioed, each with an enigmatic smile — are nestling cheek to cheek. The suggestive power of this homoerotic image, in which Sebald appears to be being seduced, via photomontage, by the dashing Egyptian film star, is breathtaking. Rather than laboriously interpret it as in any way a biographical confession, I prefer to read it as a signifier of the as yet little acknowledged playful, transgressive, and beautiful aspects of the Sebaldian queer.

Notes to the Introduction

1. Richard Sheppard, 'Dexter — Sinister: Some Observations on Decrypting the Mors Code in the Work of W. G. Sebald', *Journal of European Studies*, 35 (2005), 419–63 (p. 440).
2. Brad Prager, 'Sebald's Kafka', in *W. G. Sebald: History — Memory — Trauma*, ed. by Scott Denham and Mark McCulloh (Berlin: De Gruyter, 2006), pp. 105–25 (p. 119).
3. Claudia Öhlschläger, *Beschädigtes Leben, erzählte Risse: W. G. Sebalds poetische Ordnung des Unglücks* (Freiburg i. Br., Berlin, and Vienna: Rombach, 2006), p. 49.
4. Benjamin theorizes that *mémoire involuntaire* is a phenomenon created by capitalist society. Unlike traditional societies, where the individual is bound into collective memory by means of commemorative rituals and artefacts, capitalist society separates the individual from the collective, and causes memory to return involuntarily: 'Dieser [...] gehört zum Inventar der vielfältig isolierten Privatperson. Wo Erfahrung im strikten Sinn obwaltet, treten im Gedächtnis gewisse Inhalte der individuellen Vergangenheit mit solchen der kollektiven in Konjunktion' (Walter Benjamin, *Gesammelte Schriften*, ed. by Rolf Tiedemann and Hermann Schweppenhäuser, with the contribution of Theodor W. Adorno and Gerschom Scholem (Frankfurt a. M.: Suhrkamp, 1972–91), I: *Abhandlungen*, ed. by Rolf Tiedemann and Hermann Schweppenhäuser (1974), p. 611).
5. Ben Hutchinson, *W. G. Sebald: Die dialektische Imagination* (Berlin: De Gruyter, 2009), p. 155.
6. 'Jenseits der Grenze — Peter Handkes Erzählung *Die Wiederholung*', in *Unheimliche Heimat*, pp. 162–79 (p. 177).
7. Amir Eshel, 'Against the Power of Time: The Poetics of Suspension in W. G. Sebald's *Austerlitz*', *New German Critique*, 88 (2003), 71–96.
8. Ibid., p. 74.
9. Maya Jaggi, 'Recovered Memories. The Guardian Profile: W. G. Sebald', *The Guardian*, 22 September 2001.
10. 'Who is W. G. Sebald? Interview', Sebald in conversation with Carole Angier, in *The Emergence of Memory: Conversations with W. G. Sebald*, ed. by Lynne Sharon Schwartz (New York: Seven Stories, 2007), pp. 63–75 (p. 70).
11. Maya Barzilai, 'Facing the Past and the Female Spectre in W. G. Sebald's *The Emigrants*', in *W. G. Sebald: A Critical Companion*, ed. by J. J. Long and Anne Whitehead (Edinburgh: Edinburgh University Press, 2004), pp. 203–16 (p. 213).
12. George Mosse, *The Image of Man* (Oxford: Oxford University Press, 1996), p. 56.
13. Matti Bunzl, *Symptoms of Modernity: Jews and Queers in Late-Twentieth-Century Vienna* (Berkeley: University of California Press, 2004), p. ix.
14. Mary Cosgrove, 'Austerlitz', in *The German-Language Novel since 1990*, ed. by Stuart Taberner (Cambridge: Cambridge University Press, 2011), pp. 195–210 (p. 205).
15. Ibid., p. 206; Hutchinson, *W. G. Sebald*, p. 10.
16. Stuart Taberner, 'German Nostalgia? Remembering German-Jewish Life in W. G. Sebald's *Die Ausgewanderten* and *Austerlitz*', *Germanic Review*, 79 (2004), 181–202 (p. 181).
17. Theodor W. Adorno, *Versuch über Wagner* (Munich: Knaur, 1964), quoted in Hutchinson, *Die dialektische Imagination*, p. 1.

18. Colleen Lamos, *Devant Modernism: Sexual and Textual Errancy in T. S. Eliot, James Joyce, and Marcel Proust* (Cambridge: Cambridge University Press, 1998), p. 9.

19. J. J. Long, *W. G. Sebald: Image, Archive, Modernity* (Edinburgh: Edinburgh University Press, 2007).

20. Ibid., p. 74.

21. Ben Hutchinson, 'Bausteine 3: Sprachen', in *Wandernde Schatten: W. G. Sebalds Unterwelt*, marbacherkatalog 62, ed. by Ulrich von Bülow, Heike Gfrereis, and Ellen Strittmatter (Marbach am Neckar: Deutsche Schillergesellschaft, 2008), pp. 115–27 (p. 121).

22. Gary Schmidt, 'Sublime Melancholy: The Function of the Homoerotic in Sebald's *Die Ausgewanderten*', in *Über Gegenwartsliteratur: Interpretationen und Interventionen. Festschrift für Paul Michael Lützeler zum 65. Geburtstag von ehemaligen StudentInnen*, ed. by Mark W. Rectanus (Bielefeld: Aisthesis, 2008), pp. 297–313.

23. Barry McCrea, *In the Company of Strangers: Family and Narrative in Dickens, Conan Doyle, Joyce, and Proust* (New York: Columbia University Press, 2011), p. 3.

24. Eve Kosofsky Sedgwick, *Tendencies* (Durham, NC and London: Duke University Press, 1993), p. xii.

25. Anne Hermann, *Queering the Moderns: Poses, Portraits, Performances* (New York: Palgrave, 2000), p. 7.

26. Eric Santner, *On Creaturely Life: Rilke, Benjamin, Sebald* (Chicago: University of Chicago Press, 2006), p. 196.

27. Ibid., p. 12.

28. Michael Snedicker, *Queer Optimism: Lyric Personhood and Other Felicitous Persuasions* (Minneapolis: University of Minnesota Press, 2009), p. 4.

29. Gilles Deleuze and Félix Guattari, *Kafka: Toward a Minor Literature*, trans. by Dana Polan (Minneapolis and London: University of Minnesota Press, 1986); *Anti-Oedipus: Capitalism and Schizophrenia*, trans. by Robert Hurley, Mark Seem, and Helen R. Lane (London: Continuum, 2004).

30. Dora Osborne, 'Topographical Anxiety and Dysfunctional Systems: *Die Ausgewanderten* and Freud's *Little Hans*', in *The Undiscover'd Country: W. G. Sebald and the Poetics of Travel*, ed. by Markus Zisselsberger (Rochester, NY: Camden House, 2010), pp. 299–321 (p. 305).

31. Deleuze and Guattari, *Anti-Oedipus*, p. 2.

32. Ibid., p. 5.

33. Chrysanthi Nigianni and Merl Storr, 'Introduction', in *Deleuze and Queer Theory*, ed. by Chrysanthi Nigianni and Merl Storr (Edinburgh: Edinburgh University Press, 2009), pp. 1–10 (p. 2).

34. Verena Andermatt Conley, 'Thirty-six Thousand Forms of Love: The Queering of Deleuze and Guattari', in *Deleuze and Queer Theory*, ed. by Nigianni and Storr, pp. 24–36 (p. 25).

35. Laura Penny, 'Parables and Politics: How Benjamin and Deleuze & Guattari Read Kafka', *Theory & Event*, 12 (2009). <http://muse.jhu.edu/journals/theory_and_event/v012/12.3.penny.html> [accessed 16 December 2012].

36. Deleuze and Guattari, *Kafka*, p. 70.

37. Ibid., p. 67.

38. Ibid., p. 67.

39. Ibid., p. 68.

40. Ibid., p. 71.

41. Judith Halberstam, *In a Queer Time and Place: Transgender Bodies, Subcultural Lives* (New York: New York University Press, 2005), p. 24.

42. Snedicker, *Queer Optimism*, pp. 31, 170.

43. Anne Fuchs, *Die Schmerzensspuren der Geschichte: Zur Poetik der Erinnerung in W. G. Sebalds Prosa* (Cologne: Böhlau Verlag, 2004); Mary Cosgrove, 'Austerlitz', in *The Novel in German since 1990*, pp. 195–210; Graham Jackman, '"Gebranntes Kind"? W. G. Sebalds "Metaphysik der Geschichte"', *German Life and Letters*, 57 (2004), 456–71; Peter Morgan, 'The Sign of Saturn: Melancholy, Homelessness and Apocalypse in W. G. Sebald's Prose Narratives', *German Life and Letters*, 58 (2005), 75–92. On the significance of the concepts of generation in German culture, see Sigrid Weigel, '"Generation" as Symbolic Form: On the Genealogical Discourse of Memory

since 1945', *The Germanic Review*, 77 (2002), 264–67; *German Life & Letters*, , 59.2 (special issue): *Memory Contests*, ed. by Anne Fuchs and Mary Cosgrove (2006); and *German Memory Contests: The Quest for Identity in Literature, Film and Discourse since 1990*, ed. by Anne Fuchs, Mary Cosgrove, and Georg Grote (Rochester, NY: Camden House, 2006).

44. Morgan, 'The Sign of Saturn', p. 77.

45. Mark M. Anderson, 'A Childhood in the Allgäu: Wertach, 1944–1952', in *Saturn's Moons: A W. G. Sebald Handbook*, ed. by Jo Catling and Richard Hibbitt (Oxford: Legenda, 2011), pp. 16–41 (p. 33).

46. Deleuze and Guattari, *Kafka*, p. 68.

47. Deleuze and Guattari, *Anti-Oedipus*, p. 78.

48. Sigmund Freud, 'Massenpsychologie und Ich-Analyse', in *Kulturtheoretische Schriften*, ed. by Alexander Mitscherlich, Angela Richards, and James Strachey (Frankfurt a. M.: S. Fischer, 1974), pp. 61–134 (103–04).

49. Judith Butler, *Gender Trouble* (New York and London: Routledge, 1990), p. 86.

50. Santner, *On Creaturely Life*, p. 172.

51. Katja Garloff, 'Kafka's Crypt: W. G. Sebald and the Melancholy of Modern German Jewish Culture', *The Germanic Review: Literature, Culture, Theory*, 82 (2007), 123–40 (p. 125).

52. Ibid., p. 131.

53. See, among others, Mary Cosgrove, 'Sebald for Our Time: The Politics of Melancholy and the Critique of Capitalism in his Work', in *W. G. Sebald and the Writing of History*, ed. by Anne Fuchs and J. J. Long (Würzburg: Königshausen & Neumann, 2007), pp. 91–110.

54. Lee Edelman, *No Future: Queer Theory and the Death Drive* (Durham, NC and London: Duke University Press, 1994), p. 4.

55. Ibid., p. 5.

56. Ibid., p. 2.

57. Heather Love, *Feeling Backward: Loss and the Politics of Queer History* (Cambridge, Mass.: Harvard University Press, 2007), p. 5.

58. John Zilcosky, 'Sebald's Uncanny Travels: The Impossibility of Getting Lost', in *W. G. Sebald: A Critical Companion*, ed. by J. J. Long and Anne Whitehead (Edinburgh: Edinburgh University Press, 2004), pp. 102–20 (p. 108).

59. Ibid., p. 108.

60. Sara Ahmed, *Queer Phenomenology: Orientations, Objects, Others* (Durham, NC and London: Duke University Press, 2006).

61. R. J. A. Kilbourn, 'Kafka, Nabokov ... Sebald: Intertextuality and Narratives of Redemption in *Vertigo* and *The Emigrants*', in *W. G. Sebald: History — Memory — Trauma*, ed. by Scott Denham and Mark McCulloh (Berlin: De Gruyter, 2006), pp. 33–63 (p. 35).

62. Daniel Medin, *Three Sons: Franz Kafka and the Fiction of J. M. Coetzee, Philip Roth and W. G. Sebald* (Evanston, Ill.: Northwestern University Press, 2010), p. 85.

63. Fuchs, *Die Schmerzensspuren der Geschichte*, p. 19.

64. Öhlschläger, *Beschädigtes Leben*, p. 12.

65. Kilbourn, 'Kafka, Nabokov ... Sebald', p. 34.

66. I am grateful to Dora Osborne for this reference.

CHAPTER 1

W. G. Sebald's *Lehrjahre:*
Bourgeois Sexuality and its Discontents

Where does Sebaldian wayward, queer masculinity interact with the Oedipal structures of the German patriarchal family and of orthodox German studies? Or, to couch the question in more scholarly terms, how can a reading of W. G. Sebald's academic apprenticeship help us to understand the theoretical underpinnings of the Sebaldian queer? Sebald's very earliest critical work deals with the discontents attending on the system of patriarchal sexuality. Indeed, *Die Beschreibung des Unglücks* is riddled with discourses of perverse sexuality, unambiguously linking sex to calamity. If, as many critics have shown, the discourses that preoccupy all of Sebald's fiction — messianism, the unnaturalness of *Heimat* and the repression of memories of the Holocaust, among others — can be read from his earliest academic essays, so too can his critique of German discourses of sex, bourgeois masculinity, and modernity. This chapter reads a selection of his critical works on Sternheim, Roth, Franzos, Handke, and Schnitzler, to form a picture of Sebald as an unruly son, who in his early work demolishes the theoretical underpinnings of the patriarchal male in modernist bourgeois literature. From his earliest critical writings, through to his last published critical collection *Logis in einem Landhaus* [*A Place in the Country*], Sebald was certainly an anatomist of melancholy, but at the same time a merciless anatomist of the psychopathology of bourgeois masculinity. His academic criticism was initially informed by the language of the Frankfurt School, in particular the work of Adorno, in analysing the authoritarian structures that underlay Wilhelminian patriarchy, but also developed its own methodology that linked crises in masculinity to crises in poetics. Further, Sebald links a scornful demolition of masculinities in modernist literature to an analysis of the deforming effects of Jewish attempts to assimilate to German culture. The works analysed in this chapter trace Sebald's critical moves towards a Deleuzian 'line of flight' that tries to cross over the boundaries of German masculinity. Sebald's developing critical commitment to an ethics of brotherhood instead of an allegiance to the patriarchy draws him close to a queer and often Jewish construct of masculinity.

In his critical work, Sebald demonstrates that the family is the nexus where the political border between Austrian and Jew, and the psychic border between ego and subconscious, meet. It is this fraught conjunction that Sebald traces and retraces in his critical writing. His essay on Peter Altenberg from 1989 offers a paradigm of this link between the bourgeois family and Jewish assimilation. Sebald here asserts that the *Unbehagen* — the *discontents*, with all the Freudian overtones of that word — of the assimilated Jewish bourgeoisie are even stronger than in the Gentile variant.

> Hatten jüdische bürgerliche Familien im Assimilationsprozeß einmal die höheren Schichten erreicht, so wirkte sich in ihnen das Unbehagen an der bürgerlichen Lebensführung meist radikaler aus als in der nichtjüdischen Bourgeoisie.[1]
>
> [Once Jewish bourgeois families had reached the higher strata in the process of assimilation, discontent at the bourgeois way of life mostly affected them more radically than the non-Jewish bourgeoisie.]

In particular, Sebald holds that Jewish-Austrian literature is itself symptomatic of the liminal position that assimilated Jews held. Sons of the generation of Jews who left the ghetto for the cities of the Austro-Hungarian empire were driven to succeed in culture as well as in business, and to complete a process of assimilation, which led to the creation of a bohemia that was parasitically dependent on the bourgeoisie (*UH*, 79). Canonical modernist literary culture, in Sebald's account, is always compromised because of this parasitical relationship with bourgeois society. Thus, his critical work increasingly seeks out writers (always male) who, in his view, were and are marginalized by the German canon. These writings create a commitment to brotherliness and a set of elective affinities — *Wahlverwandtschaften* — with congenial, often Jewish, authors from previous generations. It is through these essays that Sebald's critical position leaves behind Oedipal structures and embarks on a line of flight, drawing out queer and bachelor encounters beyond the borders of Germany in the works he analyses, encounters which are later to have their counterparts in his own literary fiction.

Adorno and the Psychopathology of the Bourgeois Self

Sebald's queer line of flight begins both in his biography and in his critical work; his wayward literary affiliations can be linked to his childhood affiliation to his maternal grandfather, and his attack on the patriarchal canon of modernist literature can be linked to his distanced relationship to his father. Is the refusal of heterosexual masculinities in Sebald's work, then, traceable to a generational rage against his Nazi perpetrator father, a rage he shared with the rest of his 1968 cohort? Deleuze and Guattari condemn the reductiveness of Oedipal analyses, thereby warning us against reducing the complexity of Sebald's intellectual engagements with masculinity to this pop-Oedipal model. To the extent that Sebald can be viewed as a rebel, his generational rebellion was intellectual, beginning with a profound engagement with the works of the Frankfurt School in his undergraduate years.[2] In keeping with their principles, he rejected the *werkimmanent* [textually grounded] criticism he inherited from traditional German studies in favour of applying sociological, psychological, and biographical criteria to German texts, criteria that helped him to develop a psychopathology of the bourgeois self.[3] In his undergraduate and postgraduate work on Sternheim, he argued that the poetic inadequacies of the writer pointed towards more profound socio-political problems.

This was certainly a critical rebellion, rejecting the neutral critical stance of the perpetrator generation of academics still in power to attack their generation of writers for their linguistic and political complicity with Nazism. In this sense, then, Sebald's initial critical moves are Oedipal. Yet, as this chapter will demonstrate, the Oedipal anger behind Sebald's early attacks on assimilated Jewish writers and the Frankfurt School ideology was transformed into a far richer form of criticism that sought out those moments of brotherhood, suspension, and transgression that structure the Sebaldian queer.

To some extent, Oedipal anger and generational rebellion can be seen to inform Sebald's few public comments on current affairs. In his political anger, and also in his lack of interest in the more personally liberating aspect of the 1960s student movement, Sebald can be viewed as a classically German student rebel; Heinz Bude theorizes that the German 1968 student movement was far less one of libidinous liberation than the parallel movements in Paris or the United States, that it was rather marked by guilt and a 'laming fixation' with the history of their parents' generation.[4] As we have already seen, the modernist-inflected Sebaldian queer owes little to the gay liberation movement, and his few representations of women bear no traces either of modern feminism or of doctrines of free love or hedonism. To view his work entirely through an Oedipal lens, however, is to deny the radical critical potential that develops out of this initial generational rebellion. Peter Morgan's description of Sebald as a 'West German intellectual of the student generation', who is inescapably caught in the consciousness of the 'second generation' throughout his career, goes too far.[5] The traces of an Oedipal conflict with his father's perpetrator generation linger on principally in his occasional comments on German current affairs. In interviews, Sebald claimed that he was aware of the generational model of inherited guilt, although he claimed not to subscribe to it in its entirety, rather viewing a generational conflict as a way to understand certain events in post-war history.[6] Sebald's analysis of German politics and society remained indebted to the psychoanalytical model propounded by Alexander and Margarete Mitscherlich in *Die Unfähigkeit zu Trauern* [The Inability to Mourn] in 1967. His generational vocabulary is one that centres on the terms of collective repression, collective guilt, and the need for melancholy as a site of resistance. The profound changes in German public discourse that came with the *Historikerstreit* and reunification do not seem to have modified his essentially oppositional understanding of the dynamics of German society. Indeed, some comments draw on a version of the dialectic of Enlightenment so simplified that Sebald may at times be suspected of irony. For instance, in an interview in 1993, he dismisses the reunification of Germany in orthodox Marxist terms:

> Das hatte mit Politik wenig zu tun. Es war zunächst ein Wirtschaftsphänomen, daß halt das Geld, das hier im Westen in großen Mengen in den Kellern lag, schließlich die Mauer unterspült hat.[7]

> [That has little to do with politics. It was initially an economic phenomenon that the money, which was lying around in the cellars in great quantities here in the West, eventually undermined the Wall.]

To the interviewer's accusation that this dialectical analysis of recent history sounded somewhat naive and antiquated, he retorted that he was just stating the facts.[8] Sebald here seems indebted to a Frankfurt School-inflected reading of history that, by the 1990s, had itself fossilized into a backward, inflexible ideology.

Such indebtedness to a Freudian model and refusal to engage with the political realities of contemporary Germany can be viewed as wilful ignorance or naïveté. But Sebald is a literary artist, not a sociologist, as Hutchinson argues: his revolutionary potential, including his revolutionary queer potential, lies in his literary criticism and in his own literature, not in sporadic comments on German politics. Hutchinson argues that as an artist Sebald was able to resist the performative contradiction of critical theory, which attacks the Enlightenment without offering any alternative revolutionary potential other than enlightened criticism.[9] Sebald's poetic revolution, and his queer revolution, goes beyond being a disciple of the Frankfurt School. Sebald's work engages with aspects of critical theory without itself being critical theory, nor does it seek to continue the political aspects of Adorno's critique. This understanding of Sebald's relationship to critical theory is in keeping with Lorenz Jäger's argument that 'the doctrines of critical theory were interpreted in two different ways, on the one hand as a radical critique of existing conditions, while on the other — and this is especially true of Benjamin — they provided access to the history of German ideas'.[10] Thus, in keeping with his imaginative affiliation to his grandfather, Sebald's rebellion did not express itself by his joining the student activist APO, but rather found in critical theory a means to connect to an older culture of German ideas and literature. As indicated in the discussion of his work on Sternheim, Sebald's undergraduate and postgraduate research initially focused on attacks on what he hypostatizes as 'the bourgeois era', i.e. the culture of the 1870s to 1918, and the literature of classical modernism. Sebald enthusiastically explores Adorno's suggestion that the roots of the destruction of German culture could already be traced in pre-Nazi art movements. Adorno typically diagnoses the deformation of German culture in 'the spirit of the Berlin illustrated magazines' and the popular culture of the 1920s. For Sebald Expressionism itself is ideologically suspect on a linguistic level, as he states in the introduction to his book on Carl Sternheim:

> Abgesehen von einigen Bemerkungen Ernst Blochs, [wurde] über die ideologischen Bedingtheiten der expressionistischen Phrasierung noch nichts Verläßliches geäußert. (*Sternheim,* 10)

> [Apart from a few remarks of Ernst Bloch, as yet nothing reliable [was] said about the ideological conditioning of Expressionist phraseology.]

Sebald is not exercised by pop culture in the way that Adorno is, but rather by his perception that Sternheim, and the other writers of the bourgeois era whom he attacks, radically betray the ethics of language itself. Here Sebald passes through the door that Adorno opens up to the 'high German culture of the nineteenth century', but instead uses the door to the past to launch an attack on it.[11] Sebald is using Adorno's weaponry to attack not contemporary popular culture but the German bourgeois culture that preceded it, in which Adorno and the other critics of the Frankfurt School were educated.

Both this attack on bourgeois culture, and Sebald's ideological departure from Adorno, can be seen in the debate that Sebald attempted to open with Adorno directly. As Marcel Atze and Sven Meyer have shown in their essay 'Unsere Korrespondenz' [Our Correspondence], Sebald embarked on a direct correspondence with Adorno on the issue of a very brief note in *Minima Moralia*.[12] Here, Adorno discusses the goal of an emancipated society — an empty utopia which the student rebels filled with radical social phantasies — and concludes that it might be found in the ideal of animal-like quietude.

> None of the abstract concepts comes closer to fulfilled utopia than that of eternal peace. Spectators on the sidelines of progress like Maupassant and Sternheim have helped this intention to find expression, timidly, in the only way that its fragility permits.[13]

Sebald's letter to Adorno took issue with this note, arguing that Sternheim can only be read as a symptom of his time. He thereby positioned himself at once as the disciple of Adorno, and as a disciple who wants to go further than the master.[14] Adorno refuses to yield Sebald's point in his reply. He argues that although Sternheim's assimilation is flawed, its very failure makes it more than it 'simply is'.[15] Adorno holds open the possibility of a creative tension of assimilation in Sternheim's work, a tension that would give Sternheim's satire bite, but Sebald will not allow this. Bourgeois and assimilated literature, for Sebald, cannot provide any space for a productive utopia, even a quietist one that might seem congenial to him.

Death to the Fathers: Oedipal Trouble and Young Sebald

In keeping with this view of Sebald as an initially rebellious and wayward son, his colleague Sheppard notes that an enduring complex in Sebald's work, and one that also informs his reading, if his marginalia are indicative, is his 'problematic relationship with his father — or rather, with his image of his father and everything with which it was associated'.[16] Among Sebald's earliest essays are a series of direct theoretical engagements with the Oedipal complex and figure of the father in modernist literature. These essays critique the patriarchal structures of bourgeois society from a perspective that leans on critical theory, and further shows an awareness of the colonial structures that informed that patriarchy, while clearly rejecting feminist strategies as a possible means to demolish them. In these essays on Strindberg and Schnitzler, we see foreshadowings of the Sebaldian queer, which aligns itself to a literary form of resistance against colonialism and bourgeois patriarchy while at the same time fastidiously shrinking from femininity. Sebald's 1976 essay on modernist drama, unambiguously entitled 'Mord an den Vätern' [Father-murder], leans heavily on Freud to describe the patriarchal complex as one of the constitutive elements of bourgeois modernity.[17] If, Sebald argues, representations of the early history of paternity in modernity are grotesque or comic, as in the *commedia dell'arte*, with the ending of the bourgeois age paternity returns to 'die Gegend ihres fast unvordenklichen Ursprungs' [the area of its almost pre-conscious origins].[18] In the literature of late modernity, then, Sebald argues that the farcical history of paternity repeats itself as mythic tragedy, and we see the psychological problematic of the father metamorphose into a mythical one. 'Myth', here, is to be understood in the sense that Adorno and Horkheimer describe it in *Dialektik der Aufklärung* [*Dialectic of Enlightenment*] and Sebald uses it in *Döblin*: a brutal, fatal, and regressive power, which disintegrates the social and psychological structures governing the bourgeois order. Already in this early essay, Sebald critiques patriarchal structures without drawing an explicitly feminist conclusion (which he here dismisses as the 'usual' rhetoric of the suffragist movement). He dismisses feminist struggles by aligning feminists with the patriarchy, arguing that the 'weaker', i.e. women, mimic the language and tactics of the 'stronger' in society. Sebald thus aligns the suffragists with the dangerous resurgence of undifferentiated, brutal myth, a position far from feminist writers of the same era, such as Irmtraud Morgner or Christa Wolf, who drew on myth as a resource to structure new forms of female subjectivity. He takes particular issue with the literary reception of Bachofen's ideas of a prehistorical 'hetaerism' in society. This prehistorical matriarchy, according to Bachofen, is dispelled by the father seeking to establish his paternity and paternal law in the form of the bourgeois family.[19] Sebald reads Strindberg's play as a proto-Freudian rewriting of the *Oresteia* (Strindberg, he notes, could not have known Freud's work), and suggests that the matriarchal myth was violent enough to reassert itself of its own volition. He asserts that this strange coincidence of modern artistic representations with a period that had not yet been emancipated from myth is the 'Zeichen eines Lebens, das fremd und blindlings sich zuträgt' [sign of a life that occurs strangely and blindly].[20] Sebald's analysis links the implacable return of myth with the foundations of bourgeois society and the bourgeois self; here, as rarely later in his criticism, these foundations are revealed as explicitly gendered. Progress and civilization, in accordance with an explicit adherence to Freud and an implicit adherence to Adorno, are dialectically embroiled in their opposite, myth, and fictions of a better order inevitably dialectically contradicted by what Sebald here terms the Freudian 'reality principle'. Freud's argument in *Der Mann Moses und der Monotheismus* [*Moses and Monotheism*] that father-murder is a primordial principle of society, and that the ensuing social guilt will return, is described by Sebald as compelling despite its hypothetical character. Sebald declares Freud's argument to be convincing because of its tragic critique of civilization.

The negative dialectics and tragic view of the world espoused by Sebald in his later work is here *in nuce*, in Freudian terms. Sebald's analysis here is that of the novice eager to demonstrate his grasp of a quickly learned theory by finding evidence of it in a set of readings: a form of analysis that seeks confirmation of similarities rather than teasing out differences, as his later and more sensitive critical work does. Sebald is still far from celebrating queer brotherhood in this essay, as he here declares the brotherly ethos of the society that follows the father-murder to be a ghostly afterlife of the primordial father: 'das neue Ethos der Brüderschaft repräsentiert das Fortleben des Vaters über seinen eigenen Tod hinaus' [the new ethos of brotherhood represents the continued survival of the father beyond his own death].[21] Brotherliness as a system of morality, in this essay, is merely one more disciplinary practice of patriarchal society, not a system of male affiliation and resistance to its dictates. Sebald concludes that John Millington Synge's 1907 comedy *The Playboy of the Western World* is a clearer reading of the patriarchal complex of dominance, as it situates it within a historical society, rather than in timeless myth as the tragedians Strindberg and Ibsen attempt. He suggests that the overturning of the patriarchs had succeeded by the nineteenth century, and that the Expressionist fascination with rebellion against the father is therefore 'pubescent'.

With this dismissal of the patriarchy, and hence of Oedipal criticism, it is a short step to dismissing the 'myth' of heterosexual love, in a move showing Sebald's Foucauldian allegiance. Two of his early essays on Schnitzler are introduced by the quote 'quand le bourgeois s'amuse, on entre dans l'éternité. Les amusements du bourgeois sont comme la mort'.[22] Bourgeois Eros, in Sebald's analysis, leads only to Thanatos, and is one of the perverse turns taken by Enlightenment in its quest to create an all-powerful construct of the individual. He describes love as 'ein Teil der bürgerlichen Aufklärung und der bürgerlichen Verbesserung des Individuums in Hinblick auf eine geordnete Monogamie' [a part of the bourgeois enlightenment and the bourgeois improvement of the individual with regard to an ordered monogamy].[23] If love is divorced from sexuality in the works of German-language modernism, Sebald asserts that modernist literary heterosexuality itself expresses the pathology of the German bourgeois order, resting as it does on the repression of nature and on casting its colonial hinterland in Eastern Europe as its other:

> Die archetypischen Hetären, die bei Kafka, Broch, Roth, Musil, Thomas Mann und anderen mehr die Bildung beziehungsweise die Deformation der bürgerlichen Protagonisten beeinflussen, sind in aller Regel mit einem indefiniten Balkan assoziierte Sumpfkreaturen, die das in der Emanzipation begriffene Individuum zurückzuholen suchen in den Bereich seiner eigenen Vorgeschichte. Ihr unverwandter Blick repräsentiert eine nicht domestizierte Natur.[24]

> [The archetypical *hetairai* who influence the *Bildung* or the deformation of the bourgeois protagonist in Kafka, Broch, Roth, Musil Thomas Mann, and others, are as a rule swamp creatures, associated with an indefinite Balkan region, who attempt to call the individual back to the area of his own prehistory. Their fixed gaze represents an undomesticated nature.]

In contradistinction to this tendency, he praises Arthur Schnitzler in 'Das Schrecknis der Liebe' as a figure who is parallel to Freud in his critical analysis of bourgeois love. Writing about Schnitzler, Sebald expands on the notion of bourgeois love as a false metaphysical absolute that becomes made absolute in the works of German classicism, as a 'Voraussetzung jeder Individuation wie auch als das Mittel der Erlösung aus einem vereinzelten Dasein' [precondition for every individuation, as well as the means of redemption from a solitary existence] (*BU*, 38). Sebald makes explicit the sociopathic, indeed cruel, structures underlying this false metaphysical investment in heterosexual love, naming the principles of utilitarianism, self-interest, and disinterest in the fate of the other as inherent to it (*BU*, 38), and indeed stating that Schnitzler's scepticism about the ideal of love is also a critical commentary on the social order (*BU*, 55). Sebald therefore dismisses the foundational bourgeois trope of romantic love as an engine of deception and self-deception. In the next section, we will see how Sebald links this attack on patriarchy, so closely aligned to his own biography, to a pathology of Jewish assimilation in his debut monograph on the dramatist Carl Sternheim.

Jewish Assimilation: From Sternheim to Roth and Franzos

Written in 1969, before the essays analysed above, Sebald's attack on Sternheim's work, *Carl Sternheim: Kritiker und Opfer der wilhelminischen Ära* [*Carl Sternheim: Critic and Victim of the Wilhelminian Era*] contains the seeds of his future critical and poetic work. Indeed, already in this volume Sebald makes a link between the problems of late bourgeois literature, the rise of Nazism, and the bombing of Dresden, an aesthetic-political complex that was to preoccupy Sebald at the end of his life in *Luftkrieg und Literatur* [*On the Natural History of Destruction*]. Moreover, in keeping with the concerns of this chapter, *Carl Sternheim* is a document in which Sebald positions himself as a fearless critical rebel of the younger generation and mounts attacks on Sternheim's concept of individualism. As we have seen, Sebald both appropriates Adorno's method of cultural critique and attempts to go beyond it. The tone of the book is strident and confident, forming both an attack on Sternheim's work itself and on the generation of critics preceding Sebald who, in his estimation, provided an inadequate account of Sternheim's failings as a dramatist. Sebald's critical position is that of the pathologist, diagnosing Sternheim's work as symptomatic of the sickness of his age, but also of the pathology of Jewish assimilation. Although Sebald asserts in his introduction that 'this work stands on the side of Sternheim' (*Sternheim*, 11), he immediately quotes an author who is to become a figure of brotherliness throughout his work instead: Franz Kafka, writing about the Yiddish playwright Löwy. Sebald suggests that he will take the same brotherly attitude towards Sternheim that Kafka does to Löwy, despite his pathos-ridden prose:

> Auch sollen wir, wenn wir schon nicht ergriffen sind, seine Ergriffenheiten anerkennen und ihm die Möglichkeit des beschriebenen Unglücks erklären. (*Sternheim*, 11)

> [We should also, if we are not ourselves moved, recognize how he is moved, and explain to him the possibility of the depicted calamity.]

This affected brotherly warmth towards Sternheim is scarcely borne out by the rest of the text. Thus, while claiming solidarity with a writer praised by the Germanist academic establishment, Sebald at the same time demonstrates a truer brotherly affinity for Kafka, an affinity which, as I will show in Chapter 4, develops queer overtones.

A brief analysis of *Carl Sternheim* demonstrates the groundwork of Sebald's attack on the pathologies of bourgeois identity and sexuality that re-emerge in his later poetic works, while at the same time laying out his generational rebellion. The Sternheim book is written with little of the nuance and ambiguity that characterize Sebald's mature works. However, the psychosexual basis of German bourgeois identity and society, which overshadows Sebald's later work, is here revealed. Although Sebald pays lip service to the influence of the motors of capitalism and the cultural decadence that Adorno would diagnose in the dialectic of Enlightenment, the twinned concerns of psychosexual pathology and pathological textuality form the core of Sebald's attack. Sebald sets out a thoroughly revisionist agenda for his work, stating in the second paragraph of his study that his critical model demanded recourse to psychological and sociological categories, over and above traditional text-immanent interpretation. Sebald's overall thesis in his published master's dissertation, the argument that Sternheim worships 'bourgeois' values at the same time as he criticizes the Wilhelminian bourgeoisie, could equally be directed towards the critics whom he takes care to demolish. These critics, he claims, have 'keinerlei begriffliche Grundlagen außerhalb des herrschenden Systems' [no conceptual basis outside the dominant system]; they are de facto agreeing with the terms of Sternheim's own project (*Sternheim*, 17). This rebellion against the critical fathers appears in all of Sebald's early criticism. He thus sets himself up as an *enfant terrible*, rebelling against established academic practice with the critical tools of a younger generation. This *prise de position* notwithstanding, Sebald's concern turns out to be as much with the textuality of Sternheim's work as with the psychopathology of assimilation that he diagnoses. Sebald argues that Sternheim's work demonstrates that the more insignificant the aesthetic and ethical qualities of an artwork are, the more direct is its dependence on its social context (*Sternheim*, 19). Aesthetics and ethics are inextricably bound together in this view, and already at this point in Sebald's career, they trump his supposedly sociological concerns.

The sore point at which this pathology makes itself evident is in the unwholesome literary construct of the bourgeois individual, implicitly gendered as male. Indeed, Sebald argues that although Sternheim maintained that the concept of the 'individual nuance' was fundamental to his work, his dramatic figures are nothing but mouthpieces for Sternheim's own 'jargon' and pathologies, which in turn are identical with the pathological markers of late bourgeois society (*Sternheim*, 16). Identity is the paradigmatic bourgeois sickness that Sebald diagnoses at the heart of Sternheim's work: the identity of Sternheim's work with its own age, the identity of the critic with the work criticized, and the concept of 'personal identity' itself. Identity, for Sebald, leads to kitsch, and kitsch, he declares, is a moral as well as an aesthetic failure — 'das Böse im Wertsystem der Kunst' [the evil in the value system of art] (*Sternheim*, 28). This not only attempts to reconcile the irreconcilable contradictions in society, but also demonstrates the neurosis of the writer who produces kitsch. Here, Sebald declares his commitment to a 'rational' insight into the sociological conditions informing Sternheim's production of undifferentiated kitsch, which Sternheim has produced under the 'irrationalist' banner of 'art for art's sake'. Sebald is particularly concerned to unmask Sternheim's sacralized conception of art, which would suggest that artistic inspiration comes from a divine or metaphysical Beyond. As befits one who describes himself as a dialectical or material critic, Sebald states an intention to open up the contradictions in Sternheim's work and show that his more successful satirical works are only the more palatable flipside of an otherwise pathological oeuvre. This would indeed be an undertaking in the spirit of 1968: unmasking how social conditions are revealed by the fractures in Sternheim's work.

But Sebald's interest is not, after all, in tracing the sociological or material discontents of the Wilhelminian era per se: he takes it for granted that Sternheim's work is the product of a reality that had already become unbearable at the time without needing to delineate this in detail (*Sternheim*, 33). Without in detail quoting from Adorno (or Marcuse's) works, he operates from the basic assumption of a repressive world that does not permit a true independence of the individual (*Sternheim*, 33). The exact definition of this world that has become repressive is left to the reader to infer. Similarly, Sebald operates with an idiosyncratic and hugely compressed concept of German literary history. His declaration that after 1870 German literature turned away from formal innovation, and had instead taken on an 'irredeemably epigonal character' (*Sternheim*, 34) is backed up by a quote from Musil's *Der Mann ohne Eigenschaften* [The Man without Qualities], rather than from a work of literary history or a sociological text. Already, then, Sebald's work is as invested with creating or naming a self-reflexive network of congenial writers as it is with socio-political analysis. His analysis of Wilhelminian society remains indebted to a model that projects individual psychology onto a whole society, as when, for example, he cites the academic Gabel as proof of

> die Möglichkeit einer Geistesgestörtheit einer ganzen soziologischen Gemein-schaft [...] deren Symptomatik die Diagnose einer kollektiven Schizophrenie erlaubt. (*Sternheim*, 61)
>
> [the possibility of a mental disorder of a whole sociological community [...] whose symptomatics allow the diagnosis of a collective schizophrenia.]

Sebald further argues that ideology as collective madness of society has the same roots as the mental disorder of an individual: the inability to evaluate one's other objectively, that leads to viewing them only in one's own egocentric mirror (*Sternheim*, 62). Equally, Sebald sees Sternheim's Oedipus complex mirrored in Wilhelminian society as a whole, as it labours under

> einer Art Meta-Ödipus-Komplex [...], indem sie die Repression der patriarchal-ischen Staatsform in der Fiktion einer irrational-mütterlichen Urvergangenheit [...] kompensiert. (*Sternheim*, 63)
>
> [a kind of meta-Oedipus complex, [...] in that it compensates the repression of the patriarchal society with the fiction of an irrational-maternal prehistory.]

Once Sebald has established that society as a whole can be analysed with the tools of psychoanalysis, he returns to Sternheim's texts to diagnose oral fixations, voyeurism, and misogyny: if, Sebald argues, Sternheim is the 'doctor of the body of his time', his work in fact writes the death certificate of his time in advance. Sternheim's work is thus for Sebald at once the psychopathology of his own mind, and of the society in which it was written.

Thus, the construct of the bourgeois individual, rather than of bourgeois society, is the particular target of Sebald's critique. Sternheim's concept of the 'individual nuance', central to characterization in his work, reveals itself not only as connected with kitschy concepts of identity, but also, according to Sebald, with a destructive form of individualist capitalism: the characters who possess this *Nuance* are ruthless and repressive, but once they set their repressed drives free, they reveal the destructive forces which destroyed bourgeois society (*Sternheim*, 80) Further, Sebald equates Sternheim's concept of the 'individual nuance' with fiscal self-interest, and argues that, while Sternheim seems to claim that personal style and affectation distinguish the autonomous individual from the masses, they in fact only heighten the repressive power of society. This analysis is a straightforward Marxist one, and one that is congruent with that of Adorno and Horkheimer's *Dialektik der Aufklärung*: the more the bourgeois individual attempts to distinguish himself from his fellows, the more he falls into the militantly reactionary mould of masculinity laid out for him by bourgeois society. Once again, though, Sebald does not embark on any thoroughgoing analysis of the relationship between 'society' and literature. Instead, a sketchy critique of 'capitalism' (equated with financial self-interest) is quickly abandoned, and Sebald returns to a link between a 'fascist' distortion of language and the ideology of the bourgeois individual, which reveals itself as the ideology of the dominant self.

> Es zeigt sich, daß die 'eigene Nuance' Sternheimscher Charaktere immer schon vorher die 'eigene Nuance' einer ganzen Gruppe war. Sie hat faschistische Züge, selbst und gerade dort, wo sie von einem einzelnen als sein ureigenster Ausdruck proklamiert wird. (*Sternheim*, 46)

> [It is evident that the Sternheimian 'individual nuance' was always already the 'individual nuance' of a whole group. It has fascistic characteristics, even and particularly when it is proclaimed by an individual as his most personal expression.]

Individual bourgeois identity, then, is inextricably bound up with the language and practice of domination, and bourgeois values are epitomized in the repressive Wilhelminian patriarchy, which he names as a mythologized expression of late bourgeois reality, rather than a critical expression (*Sternheim*, 52).

Sebald's critical complex of the bourgeois individual, capitalism, and its apotheosis in fascism is certainly in keeping with the dictates of critical theory, but his overarching concern is with the way in which this complex it exposes the discontents of Jewish assimilation. Assimilation is worst for an artist, Sebald argues, because the artist must be outside society, and hence the Jewish artist is outside the milieu of assimilation. He therefore classes Sternheim with Kafka, Hofmannsthal, Kraus, and Proust as Jewish writers whose attempt at a 'second assimilation' to the dominant aesthetic meant that alienation became a central aesthetic principle of their writing. Sebald therefore diagnoses an Oedipus complex, which Sternheim suffered from to a 'greater than usual' extent (*Sternheim*, 52) as an explanation for Sternheim's overcompensation and over-identification with Wilhelminian society, an assimilation that goes as far as anti-Semitism. Sebald further argues that the ideology underlying Sternheim's work is pure abreaction. He transforms Sternheim's biography into allegory, arguing that he tries to escape from the dominance of his Jewish father through an over-identification with his German Protestant mother. Hence, he over-identifies with the 'maternal' myths of Germanicism, which forms the basis of 'pseudoconservatism'.[25] He argues that this compounds Sternheim's troubles, as the psychosexual complex of assimilation is structurally identical to that of the Oedipus complex, prevalent in that epoch in any case. The sexual crisis of the bourgeois self in late modernity and the crisis of Jewish assimilation are thus, in this early reading, identifiable with each other and imbricated in each other.

It is tempting to perform a similar biographical analysis of Sebald as critic himself. Certainly, the overdetermined Oedipus complex and attempt to affiliate himself to a German tradition which Sebald diagnoses in Sternheim finds its inverted parallel in his own writing. Sebald accuses Sternheim of a schizoid attack on tradition, and of hypocrisy. While, on the one hand, Sternheim claims to be a member of the avant-garde which demolishes all tradition, on the other, the attacks he levels on his once-admired Goethe, that he is superficial and kitschy, are in fact naming the flaws manifest in his own work (Sebald here adds drily, 'auch wenn man sie selbst etwas weniger arisch formulieren würde' [even if one would formulate them in a somewhat less Aryan fashion]; *Sternheim*, 71). Sternheim's attack on tradition, Sebald argues, becomes an expression of Sternheim's own *ressentiment* at his assimilation. This rebellion against a paternal tradition and attempt to affiliate himself to an alternative ideological tradition finds its dialectically inverted opposite in Sebald's own practice. Sebald's thesis is liberally scattered with a large number of references to Sebald's own alternative canon of German-Jewish literature and critical thought rather than to the canon of German letters. Thus, Sternheim, in Sebald's account, is at once worshipping and rebelling against a *Bildungstradition* [tradition of education or formation] to which, as a Jew, he has inadequately assimilated. Sebald, similarly, is rebelling against the selfsame tradition, but as a German is seeking to affiliate himself to the Jewish critical tradition represented by Adorno and Benjamin, and the German-Jewish literary tradition. The Oedipus complex thus serves both as a figure of literary criticism and as a constitutive element of the bourgeois self, as much for Sebald as for his literary object of criticism. The Jewish assimilation into bourgeois German society is as much a constitutive moment of that society as it is of modern Jewish literature, and Sebald consciously positions himself in that assimilation's wake.

A concern with the discontents of Jewish assimilation to bourgeois German culture can easily be read as a harbinger of Sebald's later poetic engagements with Holocaust memory and trauma, and yet there is also a distinctly queer twist to his attacks on the chimerical construct of German bourgeois masculinity to which Jewish artists are compelled to aspire. As we have seen from the 1989 essay on Peter Altenberg, this psychopathology of assimilation remained a concern of Sebald long after he had departed from any semblance of critical theory orthodoxy. Sebald's reading of the negative psychosexual effects of Jewish emancipation from the ghetto also emerges, in his 1989 essay 'Westwärts — Ostwärts: Aporien deutscher Ghettogeschichten', though in far more tender form, here looking at something akin to a Jewish 'Heimatliteratur in deutscher Sprache' [homeland literature in the German language].[26] The essay examines the sentimental memorializing of the abandoned East German ghetto by insecurely assimilated Jewish writers. The light of German bourgeois culture appears here as a chimera luring Jewish emigrants and writers out of the Eastern ghetto:

> das theologische Bild von der Erhellung der Finsternis wird dergestalt zur Metapher für den Anbruch des bürgerlichen Zeitalters, das sich als der Sabbat der Menschheitsgeschichte begreift. (*UH*, 48)

[the theological image of the lightening of the darkness thus becomes a metaphor for the dawn of the bourgeois age, which conceives of itself as the Sabbath of human history.]

Karl Emil Franzos's characters are eager to abandon the Hassidic tradition of scholarship for the German bourgeois canon of Heine, Klopstock, and Eichendorff, in an eagerness to overtake the level of education of the average European that, as Sebald comments, is reminiscent of the ape Rotpeter in Kafka's *Bericht für eine Akademie* (*UH*, 50). The 'sozusagen festtägliche Identifikation der Juden mit den deutschen, von Schiller vertretenen Bildungsidealen' [quasi-celebratory identification of the Jews with the German ideals of *Bildung*, as represented by Schiller] proved to be a lethal delusion. Yet the memory of the Holocaust is here less important to Sebald than the psychosexual dynamic of the ghetto narrative. Once again, assimilation to German culture is figured as an Oedipal process, whereby the Jewish protagonist appears to achieve an emancipation of the emotions by distancing himself from the Orthodox Jewish father in favour of a Gentile woman. In Leopold Kompert's *Der Dorfgeher*, Sebald notes the tension between Klara, the protagonist's middle-class love, and his Jewish father, whom he wants to describe to her. When the protagonist Emanuel returns to the Jewish ghetto, he forgets his 'natural relationship' to his father, and instead sees in him a stranger, whose secret being he must sound out and search through in order to prepare interesting remarks for his Klara (*UH*, 43). Bourgeois self-formation is here coded as a sexual and a textual production that, as Sebald points out, replaces Hassidic scholarship with a false Enlightenment ideal of objective scientific knowledge. It is also achieved by the sexual subjugation of women, which equally turns them into an object that bolsters the precarious bourgeois subject formation of the would-be assimilated Jew. If the path for Jewish men into German society in Franzos's work is through learning, Sebald remarks, the path for Jewish women is coded as that of 'love', or, as Sebald puts it, a fleshly transaction. Sebald here unmasks the bourgeois ideology of love, or its literary expression in the ghetto story as the emancipation of feeling, as a sordid sexual transaction, and the path to bourgeois assimilation as irretrievably gendered.

> die schönen jungen Frauen stehen natürlich für die verlorene Heimat, die häßlichen alten Männer jedoch für die Angst, daß man aller Bemühung zum Trotz noch lange nicht bürgerlich genug ist. (*UH*, 59)

> [the beautiful young women stand, of course, for the lost homeland, but the ugly old men for the fear that despite all efforts one is by far not bourgeois enough.]

The bourgeois trope of the emancipation of feeling reveals itself as the emancipation of money, and thus the ascent to German selfhood is achieved by rejecting the Jewish Orthodox father and Orthodox learning and aspiring instead to Western literature and Western capitalism. It also instates a hegemonic form of masculinity that subjugates women in its wake.

So far, Sebald's account of the tropes and structures underlying the discontents of Jewish assimilation to German bourgeois society in this essay are not dissimilar those that he detects in Carl Sternheim's work. The significance of the essay for the present study lies in its introduction of the two themes of Thanatos and brotherly or queer Eros, the tensions between which constitute much of Sebald's later poetic work. Firstly, reading *Das Christusbild*, he notes that the narrator can never really return to the ghetto, as death is in fact the natural province of the homecomer. What Sheppard names as the 'pull of Thanatos, that Max [Sebald] saw as the dominant principle behind the Symbolic Order' which underpins the German bourgeois soul is, however, counterbalanced in Joseph Roth's *Das falsche Gewicht*.[27] This, too, deals with the discontents of assimilation and deceptive hypocrisies of bourgeois love. However, Sebald here detects a moment of resistance to these ideologies in Roth's tale. Sebald declares that, in opposition to the dissolution of the bourgeois dream of love in the realist literature of the nineteenth century, which is still in thrall to the ideology of love, Roth creates 'die Geschichte einer aus allen Konventionen ausbrechenden männlichen Passion' [the story of a manly passion that breaks out of all conventions] (*UH*, 61). Sebald continues to describe how, instead of being angry at his rival for the love of the seductive Euphemia, Sameschkin, the protagonist Eibenschütz begins, in time, to love him, 'wie man einen Bruder liebt' [as one loves a brother] (*UH*, 61). Brotherly love in Roth's fictional Eastern province of Zolotograd proves a way to undermine the patriarchal logic of bourgeois manhood and heterosexual rivalry: 'In dem weit zurückliegenden Land, das dem Erzähler Roth vorschwebt, lösen sich die Herrschafts- und Besitzansprüche der Männer von selber auf' [In the far-flung land that Roth has in mind, men's claims to domination and possession dissolve of their own accord] (*UH*, 62). In this brotherly paradise, love itself is no longer an exclusive exchange; instead of the capitalist economy of calculation and sale, much is given and forgiven, and in place of the Enlightenment yearning for German bourgeois *Bildung*, a Talmudic form of learning takes place, 'das nicht auf ein besseres Fortkommen in dieser Welt, sondern höchstens auf ein gutes Fortkommen aus ihr bedacht ist' [that is not intent on better progress in this world, but at the most on a good progress out of it] (*UH*, 62). This natural way of things, Sebald concludes, still causes us to suffer, but far greater injustice and misery emanate from the so-called progress of civilization and the increase of law and order (*UH*, 63). Brotherly love literally forms the threshold to this older, more humane order of things in the lost Jewish ghetto. It is the key to resistance to the hegemonic sexualities that constitute the bourgeois order.

The language that Sebald uses to describe this moment of Jewish brotherly love in Roth is notably erotically charged — a 'passion' that 'breaks out of all conventions'. It contrasts sharply with the language with which the younger Sebald dismissed Carl Sternheim's descriptions of 'eine bereits in ihrem Entstehen von der repressiven Moral der Gesellschaft zur Perversion verurteilte Sexualität' [a sexuality which, already as it is developing, is condemned to become a perversion by the repressive morality of society] (*Sternheim*, 46). For Sebald, Roth's liminal 'manly passion' is not a product of the Freudian mechanisms of repression and neurosis, but an affect that opens the border between the bourgeois self and its discontents, and the 'natural' world of the Jewish ghetto. Daniel Boyarin has analysed the cultural significance of this manly passion on the threshold of the return to the ghetto, in

his analysis of the rise of heterosexuality and the invention of the 'manly' Jew.[28]
Like Sebald, Boyarin views the Haskalah and the end of Ashkenaz ghetto culture in
Eastern Europe with scepticism.[29] He locates Freud's construction of the Oedipus
complex precisely in its late nineteenth-century cultural context and in the context
of Freud's own biography, as a second-generation Jewish immigrant to the Viennese
bourgeoisie. For Boyarin, the move out of the ghetto and into bourgeois Viennese
society is coeval with and inescapably embroiled in the invention of the categories
of heterosexuality and homosexuality. Michel Foucault theorized that these sexual
categories were produced by disciplinary power discourses in the late nineteenth
century. As Long has shown, Sebald's critical writings 'demonstrate a sustained
engagement with Foucault at a point where French theory had yet to make any
significant impact on German studies in Britain, but evince also a desire to escape
the totalising account of power that Foucault offers'.[30] Certainly, Sebald's account
of the oppressive system of power and of the disciplining systems of gender, which
face the assimilating Jewish writer, is indeed Foucauldian, and his understanding of
the genealogy of nineteenth-century sexual practices comes directly from Foucault.
In his copy of Foucault's *Wahnsinn und Gesellschaft* [*Madness and Civilization*], for
instance, the following passage is underlined: '

> Der Sadismus ist nicht ein Name, der schließlich einer ebenso alten Praktik,
> wie der Eros ist, gegeben wurde, sondern eine massive zivilisatorische Tatsache,
> die genau am Ende des achtzehnten Jahrhunderts erschienen ist und eine der
> größten Wandlungen der abendländischen Vorstellungskraft bildet.[31]

> [Sadism is not a name finally given to a practice as old as Eros; it is a massive
> cultural fact which appeared precisely at the end of the eighteenth century, and
> which constitutes one of the great conversions of Western imagination.[32]]

The underlining suggests that Sebald derives his disciplinary understanding of
the production of modernist sexualities from Foucault, and also that, despite the
perverse practices of modernity, Sebald views Eros as a fundamental, possibly even
mythical, element of human being.

   Boyarin views the late nineteenth-century development of heterosexuality as a
process to which Freud actively contributed, by constructing the Oedipus complex
as the gateway to adult heterosexuality for the 'normal' Gentile man. Boyarin shows
how Freud's attachment to the Oedipus complex was informed by the very specific
fear of being classed as an 'unmanly' Jew by the growing misogynist and anti-
Semitic taxonomies of the 1890s. Whereas his early theories of hysteria were based
on the idea of child seduction by the father, and carried with them the potential
of a queer moment of desire, Freud abandoned them in favour of the impeccably
heterosexual theory of neurosis. Boyarin suggests that this move was allied to
Freud's anxiety about the trope of the unmanly Jew, which was in part constructed
by the disciplinary practices of bourgeois modernity which demonized the 'Eastern
Jew' as feminine, and in part arose from the genuinely different traditional
Ashkenaz ideal of manliness, that of the gentle, melancholy scholar. Thus, Boyarin
argues, for Freud, abandoning ghetto culture meant hastily discarding this queered
Jewish identity for precisely that patriarchal bourgeois structure of the self that
Sebald excoriates in his literary criticism. 'The Oedipus complex is Freud's family

romance of escape from Jewish queerdom into gentile, phallic heterosexuality', states Boyarin — not least because it is the 'fantasy of a masculinity rendered virile through both of its moments, the desire for the mother (not the father) and violent hostility towards the father'.[33]

This reading of the construction of the Oedipus complex in its cultural context of the unhappy path away from the Eastern European ghetto to a mimicry of a normative gentile heterosexuality shows the true significance of the liminal masculine passion that Sebald celebrates in Roth's work. In Sebald's account, Eibenschütz achieves the return to the 'natural' order of orthodox Jewish life and death via his transgressive queer passion for Sameschkin and refusal of the structural principles of Oedipus to which other fictional and literary representatives of assimilated Jewry fall prey. He thereby achieves an escape from the Austrian patriarchal order in which military men are supposed to be rivals for the love of women whom they ultimately subjugate. In Sebald's reading, the queer moment of passage leads to the redemption of the returning Jew by overturning the regulative order of capitalist society. 'Zum Zeichen, daß er erlöst ist, sagt der Eichmeister Singer zum Händler Eibenschütz, daß alle seine Gewichte falsch und dennoch richtig seien' [As a sign that he is redeemed, the calibrator Singer says to the pedlar Eibenschütz that all his weights are false and still correct] (*UH*, 62). Sebald ends his reading of *Das falsche Gewicht* by himself taking up the position of a queer voyeur, at once admiring and bearing witness to Eastern European Jewish manhood in the photographs of Roman Vishniak, taken in 1939. In these photographs, Sebald writes, are many 'in ihrer Tiefgründigkeit wahrhaft schönen Männergesichten' [male faces, truly beautiful in their profundity] (*UH*, 63). Sebald's eye does not linger on the beauty of the male faces, though, but instead he notes with Roland Barthes that photographs signify death, and speculates that these men almost with certainty died untimely and violent deaths. Only in literature, Sebald is suggesting here, can queer desire arrest the genocidal forward drive of history and open a door into the compassionate Jewish past.

Over the Border: Peter Handke as Case Study of Queer Masculinity and Reconciliation

This suggestive reference to the redemptive power of the queer affiliation — the homophile gaze or feeling of brotherhood — is developed further in a later essay in *Unheimliche Heimat* where Sebald views queer desire as a gateway to a timeless land of reconciliation, 'Jenseits der Grenze: Peter Handkes Erzählung *Die Wiederholung*' [Over the Border: Peter Handke's Novel *Repetition*].[34] Here, he makes explicit that such a redemption can only be found in the text itself, while writing suggestively about the power of homophile moments to open up spaces of beauty in the text itself that arrest any catastrophic conception of history. He describes Handke's novel *Die Wiederholung* as a narrative that is in itself a redemptive space for lives that have been erased by the destructive progress of history. It is worth quoting at length from this essay to understand Sebald's familial-textual idea of redemption:

> In der messianischen Tradition kommt es weniger darauf an, daß die

Getrennten einander endlich in die Arme sinken, als darauf, daß die Anstren-
gung aufrechterhalten wird, daß der Jüngere die Nachfolge des Älteren antritt,
daß der Schüler zum Lehrer und daß der fromme Erlösungswunsch, die von
Gregor in einem seiner Frontbriefe ausgesprochene Hoffnung auf die gemein-
same Fahrt in der geschmückten Osterkalesche in das neunte Land, übertragen
wird 'in die irdische Erfüllung: die Schrift'.

   Im Text der Wiederholung konstituiert sich diese Erfüllung. Das Buch ist
die Osterkalesche, in der die einander abhanden gekommenen Mitglieder der
Kobal-Familie noch einmal beisammensitzen. (*UH*, 175)

> [In the messianic tradition, it is less important that those who are separated
> finally fall into each other's arms, than that the struggle is maintained, that
> youth steps into the succession of age, that the pupil becomes a teacher, and
> that the pious wish for redemption, the hope expressed by Gregor in one of his
> letters from the front for a communal ride in the decorated Easter carriage, is
> translated 'into earthly fulfilment: writing'.
>
> In the text of *Repetition*, this fulfilment is constituted. The book is the Easter
> carriage, in which the members of the Kobal family who had lost each other sit
> next to each other once more.]

Sebald's reading of *Die Wiederholung* transforms Handke's novel, about a young
Austrian-Slovenian man's journey to the Slovenian Karst in search of the traces
of his lost brother Gregor, into a text of Jewish redemption. In his reading, Filip
Kobal's journey from Austria to Slovenia is similar to Eibenschütz's journey back
to the Zolotograd ghetto, a journey back from the patriarchal world of German
history (here, post-Nazi Austria) to an ahistorical land of peace. Moreover, Sebald's
ecstatic reading of the text equates the Slovenian people with the 'exemplary
exile people' of the Jews, and makes Filip Kobal's family their representatives
and redeemers, by a somewhat wilful reading of their 'familial mythology' (*UH*,
173). Sebald's essay interprets *Die Wiederholung* as a redemptive text in which Filip
overcomes the burden of Austrian historical inheritance not only to recover the
past, but also to deliver his Kobal family into Slovenia. Handke's text itself, Sebald
suggests, is a redemptive space:

> [es] gelingt ihm, den Text selber zu einem Schutzort zu machen in den von
> Tag zu Tag auch im Kulturbetrieb weiter um sich greifenden ariden Zonen.
> (*UH*, 178)
>
> [he succeeds in making the text itself a refuge in the arid zones which grow
> wider from day to day, even in the culture industry.]

Thus, his interpretation of Handke's Slovenia is very similar to his reading of
Roth's Zolotograd ghetto, a place of 'peaceful union' that, again, gives hope
for the redemption of 'our natural *Heimat*'.[35] Again, as with *Das falsche Gewicht*,
Sebald reads Handke's text as a journey 'von der Angst der Väter ihren Ausgang
nehmenden und über ganz Europa sich ausbreitenden Gewalt' [a violence that
proceeds from fear of the fathers and which spreads out over all of Europe] (*UH*,
170). Sebald claims that *Die Wiederholung* describes instead a voyage into a utopian,
non-patriarchal Slovenian order in which fathers play at most a subordinate role,
particularly as Filip's father is Austrian but his mother is Slovenian. Once again,
the family order serves as a metaphor for the space of history. However, although

in this essay the idea of a return to a matriarchy is coded in redemptive terms, as opposed to the mythical and hence destructive Bachofenian matriarchy present in late modernist texts, an overdetermined power of redemption is also here ascribed to a notion of brotherliness in Handke's novel. Matriarchy is redeemed both by its role as a repository of ethnic and cultural identity, here coded as both Slovenian and Jewish, and also by its closeness to brotherhood. Sebald selects the scenes in *Die Wiederholung* where Filip is united with other men for particular attention. For him, they are signs of a matriarchal utopia where people are

> ein jeder fast der Bruder des anderen. Etwas davon leuchtet auf in der Begegnung Filip Kobals mit anderen männlichen Figuren in der archaischen Landschaft des Karsts. Der ihm als Doppelgänger seiner selbst erscheinende junge Soldat von Vipava wäre hier ebenso zu nennen wie die Gestalt des Kellners aus der Wochein. (*UH*, 170)

> [each almost the brother of their neighbour. Something of this shines forth in Filip Kobal's meetings with other male figures in the archaic landscape of Karst. The young soldier from Vipava, who appears to him as a doppelganger of himself, could be named here, as well as the figure of the waiter from Wochein.]

Handke's portrait of this waiter exemplifies Sebald's conception of poetic reconciliation through brotherhood.

> Dieser Kellner, dessen Porträt mit größter Hingabe entworfen wird, ist eine veritable Imago des Ideals der Brüderlichkeit. [...] Es gehört mit zum Schönsten in der deutschsprachigen Literatur des letzten Jahrzehnts, wie die Geschichte des Kellners auf drei, vier Seiten von Handke entwickelt wird. (*UH*, 171)

> [This waiter, whose portrait is delineated with the greatest devotion, is a veritable imago of the ideal of brotherliness. [...] How Handke develops the story of the waiter over three or four pages is among the most beautiful things in German-language literature of the last decades.]

The story of the young waiter is indeed described in lyrical prose, and Filip's feelings towards him verge on the homoerotic: he thinks of the waiter constantly, more than of his parents or girlfriend, and realizes that this is a form of love. This liminal homophilia, on the border between brotherliness and queer passion, is thus clearly distinguished both from heterosexual and from filial love. Sebald comments on this privileged affect, linking it to textuality by stating that the plates which the beloved waiter flings into a stream are like the sentence arcs of the narrator, 'messages of brotherliness' (*UH*, 171). Thus, as in his reading of Roth's short story, 'brotherliness' and male love — indeed, the male/male gaze — serves for Sebald as the sign and path to a redemptive, Jewish landscape beyond history.

Sebald's attachment to a novel that describes an affective constellation of a beloved male ancestor, spectral mother, and homosexual fixation repeats a pattern that is endemic in Sebald's fiction. Discussing *Die Ausgewanderten*, Maya Barzilai points out that (illicit) homosocial desire of the German narrator for the Jewish characters whose lives he narrates lies behind and is often mediated by relations with women who are either dying or spectral. She argues that while the main protagonists of Sebald's work are male, women appear 'either as conduits of male memory or as dead mothers/lovers', so that Sebald leads us to conclude that 'in the German imagination Jewish difference continues to be configured as both feminine and homosexual'.[36] Barzilai concludes that Sebald's deployment of age-old anti-Semitic clichés of the 'queer' or 'feminine' Jew reinstates German male anxiety as the sole filter through which the past can be viewed. A similar troublesome complex of Jewish identity and, here, romanticized Slovenian otherness is at play in Sebald's interpretation of Handke.

In Handke's text, a reunion with his doppelganger (the young soldier from Vipava, mentioned above), while it is initially homoerotic, appears as a transient stage in the larger project of a reintegration of the poetic self. The section describing Filip's encounter with the soldier moves from the first to the third person, as the narrator pulls back from his fragmented, subjective first-person narration and is able to view himself as a unitary entity, a 'he' who has a describable identity. Watching the soldier from behind, the narrator writes that this self will finally be able to discover who he was, for the first time in his life. Even watching the soldier without speaking to him, Filip is able to retrieve the traumatic memory of being bullied from his childhood, and describe a reunion that reunites his fragmented self in an imagined narrative scenario.[37] Filip's poetic reunion with his childhood enemy heals those conflicts that Webber identifies as inherent in the apparition of the doppelganger, in particular, the doppelganger as symbol of the conflict between the Romantic and the real, and as symbol of the *unheimlich*, the conflict between the desire to return home and the fear of the return of the repressed.[38] At the end of *Die Wiederholung*, Filip returns to his family home, and confronts the primal scene of his parents in the marital bed. In Freudian terms, the sight of his parents in the marital bed would trigger the primal trauma of the male child, but the union of his parents now appears to the returning Filip more as a sacrament. Returning home and confronting the primal completes Filip's development from a child who resented his father's peasant origins, and wished to be entirely without origins, to a loyal son. At the end of the novel, Filip's Slovenian mother is dying, and Filip reintegrates his paternal, Austrian identity with his maternal Slovenian one.

Sebald's reading of Handke's narrative enforces upon it a messianic and Jewish model for which the text itself provides only some justification. In Handke's text, as we have seen, the encounter with the soldier, while initially homoerotic, appears as a transient stage in the larger project of a reintegration of the individual poetic self, and indeed a move away from his family of origin, which Sebald so admires in his critical essay. Thus, the novel is far more ambivalent in both its psychodynamic and its political content than Sebald's essay would indicate. It is neither a rejection of Austrian-German ancestry, nor a particularly queer or maternal text. Further, the driving affect of brotherly love also becomes less urgent towards the end of the novel, as Filip realizes he is unlikely to find convincing traces of his own brother and instead gains maturity as a poet. These distortions in Sebald's reading suggest that when Sebald characterizes Handke's entire oeuvre as 'eine möglichst weitgehende Entfernung von der deutschen Abstammung väterlichseits' [the greatest possible distancing from German descent on the father's side], this may be a projection of Sebald's own troubled relationship with his German paternal inheritance, rather than an accurate description of Handke's rich and complex poetic project (*UH*, 170). In his critical work, Sebald allows himself to be far more affirmative and polemic about the possibility of redemption than he does in his own poetic texts, as well as far more explicit about the burden of a German paternal inheritance.

Beginning the Line of Flight: Schnitzler and Incest

Brotherly love, as we have seen in Sebald's discussion on Roth and Handke, is an affect of reconciliation and compassion that can heal the wounds of history and of ethnic division. However, as he tells us in his essay on *Andreas*, sometimes the line between redemptive brotherhood and a mode of transgressive, destructive incest is very fine.

> Das Motiv der Geschwisterliebe ist in der gesamten erzählerischen Literatur des 19. Jahrhunderts von zentraler Bedeutung, sowohl als Chiffre erotischer Utopie als auch als das Exempel für die durch nichts mehr gutzumachende Transgression.[39]
>
> [The motif of sibling love is of central importance in the entirety of nineteenth-century narrative literature, as a cipher for erotic utopia as well as the example for the utterly irredeemable transgression.]

This liminal idea of incest also appears in Sebald's essay on Schnitzler, 'Das Schrecknis der Liebe: Zu Schnitzlers *Traumnovelle*' [The Terror of Love: On Schnitzler's *Dream Story*], which touches on the disruptive potential of incest to undermine the repressive edifice of bourgeois love. The main argument of the essay forms a part of Sebald's attack on the psychopathology of the bourgeois self; it declares that bourgeois love is a form of secularized metaphysics that is at odds with the utilitarian ethos of the capitalist nineteenth century. Schnitzler's work provides particularly important evidence for the growing *fin-de-siècle* scepticism about bourgeois love, he argues, and for how the romantic, military masculine ideal that dominated the nineteenth century was increasingly undermined by the twin threats of the marketization of sex and of syphilis. While Schnitzler reflected the conventional patriarchal ideas about love in his private papers, Sebald argues that his literary texts go beyond convention to function as case studies similar to those of Freud. Sebald argues that Schnitzler's interest in the disruptive figures of the hysterical woman, the masturbating child, the Malthusian couple, and the perverse adult becomes a criticism not only of the ideal of love, but also of the whole of society. To these four totemic figures of disruptive sexuality, a fifth could be added, that of the incestuous siblings, who are hinted at but not explored further in the essay. The hint emerges in Sebald's analysis of Schnitzler's *Traumnovelle*, where he devotes a section to a picture of a man in uniform painted by Marianne's missing brother, who is now 'somewhere abroad' (*BU*, 46). Sebald writes that this portrait contains a fetishistic value, equal to the fetishistic value of Gregor Samsa's portrait of the woman in furs in *Die Verwandlung* [*The Metamorphosis*], to which Gregor clings when his parents are clearing out his room. For Sebald, Schnitzler's photograph is significant because in the *Traumnovelle* it is linked to an amorous adventure with a chevalier in uniform. Sebald suggests that the fetishization of the uniformed man represents a form of imperial nostalgia, a yearning for an *ancien régime* that is now in fact past; the last gasp of the authoritative man in uniform is the *flâneur* with his fetishistic apparatus of the cane (*BU*, 49). Thus, he suggests that the photo represents the bourgeois woman's typical desire for 'vom Geschichtsverlauf relegiertes männliches Wesen' [a male being who has been relegated by the course of history] (*BU*, 48). Sebald comments that the picture demonstrates 'daß die größte Sehnsucht auch immer die unstatthafteste ist' [that the greatest yearning is always also the least permissible] (*BU*, 47). Sibling incest here seems to be one more distasteful manifestation of the perversions of sexuality in late bourgeois society, and one more proof of the frailty of the patriarchal ideal of love, not dissimilar to the growth in prostitution also caused by the hypocrisies of bourgeois marriage.

However, Sebald does not end his analysis of the picture here, and its significance goes beyond that of a cypher for a bankrupt ideology. As we know from his earlier essay on Ernst Herbeck, by the time of writing this essay Sebald had already engaged with Deleuze and Guattari's *Kafka: Towards a Minor Literature*, which begins with a discussion of this very portrait in *Die Verwandlung*. Sebald particularly invites a connection to Deleuze and Guattari through his reference to Gregor's fetishistic portrait of a woman in furs. Deleuze and Guattari characterize the scene where Gregor clings to this picture, while listening to the sound of his sister's violin, as a moment that shows the difference between 'a plastic and still Oedipal incest with a maternal photo and a schizo-incest with the sister'.[40] Deleuze and Guattari then go on to define schizo-incest as 'a desire that straightens up or moves forward, and opens up to new connections, [...] deterritorialization'.[41] Sebald's description of the portrait of a man in uniform leaping down a hill suggests that Schnitzler's picture also contains both of these meanings: Marianne's overt patriarchal or Oedipal desire for a military chevalier, but also an incestuous desire for the artist-brother who painted the picture and who has managed to escape beyond the boundaries of Vienna. The leaping man may be confined within an imperial uniform, but his undisciplined movement suggests that, like Marianne's brother, he may be moving away from the disciplinary gestures of military masculinity and attempting a line of escape. In Sebald's reading, the warlike portrait only ostensibly binds the young woman Marianne back into the Oedipal patriarchy of *fin-de-siècle* Vienna, where desire's object is ultimately death alone, while still containing the disruptive possibility of a form of liberation thanks to an incestuous connection with the deterritorialized artist brother.

In this chapter, we have seen how Sebald's line of escape away from German patriarchy and towards the borders of masculinity, over which Jewish identity and queer love lie, developed in the first stages of his critical career. His youthful commitment to a politicized literary analysis informed by Adornian dialectics combined with a critical attack on patriarchy in modernist literature. Sebald attacked not only the literary construct of the German male, but also the psychopathology of Jewish assimilation to German patriarchal culture, visible in the writings of writers like Sternheim. His later critical essays explore alternative models of masculinity that refuse to continue the patriarchal reproduction of bourgeois society, and instead cross the boundary of the ghetto, in Roth and Franzos, and of Slovenia in Handke, to seek out a form of brotherly love there. These essays delineate literary utopias where brotherly love and desire cross. Even in his essay on Schnitzler, which roundly attacks the hypocritical construct of bourgeois love and late bourgeois masculinity, traces of his reading of Deleuze and Guattari can be seen, which promise a line of escape from these repressive Oedipal structures. By the time that he had published *Die Beschreibung des Unglücks* and *Unheimliche Heimat* — the early 1990s — and started on his own poetic project, Sebald was no longer the Adornian son rebelling in step with the rest of his generation (which also includes Peter Handke) against the toxic Nazi legacy in modernist literature and in the Germanist establishment. Instead, he has worked out elements of a non-Oedipal Eros of resistance that is saturated with brotherly affects, at times troubled by the temptation of incest, frequently Jewish and often queer. It is now time to turn to his poetic texts to see how this sexuality manifests itself as a moment of resistance in what is, after all, not so Thanatic a poetic project.

Notes to Chapter 1

1. Sebald, 'Peter Altenberg — Le Paysan de Vienne', in *Unheimliche Heimat*, pp. 65–86 (p. 79).
2. Sebald acquired and intensively studied works by Adorno, Benjamin, Bloch, Horkheimer, and Marcuse as a student. *Minima Moralia* was of particular importance for him. Richard Sheppard, 'The Sternheim Years: W. G. Sebald's *Lehrjahre* and *Theatralische Sendung* 1963–75', in *Saturn's Moons: A W. G. Sebald Handbook*, ed. by Jo Catling and Richard Hibbitt (Oxford: Legenda, 2011), pp. 42–80 (p. 53).
3. Ibid., p. 62.
4. Heinz Bude, *Bilanz der Nachfolge: Die Bundesrepublik und der Nationalsozialismus* (Frankfurt a. M.: Suhrkamp, 1992), pp. 88–89.
5. Morgan, 'The Sign of Saturn', p. 81.
6. Maya Jaggi, 'Recovered Memories'.
7. Marco Poltronieri, 'Wie kriegen die Deutschen das auf die Reihe? Ein Gespräch mit W. G. Sebald', in *W. G. Sebald* (Porträt 7), ed. by Franz Loquai (Eggingen: Isele, 1997), pp. 138–44 (p. 140).
8. Ibid., p. 139.
9. Hutchinson, *W. G. Sebald*, p. 19.
10. Lorenz Jäger, *Adorno: A Political Biography*, trans. by Stewart Spencer (New Haven: Yale University Press, 2004), p. 180.
11. Ibid., p. 180.
12. Marcel Atze and Sven Meyer, '"Unsere Korrespondenz": Zum Briefwechsel zwischen W. G. Sebald und Theodor W. Adorno', in *Sebald: Lektüren*, ed. by Marcel Atze and Franz Loquai (Eggingen: Edition Isele, 2005), pp. 17–38.
13. Theodor W. Adorno, *Minima Moralia: Reflections on a Damaged Life*, trans. by E. F. N. Jephcott (London: Verso, 2005), p. 157.
14. 'Unsere Korrespondenz', p. 12. Translation mine.
15. Ibid., p. 14.
16. Sheppard, 'Dexter — Sinister', p. 419.
17. Sebald, 'Mord an den Vätern: Bemerkungen zu einigen Dramen der spätbürgerlichen Zeit', *Neophilologus*, 60 (1976), 432–41.
18. Ibid., p. 432. Translation mine.
19. Ibid., p. 433.
20. Ibid., p. 435.
21. Ibid., p. 437.
22. W. G. Sebald, 'Die Mädchen aus der Feenwelt — Bemerkungen zu Liebe und Prostitution mit Bezügen zu Raimund, Schnitzler und Horvath', *Neophilologus*, 67 (1983), 109–17, and 'Das

Schrecknis der Liebe: Zu Schnitzlers *Traumnovelle*', in *Die Beschreibung des Unglücks*, pp. 38–60 (p. 38).

23. Sebald, 'Die Mädchen aus der Feenwelt', p. 112. Translation mine.

24. Ibid.

25. Sebald quotes extensively from *The Authoritarian Personality* at this point to support his argument, a quotation that perhaps leads him into what is one of the few unreservedly positive appraisals of the bourgeois tradition in his entire work. 'Die wilhelminische Gesellschaft kompensierte im Kult der germanischen Urvergangenheit den Verlust ihrer tatsächlichen, positiv bürgerlichen Tradition, der von der Repression einer autoritär-patriarchalischen Staatsform erzwungen worden war' [Wilhelminian society used the cult of a Germanic prehistory to compensate the loss of its real, positive bourgeois tradition, which was forced by the repression of an authoritarian and patriarchal state structure] (*Sternheim*, p. 52). The 'positive bourgeois tradition' referred to here is not further explicated, but the formulation seems to be far from the ethical position of eccentric melancholy acknowledged as a constitutive element in Sebald's work by many critics.

26. *Unheimliche Heimat*, pp. 40–64 (p. 40).

27. Sheppard, 'Dexter — Sinister', p. 442.

28. Daniel Boyarin, 'Freud's Baby, Fliess's Maybe: Homophobia, Anti-Semitism, and the Invention of Oedipus', *GLQ*, 2 (1995), 115–47.

29. Matti Bunzl, 'Jews, Queers, and Other Symptoms: Recent Work in Jewish Cultural Studies', *GLQ*, 6 (2000), 321–41 (p. 330).

30. Long, *Image, Archive, Modernity*, p. 16.

31. Michel Foucault, *Wahnsinn und Gesellschaft: Eine Geschichte des Wahns im Zeitalter der Vernunft*, trans. by Ulrich Köppen (Frankfurt a. M.: Suhrkamp, 1972), p. 367.

32. Michel Foucault, *Madness and Civilization: A History of Insanity in the Age of Reason*, trans. by Richard Howard, with an introduction by David Cooper (London: Routledge, 2001), p. 199.

33. Boyarin, 'Freud's Baby, Fliess's Maybe', p. 134.

34. *Unheimliche Heimat*, pp. 162–78.

35. See Helen Finch, 'Die irdische Erfüllung: Peter Handke's Poetic Landscapes and W. G. Sebald's Metaphysics of History', in *W. G. Sebald and the Writing of History*, ed. by Anne Fuchs and J. J. Long (Würzburg: Königshausen & Neumann, 2007), pp. 179–97.

36. Barzilai, 'Facing the Past and the Female Spectre', p. 215.

37. Peter Handke, *Die Wiederholung* (Frankfurt a. M.: Suhrkamp, 1986), p. 256.

38. Andrew J. Webber, *The Doppelgänger: Double Visions in German Literature* (Oxford: Clarendon, 1996), pp. 3ff.

39. 'Venezianisches Kryptogramm: Hofmannsthal's *Andreas*', in *Die Beschreibung des Unglücks*, pp. 61–77 (p. 71).

40. Deleuze and Guattari, *Kafka*, p. 3.

41. Ibid., p. 4.

CHAPTER 2

Bachelors in Feather Boas:
Masculinity Gone Astray

The Beast with Two Backs at Covehithe

Sebald's critical writing may be saturated in sexuality, but his poetic writing at times shrinks fastidiously from sex, as from something dark or grotesque. *Die Ringe des Saturn* presents an explicit condemnation of sexual intercourse in an intertextual quote from Jorge Luis Borges's short story 'Tlön, Uqbar, Orbis Tertius':

> Bioy Casares erinnerte demzufolge, einer der Häresiarchen von Uqbar habe erklärt, das Grauenerregende an den Spiegeln, und im übrigen auch an dem Akt der Paarung, bestünde darin, daß sie die Zahl der Menschen vervielfachen.
>
> [Bioy Casares then recalled the observation of one of the heresiarchs of Uqbar, that mirrors and copulation are abominable, because they increase the number of mankind.] (*RS*, 90; *RSe*, 70)

In *Die Ringe des Saturn*, the Sebaldian narrator calls up this intertextual reference while remembering a walk on the cliffs of Covehithe, where he sees 'ein Mann, ausgestreckt über dem Körper eines andren Wesens, von dem nichts sichtbar war als die angewinkelten, nach außen gekehrten Beine' [a man stretched full length over another body of which nothing was visible but the legs, spread and angled] (*RS*, 88; *RSe*, 68). This ghastly, seemingly cannibalistic vision reveals itself as something almost as uncanny, the beast with two backs:

> Ungestalt gleich einer großen, ans Land geworfenen Molluske lagen sie da, scheinbar ein Leib, ein von weit draußen hereingetriebenes, vielgliedriges, doppelköpfiges Seeungeheuer, letztes Exemplar einer monströsen Art, das mit flach den Nüstern entströmendem Atem seinem Ende entgegendämmert.
>
> [Misshapen, like some great mollusc washed ashore, they lay there, to all app-earances a single being, a many-limbed, two-headed monster that had drifted in from far out at sea, the last of a prodigious species, its life ebbing from it with each breath expired through its nostrils.]

The monstrous and Thanatic dimensions that this simple act of heterosexual inter-course takes on in *Die Ringe des Saturn* can be explained when we consider Sebald's critical attacks on reproductive sexuality. Indeed, copulation has also been associated with the monstrous earlier in the book, when the Sebaldian narrator complains that in today's 'nature' television programmes, one is more likely to see some monster at the bottom of Lake Baikal coupling than a normal blackbird (*RS*, 33; *RSe*, 22). Sebald also alludes to this monstrous aspect of human reproduction in his essay on Elias Canetti, where he notes that the metabolism of nature is just as monstrous a force of oppression as human systems of power. Both procreation and fatherhood, Sebald argues, play their part in this universal system of repression, to which victims of power such as Canetti are particularly sensitive. 'Die natürliche Prokreation, die Liebe, ist ihnen ein illusionärer Trost' [natural procreation, love, is an illusory consolation for them], Sebald claims.[1] Far from offering consolation, procreation is part of the natural machinery of oppression, as it occurs in the interior of nature's all-encompassing, monstrous digestive system. Human reproduction is therefore linked not to any beautiful natural order, in this essay, but to a destructive, Thanatic one. Sebald argues that this view leads Canetti to hope for redemption rather than reform in his political writings, and to maintain an implacable opposition to death. If a sexuality that leads to redemptive hope is possible, it does not encompass heterosexual copulation.

At Covehithe, the woman, conventionally positioned underneath the man, appears as something inhuman, a being that is headless and abject. The man's foot twitches like that of a just-hanged man, suggesting that the act of heterosexual copulation is indeed a *petit mort*. It renders copulation an act of punishment not unlike the dissection of Aris Kindt subsequent to his execution, which is a central concern of the first section of *Die Ringe des Saturn*. But is this monstrous scene at Covehithe, as Christian Moser suggests, a general recoiling from the 'atavistic, brutish and violent elements inherent in the human act of love', or does it specifically recoil from heterosexual copulation?[2] The merging of the lovers is so disturbing that the liminal space of the cliff becomes uncanny and unreal to the Sebaldian narrator. Musing on the scene later, the Sebaldian narrator wonders whether he has not entirely imagined it. He compares this possible invention to the idealist constructions invented by the heresiarchs of Uqbar in Borges's short story, which are in danger of blotting out the real world.[3] 'Tlön, Uqbar, Orbis Tertius' becomes a figure for two forms of redemption in Sebald's work. Firstly, Sebald uses Borges's story to hint at the redemptive potential of memory in the face of the destruction of the material world.[4] In Borges's imaginary world of Tlön, things 'tend to grow vague or "sketchy," and to lose detail when they begin to be forgotten', but memory can save objects from destruction, even the memory of beasts such as horses or birds.[5] This conceit explains the maxim cited by Bioy Casares, that mirrors and copulation are abominable. Mirrors create a world of destructive illusion, and are therefore to be resisted in favour of the redemptive power of memory. The imperative to resist copulation, or fatherhood, as Borges's second version of the maxim has it, is equally critical to Sebald's project of resisting the totalizing, idealist labyrinth of Enlightenment that Tlön symbolizes.

In the previous chapter, I traced Sebald's resistance to the bourgeois order and the bourgeois family in his early critical works. In this chapter, I show how a queer imperative to resist heterosexual copulation and marriage runs through his critical essays and in *Die Ringe des Saturn*, a text that is almost entirely populated by melancholy bachelors who do indeed resist fatherhood and reproduction.

Sebald's bachelor poetics, as already indicated in the previous chapter, are indebted to Deleuze and Guattari's *Kafka: For a Minor Literature*. Further, as we saw in the introduction, Sebald's poetics, with its commitment to melancholy and refusal of futurist utopias, as well its rejection of any semblance of the bourgeois novel plot of marriage and a happy ending, has a superficial family resemblance to the negative or 'pessimistic' queer theories of Butler and Edelson. In Sebald's 1980 book on Döblin, his criticism approaches just such anti-reproductive theories by suggesting that in Döblin's early short story 'Der schwarze Vorhang' the author views homosexuality, in an almost monastic fashion, as a 'purer' instinct that renounces procreation. In this short story, the young Johannes is revolted by heterosexual copulation, and seeks to flee from it into a 'purer' literature. Sebald interprets the term 'purer' to refer to a homosexual relationship, one that refuses procreation in keeping with the yearning of natural philosophy (*Döblin*, 126). Sebald argues that, thanks to Döblin's seduction by a fatalistic mythology of death, and thanks to the taboo surrounding homosexuality in German culture of his time, such homosexual yearnings can only find literary expression in violent murder of a partner. Sebald here suggests that, within the natural philosophical system whereby nature's own order is allowed to speak autonomously rather than being dominated by mankind, homosexuality may be a means to open a redemptive natural philosophical hope that the way downwards may lead up (*Döblin*, 127). These early suggestions that a life of letters may lead to the possibility of redemption, and of a form of queer masculinity linked to the renunciation of reproduction and a fear of heterosexuality, appear again and again in Sebald's own fiction. Here, I demonstrate the significance of Sebald's commitment to the figure of the non-reproductive bachelor and to a schizoid poetics that leans on the theories of Deleuze and Guattari.

Minor Literature and the Desire of the Bachelor: Schizo-poetics of Resistance

Sebald's fiction develops the themes of the refusal of reproduction, the *horreur des femmes*, and bachelorhood. The bachelor is a frail and disintegrative structure, and his resistance is often non-heroic. Therefore, Sebald's bachelors figure their resistance not through the heroic structures of the realist novel, but through decentred, plural poetics. Therefore, if bourgeois constructs of masculinity and totalizing myths of dominance and destruction close off hope for redemption, schizoid poetics can be a means of decentring and resisting such oppressive structures. The potential of schizophrenia for resistance emerges in Sebald's 1983 essay on Handke's *Die Angst des Tormanns beim Elfmeter* [*The Goalie's Anxiety at the Penalty Kick*], a novel about the mental deterioration of a schizophrenic goalkeeper.[6] Sebald here both analyses Handke's radical affinity for the decentredness of the psyche, and praises Handke for avoiding too great an identification with schizophrenic individuals. He then embarks on speculation that the radical alienation inherent in schizophrenia may be a natural or at least logical reaction to mechanisms of domination. Among these mechanisms, Sebald counts the phenomena of language itself, an alienating society, the *langueur* of the Austrian provinces, an excessive sensitivity, and not least artistic creativity. Schizophrenia then becomes a privileged position of insight and art, at once a position of extreme danger and of extreme truth.

> Die Pathographie der Erzählfigur und die Biographie des Erzählers treffen sich so in dem angesichts der gesellschaftlichen Normalität illegitimen Dasein von Krankheit und Kunst, die auf verschiedene Weise an das erinnern, was in den Kindern zugrunde gerichtet wird. (*BU*, 130)

> [The pathography of the protagonist and the biography of the narrator meet in the existence of sickness and art, which is illegitimate in the view of social normality, and which both recall, in different ways, that which is destroyed in children.]

With this concluding passage, Sebald draws a link between mental illness and art, while connecting them to the traumas of childhood. This move demonstrates the persistence of a Freudian understanding of the traumatic formation of culture in his thought. Nonetheless, Sebald's work on Herbeck in the same volume suggests a still stronger affinity with the poetics of schizophrenia. Sebald here describes the language of the schizophrenic as diametrically opposed to ordered language, and indeed as something that that represents hope for resistance in the face of society's progression towards catastrophe (*BU*, 140). Following this argument, he suggests that the fragmented psyche of the schizophrenic is the pendant to the destructions wrought in the individual by history:

> Die von der Geschichte quasi auf eigene Faust veranstalteten Katastrophen haben ihr genaues Korrelat nicht mehr in einem sinnvollen bürgerlichen Bildungsroman, sondern in den Zerstörungen, die die Geschichte im einzelnen hinterläßt. (*BU*, 142)

> [The catastrophes which are caused by history on its own, so as to say, no longer have their exact correlate in a meaningful bourgeois *Bildungsroman*, but in the particular destructions that history leaves behind.]

The *Bildungsroman* genre describes a normative novel of formation of a young man who embarks on a series of erotic and artistic wanderings before his successful reintegration into bourgeois society.[7] Sebald here argues that inherited genres of bourgeois writings cannot access the insights delivered by the poetic truth of schizophrenic textuality.

It might seem, with the totalizing reference to the 'destructions of history', as though we are back to Sebald's poetics of destruction, which views the human as another suffering object among many that is subject to 'die gegenwärtige Situation [...], in der die technische Progression sich bereits teleologisch an der Katastrophe orientiert' [the present situation [...] in which technical progression already orientates itself teleologically towards catastrophe] (*BU*, 140). But Eric Santner is right when he suggests that 'Sebald's preoccupation with homoerotic desire' is often in some way connected to the natural history of destruction in his work:

> Isn't there a kind of oscillation in Sebald's universe between homoerotically charged male bonding and an obsession with the end of the world? Or rather, aren't Sebald's narrators constantly forming bonds with other men by way of a shared sense of ruination and desolation?[8]

Santner here suggests that homoerotic or homosocial bonds oscillate unstably between being a product of destruction and resistance both to that destruction and to the totalizing seduction of apocalyptic thinking itself. Theoretical seeds of such an idea are to be found in the Herbeck essay, where Sebald, returning to Alexander and Margarete Mitscherlich's model of a fascistoid family, argues that Herbeck's poetry gives the idea of

> Faschismus als einer Familienangelegenheit, die sich sowohl zur Krankheit des einzelnen als auch, auf der Ebene der Geschichte, zum Fiasko eines Weltkriegs auswachsen kann (*BU*, 142).
>
> [fascism as a family affair, which can grow into the sickness of the individual as well as, on the level of history, to the fiasco of a world war.]

In Herbeck's poetry, Sebald sees a horror of the mania for collective identity that leads at once to the cult of the nuclear family and to nationalist fascism. This is combined in Herbeck's work with the theme of frustrated heterosexual love for the erotic figure of a lady. Here, Sebald draws on Deleuze and Guattari's theory to suggest that there is nothing left for frustrated lovers such as Herbeck — and Gregor Samsa, Sebald adds — but to become bachelors. In their *Kafka: Toward a Minor Literature*, Deleuze and Guattari draw out the sexual-political significance of the bachelor, which is part of a schizoid formation that resists the Oedipal model of the psyche.[9] 'With no family, no conjugality, the bachelor is all the more social, social-dangerous, social-traitor, a collective in himself'.[10] For Deleuze and Guattari, the bachelor-machine represents an advanced staging point on the line of flight.

Sebald therefore views Herbeck's writing as a schizo-poetics in this Deleuzian sense. *Die Ringe des Saturn*, with its parade of melancholy bachelors, also demonstrates aspects of schizo-poetics. Judith Ryan has shown how the narrative of *Die Ringe des Saturn* conforms to Deleuze and Guattari's description of a Kafkaesque 'rhizomatic text'. She notes that the narrator demonstrates a kind of movement that depends at once on 'lines of articulation' and 'lines of flight', and the book that results from it is one that is structured by 'principles of connection and heterogeneity'.[11] In keeping with the non-linear, rhizomatic structure of Kafka's writing, which Deleuze and Guattari state can be entered at any point, Sebald's lines of flight, I argue, do not follow the sequence outlined in *Kafka* in any particular order. The 'intensity' of the Sebaldian bachelor's desire both incorporates and resists incestuous and homosexual desire, at different times. Many of Sebald's bachelors are melancholy, several ill, or in pain; not a few are preposterous. Nonetheless, as Deleuze and Guattari tell us, although the bachelor existence is self-contradictory and often a failure, these melancholy facts do not alter its potential for resistance.

> Undoubtedly, it has its problems, its weaknesses, such as its moments of lowered intensity: bureaucratic mediocrity, going around in circles, fear, the Oedipal temptation to lead the hermit's life [...] and, even worse, the suicidal desire for self-abolition. But even with these downfalls, it is a production of intensities [...] He is the deterritorialized, the one who has neither 'center' nor 'any great complex of possessions'.[12]

This summary of the potential of the bachelor closely corresponds to Sebald's own conception. Thus, writing on Herbeck, Sebald directly paraphrases Deleuze and Guattari, writing that bachelor existence is the 'Ausdruck eines Verlangens, das die inzestuöse Sehnsucht an Weite und Intensität noch übertrifft' [expression of a desire that outdoes the incestuous longing in breadth and intensity] (*BU*, 147). 'Intensity', in Deleuze and Guattari's understanding, is a mode that goes beyond mimesis to become pure expression of that which is ordinarily oppressed by Oedipal society. Herbeck as bachelor-poet produces such intensity, and is a frail figure of resistance to and escape from such oppressive structures, both the Oedipal structures of bourgeois subjectivity and the patrilineal inheritance associated with the Nazi past and his fascistoid family. (Here, we may see a link to Sebald's own troubled relationship to his father, and to his father's involvement with the Nazi party.) Sebald comments that Herbeck's bachelor art is a means of accessing a radically decentred poetics, akin, Sebald says, to Schönberg's twelve-tone compositions, suggested as an alternative to polyphonic and homophonic hierarchies (*BU*, 145). Instead of such hierarchical compositional structures, Herbeck's intense art restores to each word its aura. Therefore, Sebald's Herbeck is a key figure in understanding the Sebaldian complex of sexuality, subjectivity, and poetics. Herbeck's poetic vision also corresponds to his 'extreme sensibility', achieved through suffering the pain of mental illness (*BU*, 147). Bachelor art, then, restores the auratic quality to art; it is in itself an attempt at restitution, but one that takes its toll on the bachelor artist. Herbeck combats his experience of suffering with his 'dream of becoming smaller', and as Hutchinson comments, this combination of suffering and the dream of diminution is key to achieving clarity of vision throughout Sebald's work.[13] Further, the sexual pathologies that Sebald detects in Herbeck's schizoid poetics also inform the larger political dimension of Sebald's own work which, though it frequently finds its *Glück im Winkel* (happiness in a niche), is still drawn both to the larger political dimension and to the bachelor desires that lie behind Herbeck's work.

These bachelor desires find literary expression when, in the 'All'estero' section in *Schwindel. Gefühle.*, Herbeck appears as a figure on loan, rather than as the object of Sebald's literary criticism. There is a lightly homosexual overtone to the Sebaldian narrator's decision to visit Herbeck, as he makes the decision in the same minute that he impetuously decides to travel to Venice on the night train, an intertextual echo of Gustav von Aschenbach's sudden and homophile decision to travel to Venice in Mann's *Der Tod in Venedig*, as we will see in Chapter 4. The family themes that occur in Sebald's discussion of Herbeck's work reappear in his presentation of Herbeck's life story in *Schwindel. Gefühle.*: his nervous illness is causally linked to his family life, in particular his father, and indeed to his forced service in the military in the Second World War (*SG*, 45; *V*, 38). The narrator's excursion with the bachelor-poet Herbeck up into Burg Greifenstein becomes a literal line of flight for both:

> Viel hätte, glaube ich, an diesem Vormittag nicht gefehlt, und wir hätten beide das Fliegen gelernt, oder ich zumindest, was man braucht für einen anständigen Absturz.

[That morning, I think, we were both within an inch of learning to fly, or at least I might have managed as much as is required for a decent crash.] (*SG*, 49; *V*, 42)

This sentence carries overtones of the legend of Icarus, but also of the perennial Sebaldian utopian topos of flight. Returning down into the village, they hear the singing of children, which moves Herbeck to say, 'Es klingt sehr schön durch die Luft und erhebt einem das Herz' [That is a very fine sound, borne upon the air, and uplifts one's heart] (*SG*, 52; *V*, 44). We are reminded that music causes the bent head to lift, in Deleuze and Guattari's schizo-poetics.[14] Herbeck's line of flight is also a flight backwards into childhood, but a mythical, prelapsarian childhood, akin to Sebald's vision of Handke's Slovenia (which Handke terms *Kindschaft*, or 'childscape'), rather than any historical socialization via patriarchy and Nazi oppression. If the essay on Herbeck is the only time when Sebald directly refers to Deleuze and Guattari, Herbeck both as writer and as fictional figure on loan is the prototype of Sebald's melancholy bachelors, with his yearning for *Kindschaft*, his solitary voyage, his production of intensities via a schizo-poetics, and his line of escape from the fascistoid structures of the Oedipal family.

Die Ringe des Saturn

More than any of Sebald's texts, *Die Ringe des Saturn* is populated by the figure of the melancholy bachelor, sometimes an artist, sometimes queer, sometimes halfway between revenant and saint. These figures are part of the post-apocalyptic landscape of the novel, and as such, may be viewed as merely poetic instances among many that create the critique of history and poetics of landscape contained in the novel. Yet it is worthwhile paying particular attention to these often preposterous and failed figures. Hutchinson has shown that through them, particularly through Edward Fitzgerald and Swinburne, Sebald calls attention to the destructive process of writing and the futility of trying to erect a bulwark of poetics against the erosions of time.[15] The bachelors of *Die Ringe des Saturn* occupy a space between what Deleuze and Guattari (drawing on Proust) call a homosexuality which operates under the sign of Saturn, a homosexuality 'which is Oedipal, exclusive, and depressive', and an anti-Oedipal schizoid homosexuality, for, while they are melancholy, these bachelors also embody particular attempts to resist the Oedipal imperatives of bourgeois society.[16] It is less the case that their writings are the means whereby they undertake this resistance, but rather their bachelor condition allows them to produce such resistant writings in the first place: bachelor writings are minor literatures. Indeed, to return to 'Tlön, Uqbar, Orbis Tertius', Borges has provided the template for such bachelors in the figure of Herbert Ashe: 'In life, Ashe was afflicted with unreality, as so many Englishmen are; in death, he is not even the ghost he was in life [...] I understand that he was a widower, and without issue'.[17] Like Sebald's melancholy bachelors, he finds solace in an emotionally repressed homosociality: 'My father had forged one of those close English friendships with him (the first adjective is perhaps excessive) that begin by excluding confidences and soon eliminate conversation'.[18] In this section, I examine how the bachelor's refusal of heterosexual love contributes to Sebald's concepts of a literature of resistance and a rejection of heteronormative reproduction.

Bachelors comic: Swinburne

As Borges's lugubrious portrayal of Ashe suggests, not all literary bachelors are wholly framed in terms of tragic melancholy, and certainly not all in *Die Ringe des Saturn*. Indeed, Adrian Daub suggests that 'Sebald's task in *The Rings of Saturn* is thus the task he inherited from Thomas Bernhard: how to remain melancholic in a self-ironizing world'.[19] There is thus an inherent comedy to some of Sebald's bachelors, perilously poised between the ethical impulse to maintain melancholy as a mode of resistance and the ironizing effects of history that renders all their strivings vain and their gentle, unproductive eccentricities ludicrous. The Sebaldian bachelor-narrator himself (here, unlike in *Die Ausgewanderten*, no mention is made of a wife) is a figure whose lugubrious melancholy reaches a note of iconic comedy in the scene where he grapples with an inedible plate of fish and chips (parodied in *Private Eye*, and picked up on by the English press with a tart 'What a lemon!').[20] Indeed, the comic moments at times threaten to topple into kitsch. Thus, in the second section, we read of the narrator's bachelor neighbour Frederick Farrar and his sisters Violet, Iris, and Rose. Entirely in the mode of Deleuzian schizo-incest, we are told that Farrar grew up amid the care and attention of his three beautiful sisters, before, in 1914, his world was shattered by the terrible pains of separation when he was sent to boarding school (*RS*, 63; *RSe*, 46). Farrar's resentment at the separation, already politically overdetermined by virtue of the year in which it occurs, is heightened by having to hear a patriotic speech by his headmaster about the background and higher purpose of the war, which had broken out during the holidays. At this moment, he hears the unforgettable sounds made by a boy cadet called Francis Browne, who is playing the bugle. The boy cadet, whose name marks him as kin of the text's guiding spirit Thomas Browne, and also of Edward FitzGerald's unrequited love William Browne (discussed below), plays the Last Post of the dying bourgeois age as it tumbles into the cruelty of the First World War. Farrar, who dutifully follows his father's orders and becomes a judge, is here caught between the odious patriotic system that reproduces its own patriarchal oppression, and the melancholic music of the 'unforgettable' cadet. Thus far, Farrar seems a perfect exemplar of the dialectic of oppression and melancholic resistance, hearing the siren call of erotic yearning and loss from the uniformed boy (not unlike the uniformed cadet in the portrait belonging to Schnitzler's heroine, or indeed the musical call of Gregor Samsa's sister on the violin), but conforming to the patriarchal pressure to reproduce the bureaucratic structures of oppression of the bourgeois age. Farrar spends his life in lawyers' chambers and courts of law, the legal mechanics of government domination. His life, in keeping with the theme of combustion burning through the text, comes to an end when his cigarette lighter sets his nightshirt alight. Here the comic aspect of the bachelor threatens to overcome the melancholic or tragic, and the perilous threat of Sebaldian 'black kitsch' comes close when we are told that he spends his last years breeding rare roses and violets — 'Daß auch die Iris zu seinen besonderen Vorlieben zählte, brauche ich eigentlich kaum anzufügen' [I need hardly add that the iris was also one of his favourites] (*RS*, 63; *RSe*, 47). The elderly bachelor's *Glück im Winkel* approaches floral kitsch as much as it does an incestuous obsession with his sisters.

Similarly, 'poor Algernon' Swinburne cuts a somewhat ludicrous figure, his comic physicality at all times visible through his melancholic mien in Sebald's depiction. Hutchinson correctly shows how Sebald links Swinburne's self-destructive practice of literature with the longer history of destruction, by introducing him to the narrative while describing the natural destruction of Dunwich by tidal erosion, on the one hand, and by linking his date of birth and familial ancestry with the suffering of the Chinese people during the Opium Wars and the fall of the Chinese empire, described earlier in the chapter.[21] Swinburne demonstrates a tragic relationship to literature and a suffering relationship to his body, despite his early literary success:

> Erst als die Hoffnung auf einen Heldentod endgültig an seinem unterentwickelten Körper gescheitert war, warf er sich rückhaltlos in die Literatur und damit in eine vielleicht nicht minder radikale Form der Selbstzerstörung.
>
> [Only when all hope of dying a hero's death was gone, thanks to his under-developed body, did he devote himself unreservedly to literature and thus, perhaps, to a no less radical form of self-destruction.] (*RS*, 196; *RSe*, 163)

Swinburne's break with the heteronormative line of descent and military inheritance of his ancestors — who had been courtiers, commanders, warriors, puissant landlords, and explorers — takes place as much in the patriarchal fantasies of his biographers as in his own eccentric life. Sebald tells us that his biographers long wondered how to account for the phenomenon 'wie aus solch lebenstüchtigen Geschlechtern ein beständig in der Gefahr des Nervenzusammenbruchs schwebendes Wesen hervorgehen konnte' [how a family so adept at life should have produced a scion forever on the verge of a nervous breakdown] (*RS*, 195; *RSe*, 162). Thus, Swinburne's vaporous and nervous affect and somewhat monstrous appearance queers the stern line of Darwinian descent, breaking with the repressive logic of origin and inheritance. Instead, these biographers attribute to him a magical origin, viewing him as 'ein jenseits aller natürlichen Möglichkeit, gleichsam aus dem Nichts entstandenes epigenetisches Phänomen' [an epigenetic phenomenon sprung from the void, as it were, from beyond all natural possibility] (*RS*, 195; *RSe*, 162). The author of the poem 'By the North Sea', which is a literary contribution to the natural history of destruction, thus breaks with the laws of nature and reproduction in his own person.[22] Further, his own life is only preserved through the devotion of his friend, Watts-Dunton, who protects him from any nervous excitation in suburban exile, where the two bachelors live a secluded life conducive to literary production. Finally, one of Swinburne's visitors comments that the elderly poet puts him in mind of the grey silkworm *Bombyx mori* (*RS*, 198; *RSe*, 165). Thus, the Swinburne figure gathers together several of the key themes of the entire text — erosion on the North Sea coast, oppression and decay in the Chinese empire, silk production — with the life of the bachelor-poet, resistance to marriage in favour of homosociality, and courting self-destruction in the cause of literary production.

However, notwithstanding Swinburne's conformity to the classic traits of the Sebaldian bachelor, the comic aspects of his portrayal at all times cast his melancholic characteristics and any queer resistance into ironic relief. Swinburne is brought into the narrative when he associates the green glow of the sea at Dunwich with the palace of Kublai Khan. Notably, however, the Sebaldian narrator casts doubt on precisely this form of historical association, so central to his own literary practice, by calling the veracity of the source study for this incident 'questionable' (RS, 193; the word is not translated in the English). Swinburne appears more as a lugubrious counterpart to the tragic bachelors with whom Sebald shares a *Wahlverwandtschaft*. He is implicitly allied with the comic Sebaldian bachelor who is so disappointed in his fish and chips, rather than with suffering figures such as Robert Walser or Herbeck who exemplify the martyrdom inherent in heroic bachelorhood. Several times, Sebald emphasizes his comical physical aspect, such as his physical fragility, his 'ungeheuer große[r], ja überdimensionale[r] Kopf' [extraordinarily large, indeed outsize head] (RS, 195; RSe, 162), and his antic manner, 'mit flatternden Händen gleich einem aufgescheuchten Falter' [flapping his hands flitted about [...] like a startled moth] (RS, 198; RSe, 165). Equally, his early literary effusions are described with some archness: Sebald describes how he is laid low

> von den phantastischen Kunstgesprächen in den Salons der Präraffaeliten und der Geistesanstrengung bei der Komposition seiner mit wundervollem poetischen Bombast ausstaffierten Tragödien und Dichtungen.

> [by the dazzling conversations on art in the Pre-Raphaelite salons, or by the mental strain of composing his own verse and tragedies, overflowing with wonderful poetic bombast.] (RS, 192; RSe, 160)

Sebald's sly usage of the word 'Wunderpoet' to describe the elderly Swinburne, and his description of Swinburne's bathetic descent from a fiery young would-be *beau sabreur* of bourgeois literature to meek elderly patient in suburban exile, adds to the sense that Swinburne is in some sense not to be taken seriously. This is a sense that was shared by many of Swinburne's contemporaries, most notably Oscar Wilde, who summed up his career acidly:

> Mr. Swinburne once set his age on fire by a volume of very perfect and very poisonous poetry. Then he became revolutionary, and pantheistic, and cried out against those who sit in high places. Then he returned to the nursery, and wrote poems about children of a somewhat over-subtle character.[23]

Clearly, Wilde disapproved of Swinburne's turn from revolutionary to domesticated poet, a man who 'manages to combine with his patriotism a strong affection for the Tory party' and finds this turn indicative of a failure to resist literary and political hegemony.[24] Wilde may have felt Swinburne's betrayal all the more keenly because Swinburne's early literary works, the 'poisonous poetry' which was 'decked out with bombast', was remarkable for its radically queer character. Whereas Sebald only makes reference to two of Swinburne's works, the melancholic 'By the North Sea' and also 'Atalanta in Calydon', there was a considerably more sexually transgressive tone to many of his works than Sebald records: Thaïs E. Morgan laconically states 'Swinburne explores a range of transgressive perversities, including hermaphroditism and androgyny among sado-masochism, lesbianism, and necrophilia, as part of his avant-gardist agenda during the early and mid-1860s'.[25] Indeed, not only Oscar Wilde and contemporary critic Robert Buchanan, who anathemized Swinburne as an 'intellectual hermaphrodite',[26] but also recent critics such as Morgan and Richard Dellamora view Swinburne's poetic programme as anti-Oedipal. They describe his programme as one of 'male aesthetes interested in extending the boundaries of masculinity',[27] and of 'imagining other ways of being a man in Victorian England'.[28] Poems of Swinburne's such as 'Hermaphroditus' and 'Anactoria' are particularly concerned with hermaphrodism and androgyny, with an aesthetics that transgresses dual gender binaries and 'both parodies and disparages conventional sexuality while celebrating bisexual fantasy and experience'.[29] Indeed, Dellamora goes so far as to suggest that these poems 'provide the utopian basis of a transformation both of culture and of personal existence'.[30]

In *Die Ringe des Saturn*, neither Swinburne's early excess of polymorphously perverse passion nor any fully utopian basis of homosexual transformation is included in the text. Sebald takes up his account after Swinburne's nervous breakdown of 1879, after which time he had renounced his early 'Whitmania' and, as Wilde jeered, become respectable.[31] Thus, Sebald's older Swinburne behaves like a well-behaved child, not like a sexual revolutionary, and Sebald domesticates the disruptive sexual potential of his earlier work into a dutifully sexless relationship with his fellow-bachelor, Watts Dunton (*RS*, 198; *RSe*, 165). Instead of delivering the utopian promise detected by Dellamora, Sebald's Swinburne story ends on the theme of memory and the Benjaminian retrieval of images from the past, as Swinburne retreats into a reminiscence of his great-aunt's: 'diese eineinhalb Jahrhunderte in die Vergangenheit zurückreichende Erinnerung' [this memory that goes back a century and a half into the past] (*RS*, 199; *RSe*, 166). Swinburne is a queer bachelor indeed, but the sexual excess and utopian potential of his work is subjugated, in *Die Ringe des Saturn*, to Sebald's poetics of memory and destruction. In this context, the constant emphasis that Sebald places on the ridiculous appearance of Swinburne's large head and mound of fiery hair, his childish manners and infantile body, appear to present less the libidinous space of homosexual or polymorphous desire present in Swinburne's own writings, than characteristics of Deleuze and Guattari's 'childhood blocks' of deterritorialization.[32] Deleuze and Guattari call this 'a becoming-child of the adult taking place in the adult, a becoming-adult of the child taking place in the child, the two in contiguity'.[33] Such behaviour is linked to the 'mannerism of politeness', evident in Swinburne's docile acquiescence to Watts Dunton. They term this mannerism 'schizo-buffoonery', a phrase appropriate to Swinburne's childish clowning, and suggest that 'it can be a way of saying "Shit" to the authorities'.[34] So Sebald's bachelor Swinburne does resist reterritorialization, just as he has resisted the oedipal imperative to procreate; such resistance, though, is produced within the text of *Die Ringe des Saturn*, rather than by intertextual reference to Swinburne's own poetic production.

Bachelors tragic: Le Strange

Bachelorhood can also demonstrate the symptoms of a traumatized response to the horrors of history, as shown in the antics of the appropriately named Major George Wyndham Le Strange. Le Strange, as an English-language newspaper cutting purportedly reproduced in *Die Ringe des Saturn* tells us, becomes a 'virtual recluse', who withdraws to his estate in Henstead, Suffolk after his tank regiment liberated Bergen-Belsen on 14 April 1945. According to the cutting, he 'left his vast estate' to his housekeeper 'on condition that she dined with him in silence every day' (*RS*, 81; *RSe*, 63). The Sebaldian narrator does not make explicit in words the traumatic connection between Le Strange's participation in the liberation of Bergen-Belsen and his subsequent melancholy bachelor habits. In the German edition of the text, instead, the reader is faced with the trauma in the form of an image as, between the end of page 77, concluding 'das am 14. April 1945' [that on the 14th of April 1945], and the beginning of page 80, 'das Lager von Bergen-Belsen befreite' [liberated the camp at Bergen-Belsen], Sebald interposes an archival photograph of trees and bodies covered by blankets (*RS*, 78–79).[35] The position of this image in the sentence leads the reader to suppose that it does indeed represent Bergen-Belsen; it also traumatizes the readers by confronting them with the explicit image before the narrative has told them what they are seeing. Daub argues that this picture performs as an 'irruption that allows for the shock, the mystery, and the sheer incomprehensibility of what Major Le Strange saw'.[36] However, as Daub's research shows, the newspaper cutting is almost certainly a forgery of Sebald's, and hence the image itself — an unusually explicit reference to genocide in Sebald's work — loses in authenticity or indexical value.[37] Rather than serving a documentary function, he argues, the image reproduces the well-documented shock that Sebald claims to have experienced when shown footage of the liberation of concentration camps as a teenager. Daub argues that the name 'George Wyndham Le Strange' resembles a rearrangement of 'Winfried Georg Sebald', and that thus 'the major is none other than Sebald visiting the site of his "initiation" into the Holocaust'.[38] If we are to follow this logic, then, perhaps all of the bachelors in *Die Ringe des Saturn* can be seen as representatives of the figure of 'W. G. Sebald', re-enacting his personal and political trauma on a domestic scale, while, as with the figure of Swinburne, also comically satirizing his melancholy response to those traumas. Le Strange's bachelor antics, like Swinburne's, go beyond a melancholy retreat from the traumas of history. The narrator lists a series of incredible stories that circulate about Le Strange in later years, of which he says, 'Was ich von solchen Geschichten halten soll, das ist mir bis heute nicht klar' [To this day, I do not know what to make of such stories], thereby provoking the reader to interpret them (*RS*, 83; *RSe*, 64). One of these myths states that he retreats to a cave in his garden and sits there like the holy St Jerome in the desert, emphasizing the sacred status of the melancholy bachelor. Another states that he is constantly surrounded by winged creatures, which reminds us not only of St Francis preaching to the birds, but also of the 'becoming-animal' which Deleuze and Guattari tell us is one of the possible means of escape for the bachelor, a 'creative line of escape that says nothing other than what it is'.[39] Furthermore, though, we are told that Le Strange's skin turns an unnatural olive-green, marking him as an 'epigenetic phenomenon' like Swinburne rather than a 'natural' human animal. Once his wardrobe has worn out, he decks himself in clothes taken from chests in his attic. The image of the melancholy bachelor attired in preposterous bygone finery, such as the canary-yellow frock coat, carries with it a whiff of camp, of gender performativity. These camp garments are not unlike the dashing feather boa sported by Edward FitzGerald while aboard his yacht, the *Scandal*, and FitzGerald is perhaps the most significant of the bachelors of *Die Ringe des Saturn*, as he combines both the comic and tragic aspects of melancholy bachelorhood in a mode of queer literary resistance.

Bachelors poetic: Edward Fitzgerald

Edward FitzGerald, composer-translator of The Rubá'iyát of Omar Khayyam, is the counterpart to Swinburne's antic bachelor in *Die Ringe des Saturn*, whose synthesis of the tragic and the comic results in a genuinely radical poetic production. Both Swinburne and FitzGerald are described by their yearning relationship to a textual Orient; Sebald introduces both in the text as scions of dynastic aristocratic families, against whom they rebel by their eccentricity, literary pursuits, and affection for men; both turn to literary pursuits, but ones which are detrimental to their mental health, and both are in some way 'unfitted for general society', seeking solace in literature and the sea.

The comic Swinburnian themes thus act as a prelude for the melancholic FitzGeraldian ones later in the text. FitzGerald, like Swinburne, is born into the privilege of the colonial classes, but unlike Swinburne he reacts with explicit horror against such privilege, creating a literature that resists colonial oppression by translating the poetry of mediaeval Persia into English. FitzGerald hereby creates a bridge of respect between the two cultures, and challenges what Long calls 'a mode of colonial subjectivity' that views itself 'as occupying a privileged position at the heart of an extensive empire'.[40] Such a mode of subjectivity, as Long has shown, is grounded in a panoptical model of oppression that administrates, categorizes, and dominates all that it surveys. By contrast, FitzGerald's loving translations of the Rubá'iyát become the medium in which he makes good the depredations perpetrated by the property-owning classes; as Hutchinson says, FitzGerald's resistance manifests itself in literature.[41] Although he embarks on countless failed literary projects, the Rubá'iyát is his sole success. His English verse is in itself a literature of restitution, which erases the tyranny of the authorial subject over his material in the process of writing, in favour of allowing the language of poetry to speak for itself. Sebald tells us that this abrogation of the Orient allows a literary reconciliation that is also political:

> Die von ihm zu diesem Zweck ausgesonnenen englischen Verse fingieren in ihrer scheinbar absichtslosen Schönheit eine jeden Anspruch von Autorschaft weit hinter sich zurücklassende Anonymität und verweisen, Wort für Wort, auf einen unsichtbaren Punkt, an dem das mittelalterliche Morgenland und das erlöschende Abendland einander anders als im unseligen Verlauf der Geschichte begegnen dürfen.

[The English verses he devised for the purpose, which radiate with a pure, seemingly unselfconscious beauty, feign an anonymity that disdains even the least claim to authorship, and draw us, word by word, to an invisible point where the mediaeval orient and the fading occident can come together in a way never allowed them by the calamitous course of history.] (*RS*, 238; *RSe*, 200)

FitzGerald's renunciation of authorial literary practices in favour of a literature that opens up an alternative course to the history of relations between Occident and Orient is a clear rebellion against the colonial practices of his ancestors and class. As Hutchinson says, Sebald leaves no doubt that he understands FitzGerald's eccentric habits as resistance against his own class.[42] The source text for much of Sebald's biographical material on FitzGerald, Peter de Polnay's *Into an Old Room: The Paradox of Edward FitzGerald* (1950), makes the Anglo-Norman nature and influence of his class background explicit. De Polnay ascribes FitzGerald's deterritorialized imagination to his Irish origins, writing that FitzGerald's Irish background allowed him to 'let his eye roam as far as the little tree near to the hedge beyond the garden and at the same time to see the minarets of Khorassan'.[43] Indeed, FitzGerald's Anglo-Norman background also displays a hybridity between Protestant and Catholic origins, since, despite his Protestant parents, he numbered among his ancestors Irish Catholic rebels against British occupation.[44] Cultural hybridity in the wake of colonial domination has been posited by many theorists, chief among them Homi Bhabha, as a form of existence that offers a productive challenge to colonial domination. 'Hybridity begins to become the form of cultural difference itself, the jarrings of a differentiated culture whose "hybrid counter-energies", in Said's phrase, challenge the centred, dominant cultural norms with their unsettling perplexities generated out of their "disjunctive, liminal space"', writes Robert Young.[45] Drawing on Mikhail Bakhtin and Stuart Hall, Young suggests that hybridity allows for a particular form of polyvocality, indeed an interrogative language, which produces 'a hybridized, critical speech', or, in Bakhtin's description of the hybridized novel, 'an artistically organized system for bringing different languages in contact with one another'.[46] Such theories help us to understand Sebald's understanding of the complex interrelation of FitzGerald's hybrid ancestry and his hybrid poetic work, and how, in creating an imaginary interaction of cultures 'in a way never allowed by the calamitous course of history', FitzGerald's verse, merging English and Persian, mobilizes a cultural resistance enabled by his own hybrid background. Such hybrid prose is in keeping with his early literary efforts; Sebald describes him as occupied

> mit seiner in die verschiedensten Sprachen ausschweifenden Lektüre, mit dem Schreiben unzähliger Briefe, mit Notizen zu einem Lexikon der Gemeinplätze, mit dem Zusammentragen von Worten und Phrasen für ein komplettes Glossarium der Sprache der Seefahrt und des Seelebens sowie mit der Zusammenstellung von *scrap-books* jeder nur erdenklichen Art.

> [with reading, in a variety of languages, with writing countless letters, with making notes towards a dictionary of commonplaces, with compiling a complete glossary of all words and phrases relating to the sea and to seafaring and with pasting up scrap books of every conceivable description.] (*RS*, 237; *RSe*, 200)

These literary activities cover a wide range of marginal and minor literary modes privileged by Sebald's poetics, most notably the *bricolage* of FitzGerald's scrapbooks. The significance of the practice of *bricolage* for Sebald has been widely documented; Sheppard notes that his annotations to the 1973 Suhrkamp paperback edition of Claude Lévi-Strauss's *La Pensée sauvage* (*Das wilde Denken*) 'indicate that he was particularly drawn to Lévi-Strauss's concept of "bricolage (Bastelei)" (p. 29 — heavily underlined) because he felt that this aleatory technique was still capable of generating auratic art', while Fuchs argues that, in *Austerlitz*, *bricolage* is a key element of Sebald's mnemotechnics.[47] FitzGerald's literary practices, then, correspond closely to Sebald's own literary ideals, in privileging the *Nebeneinander* over the principle of hierarchy. They thereby refuse the hegemony of the author over the work as well as that of his own colonizing culture over the Persian culture that he translates.

The history of colonialism plays a strong part in the FitzGerald narrative, and in Sebald's construction of his queerness. Topographically, Boulge Park, where FitzGerald was born and died, borders on an imaginary Persia — in Sebald's interpretation of De Polnay's metaphorical assertion, this border in FitzGerald's imagination becomes one magically realized in the text. 'Jenseits des Blumengartens erstreckte sich bis an den Weltrand, wo die Minarette von Khorasan aufragten, ein gleichmäßig grüner und vollkommen leerer Park' [Beyond the flower garden an even green park, utterly deserted, extended to the very edge of the world, where the minarets of Khorasan soared] (*RS*, 247; *RSe*, 208). The narrator, though, enters Boulge Park via another border, across the agrarian land which borders on Boulge. Cornilis de Jong, a chance-met traveller, tells the narrator that he wishes to purchase the farmland in order to invest monies made from sugar-beet plantations. Thus, Boulge lies between, on the one hand, an imaginary mediaeval Persia, and a territory that will soon serve to increase the profit made by eighteenth- and nineteenth-century European sugar barons by means of a slave economy. Boulge thus borders both on a reconciliation with the repressed Orient, and with the continuation of its colonial oppression. The roots of this oppression can be found in FitzGerald's own ancestral family, which, like the Swinburnes, has counted among the wily winners of history. Sebald characterizes the Anglo-Norman culture of FitzGerald's ancestors by their repressive and greedy practices of colonialism:

> Das über Generationen hinweg durch [...] die rücksichtslose Unterwerfung der einheimischen Bevölkerung und eine kaum weniger rücksichtslose Heiratspolitik geschaffene Familienvermögen [...] bestand, abgesehen von den Besitzungen in England, in erster Linie aus den schier unübersehbaren irischen Ländereien, aus der gesamten, auf diesen Ländereien sich befindenden beweglichen und unbeweglichen Habe sowie aus einer sich nach Tausenden zählenden, zumindest in der Praxis noch so gut wie leibeigenen Bauernschaft.

> [The family fortune, amassed over generations [...] by ruthless subjection of the local people and by a no less ruthless marriage strategy [...] consisted principally, apart from properties in England, of their vast land holdings in Ireland, together with the goods and chattels, and hosts of peasants who were effectively no more than their serfs.] (*RS*, 234; *RSe*, 197)

The reference to the FitzGeralds' enserfed tenants draws a link to the other colonial practices exposed and condemned throughout *Die Ringe des Saturn*, such as those in China and in the Congo. The FitzGeralds' 600-year-old colonial practices thus demonstrate that Sebald's natural history of destruction starts prior even to what Long refers to as the 200-year '*époque de longue durée*' of modernity in Sebald's work, an analysis which sees modernity in Sebald's work as featuring 'patterns of continuity that can be traced through European history from the early nineteenth century to the present'.[48] Colonial practices, like Oedipal structures, have deeper historical roots.

As De Polnay's account shows, FitzGerald seeks a life of bachelor seclusion to expiate his inherited feudal guilt. Because of the revulsion that he has felt against his class from his childhood, he eschews the dungeon-like family manor in favour of the liminal position of a tiny two-roomed cottage on the edge of the park (*RS*, 237; *RSe*, 199). FitzGerald prefers elective affinities with distant and long-dead writers, such as Khayyam and Mme de Sévigné, to participating in the material customs of his class, such as funerals or 'das Ritual des gemeinsamen Tafelns', literally the 'ritual of the common table' (*RS*, 240; *RSe*, 202). Queer theorist Ahmed points out that a kitchen or dining table is a 'kinship object', where the work of conventional genealogy takes place, closing down relationships to the social form of heterosexual reproduction. The utterances that take place at the table, Ahmed argues, perform the work of alignment, positioning 'the child as the not-yet adult by aligning sex (the male body) and gender (the masculine character) with sexual orientation (the heterosexual future). Through the utterance, these not-yet-but-to-be subjects are "brought into line" by being "given" a future that is "in line" with the family line'.[49] The dining table, she argues, denies any affinities other than those that bind heterosexual couples together into 'social ones' designed to reproduce familial genealogy; it most certainly does not have any room for such eccentric elective affinities as FitzGerald's.

Given that he rejects the orienting function of communal dining, it is no wonder that Sebald's FitzGerald is explicitly marked as homosexual, thus refusing to perpetuate the oppressive dynastic politics of his clan and produce another generation of rapacious aristocrats. Instead, and in keeping with the sister-oriented nature of the deterritorialized bachelor, Sebald notes that Fitzgerald's strongest family affinity is an affective link to his sister Andalusia, as she, like FitzGerald, is beset by what he terms the blue devil of melancholy. Although neither Sebald nor De Polnay explicitly links FitzGerald's homosexuality to his overbearing mother in vulgar-Freudian fashion, the implicit link is most certainly present, with Mary FitzGerald described as possessing a 'terrifying bust', who causes her husband to dwindle to a contemptible figure (*RS*, 234; *RSe*, 197). Like Le Strange, again, FitzGerald has a camp aspect, as revealed in his endearing description of FitzGerald's sole concession to the elegance expected of a yacht owner, 'die lange weiße Federboa, die er, wie berichtet wird, gerne am Deck anlegte, und die, von weitem sichtbar, hinter ihm herwehte im Wind' [the long white feather boa which he reportedly liked to sport on deck and which fluttered behind him in the breeze, visible at a good distance] (*RS*, 242; *RSe*, 204). Sebald's queer FitzGerald conforms in no small measure to the clichés of effeminate homosexuality current in the 1950s, when De Polnay finished his account. Yet De Polnay uses Havelock Ellis's *Studies in the Psychology of Sex* for his starting point when discussing FitzGerald's homosexuality, and his view, it would seem, is closer to the textual construction of poetic queerness in Sebald's text. 'There cannot be the slightest doubt that intellectual and artistic abilities of the highest order have frequently been associated with a congenitally inverted sexual temperament', argues Havelock Ellis, and agrees 'that the method of arguing the existence of homosexuality from the presence of feminine traits must be decisively rejected'.[50] FitzGerald's queerness is compounded with his literary resistance, by his refusal to arrogate either an authorial or a reproductive subject position to himself; Sebald here glances at vulgar-Freudian pathologies of queerness, but does not succumb to them.

Sebald paints FitzGerald's bachelor isolation and sexual repression as well-nigh complete; he does not engage in any physical sexual encounters, and instead is unrequitedly in love with a 'kind of ideal', his close friend William Browne. Sebald tells us, 'Die Liebeserklärung, die FitzGerald wahrscheinlich nie zu machen wagte, findet sich erst in dem Beileidsbrief an die Witwe' [the love which FitzGerald probably never dared to declare was not expressed until he wrote his letter of condolence to Browne's widow] (*RS*, 240; *RSe*, 202). In fact, De Polnay cites Havelock Ellis here, who records merely that FitzGerald wrote to Mrs Browne that he 'used to wander about the shore at night longing for some fellow to accost me who might give some promise of filling up a very vacant place in my heart'. While this is certainly queer, this is not quite an direct romantic declaration of love for Browne.[51] Thus, whereas Sebald's account of Swinburne erases much of his textual libido, here he embellishes and romanticizes the nexus of hybridity and queerness, thereby underlining FitzGerald's outsider and bachelor status. Indeed, De Polnay suggests that FitzGerald's poetry of reconciliation comes precisely from the denial of his homosexuality: 'It is feasible that if he had led an actual and active sex life the Rubá'iyát might never have been translated'. Unlike De Polnay, Sebald does not deal in a Freudian economy of repression. He makes of FitzGerald's homosexuality a romantic literary inspiration, whereas both De Polnay and his source, Havelock Ellis, suggest that he was more or less unaware of his true sexual feelings, which appear 'never to have reached full and conscious development'.[52] Further, Sebald neglects to mention FitzGerald's unhappy, and swiftly dissolved marriage, which is attested by both Havelock Ellis and De Polnay: 'He felt himself called on to marry, very unhappily, a woman whom he had never been in love with and with whom he had nothing in common', writes Havelock Ellis, attesting to the historical FitzGerald's willingness to conform to social mores. Thus, Sebald's narrative makes of FitzGerald a somewhat queerer bachelor and exile from his social class than his source material would suggest. The openly queer interpretation which Sebald makes of De Polnay's and FitzGerald's texts mirrors the queer interpretation that the Sebaldian narrator himself puts on his parting from Cornelis de Jonge, at the edge of Boulge Park: the part with 'einer gewissen, von ihm, wie es mir schien, erwiderten Herzlichkeit' [with a warmth which it seemed he returned] (*RS*, 232; *RSe*, 195). As we have noted, Sebald represents FitzGerald's poetics as a mirror of his own; other elements of the FitzGerald narrative further echo those of the Sebaldian narrator in *Die Ringe des Saturn*, including the trip to Holland to gaze at an Old Master, his dislike for the exploitation of the natural world by human civilization, his experience of the act of writing as a colloquium with the dead, and his preference for communing with works of art 'in the Theatre of one's own Recollections' (*RS*, 244; *RSe*, 205). If FitzGerald devotes his early life to drawing out *Wahlverwandtschaften* with long-dead writers, so Sebald marks a *Wahlverwandtschaft* with FitzGerald in turn, creating in FitzGerald an ally in his poetic methodologies, his lamenting the destruction of the natural landscape, and his literary resistance to Oedipal and political structures of domination.

Sea- and Love-Life: Barques and Bachelor Heterotopias

As we have seen, although Sebald's melancholy bachelors resist the heteronormative, Oedipal forces of society, they put up at most passive or literary resistance to the forces of oppression in modernity. However, at times they construct spaces of queer utopia that are something slightly more than a mere *Glück im Winkel*. FitzGerald's route of escape from the normative values of his class is taken on board ship. *Die Ringe des Saturn*, as a book describing a coastal walk, is inherently concerned with the sea, sea vessels, sea voyages, and sea battles. Cosgrove points out that 'Sebald's narrator is never far from the sea — it provides the epic backdrop to his local wanderings, lending his regional travels a cosmic dimension and connecting him to world history'.[53] Warships often participate in the catastrophic progress of modernity, and in the account of the battle of Sole Bay that opens Section IV, demonstrate the inadequacy of historiography to represent this bloody and inconclusive catastrophe. Equally, the *Mont Blanc* on which Joseph Conrad crosses the Atlantic Ocean is implicated in colonial exploitation (*RS*, 133; *RSe*, 110). Ocean liners turn up in others of Sebald's works, as engines of exile, for instance, in *Die Ausgewanderten*. They also appear in *Austerlitz*, where they function as destructive engines of modernity and of separation. It is hearing a radio report about the sea steamer *Prague* that makes Austerlitz recall that it was this liner that brought him away from the Continent towards lifelong exile in Britain. The motif of the ocean liner appears with most savage irony where Austerlitz describes the parody of a spa town performed in Theresienstadt for the benefit of the Red Cross, where the residents appear to gather every evening on the battlements 'beinahe so wie Weltreisende auf einem Ozeandampfer, ein alles in allem beruhigendes Schauspiel' [as if they were passengers enjoying an evening stroll on the deck of an ocean-going steamer] (*A*, 349; *Ae*, 341). The night after visiting Terezín, too, Austerlitz sees a vision of a desolate semi-marine landscape around the northern Czech city of Dux, where the power stations appear like ominous ships (*A*, 295; *Ae*, 285). The image of the steamship is doubly laden, though: it is also a figure of escape for Austerlitz's mother Agáta. When banned by the Nazis from performing in public or moving freely through Prague, she says she only now understands how wonderful it is to stand on a river steamer without a care in the world (*A*, 251; *Ae*, 243). In a further liberating manifestation, a steamship also features in FitzGerald's idyllic courtship of William Browne.

The conceptual distinction between warship or steamship and a yacht such as FitzGerald's *Scandal* is also apparent in Sebald's essay on Ernst Herbeck, where he distinguishes between the ocean liner as the engine of bourgeois society, and the makeshift raft as the last resort of the schizoid bachelor. Here, he directly quotes Deleuze and Guattari on Kafka's bachelor:

> Seine Reise ist nicht die stolze Fahrt des Bürgers auf einem Schiff übers Meer 'mit viele Wirkung ringsherum', sondern die Schizo-Reise 'auf seinen paar Holzstückchen in den Wellen, die sich noch selbst gegenseitig stoßen und herunterdrücken.' (*BU*, 147)[54]

> [His journey is not the proud travel of the bourgeois on a ship over the sea 'with great effect, round about', but the schizo-voyage 'on a few planks of wood that even bump against and submerge each other'.]

As we have seen, Sebald suggests that Herbeck is one of these schizoid bachelors, making his way out on a solitary voyage of the bachelor that inevitably results in him going through a succession of metamorphoses that makes him ever smaller, and his position ever more painful. This double potential of the boat, for bourgeois oppression and bachelor route of escape, is described by Foucault as a 'heterotopia':

> the boat is a floating piece of space, a place without a place, that exists by itself, that is closed in on itself and at the same time is given over to the infinity of the sea and that, from port to port, from tack to tack, from brothel to brothel, it goes as far as the colonies in search of the most precious treasures they conceal in their gardens, you will understand why the boat has not only been for our civilization, from the sixteenth century until the present, the great instrument of economic development [...] but has been simultaneously the greatest reserve of the imagination. The ship is the heterotopia par excellence.[55]

The heterotopia is omnipresent in Sebald's work, with its doubled quality of oppression and utopia. Öhlschläger argues that in Sebald, heterotopias are mostly negative spaces, demonstrating the way in which systems of oppression exclude people as they immure them, as does the Palais de Justice in Brussels.[56] However, the heterotopias in *Die Ringe des Saturn* are not stable counter-spaces to the ordered world of modernity, but rather 'obligatory points of passage that form the basis of an alternate mode of the ordering of these conditions'.[57] They are only viewed as heterotopia by virtue of their relation to the space around them. This explains the strange transformation, in *Schwindel. Gefühle.*, of the Martinsheim old people's home into a ship, while the narrator is visiting Ernst Herbeck:

> Es war, als blickte man auf ein wogendes Meer. Das Festland, schien mir, war bereits hinter dem Horizont versunken. Ein Nebelhorn dröhnte. Weiter und weiter zog das Schiff auf das Wasser hinaus.

> [It was like looking upon a heaving sea. The mainland, it seemed to me, had already sunk below the horizon. A foghorn droned. Further and further out the ship plied its passage upon the waters.] (*SG*, 53; *V*, 45)

Steamship and retirement home transform into each other because both function as heterotopias, though of different kinds: Foucault tells us that retirement homes [...] are, as it were, on the borderline between the heterotopia of crisis and the heterotopia of deviation since, after all, old age is a crisis, but is also a deviation since in our society where leisure is the rule, idleness is a sort of deviation.[58]

The heterotopia of the boat, with its imaginative possibilities, becomes transformed into the heterotopia of deviation; heterotopias do not redeem or lift the rules of society, as do utopias, but rather make its mechanisms of domination plain. The story of the old people's home/ship is encapsulated in the narrative of the Sebaldian narrator's excursion with Herbeck, where the possibility of flying seems nigh: a reminder that their possibility of escape borders on death.

In Sebald's fiction, riddled as it is with heterotopias, transcendence is a desire but not a concrete possibility, and the desire of the bachelor, his line of flight, leads more often to impossible pain rather than to a possible alternative social order; imaginary utopias, such as the garden at Boulge, which touches mediaeval Persia, are rare throughout Sebald's fiction. Persian gardens, Foucault tells us, are classic heterotopias: 'the garden is the smallest parcel of the world and then it is the totality of the world. The garden has been a sort of happy, universalizing heterotopia since the beginnings of antiquity'.[59] In the tormented journey of the narrator in *Schwindel. Gefühle.*, it is in the garden at Verona that the narrator finds a rare moment of peace and encounters the eternity of the yew trees, rather than the death that surrounds him in Venice (*SG*, 81; *V*, 70). In an earlier chapter of *Die Ringe des Saturn*, the meeting of Western colonial power and oriental garden is a more typically unhappy one: British and French troops destroy the enchanted garden of Yuan Ming Yuan in a frenzy of racist violence. This garden was, prior to its destruction, a classic Foucauldian heterotopia, and moreover one where nature and human art are reconciled: 'die ganze unbegreifliche Pracht der Natur und der von Menschenhand in sie eingebetteten Wunder sich spiegelte in den dunklen, von keinem Lufthauch bewegten Gewässern' [the whole incomprehensible glory of Nature and of the wonders placed in it by the hand of man was reflected in dark, unruffled waters] (*RS*, 174; *RSe*, 144). The boats of the Sebaldian bachelor cannot represent stable counter-spaces to the bourgeois order, any more than gardens can, but undertake brief, fraught excursions along its margins. In *Nach der Natur*, in the second last canto, Sebald tells us

> vor hundert | Jahren verschwand hier | Edward Fitzgerald, der Übersetzer | Omar Khayyams. In schon fortgeschrittenem Alter | bestieg er eines Tages sein Boot, segelte mit festgebundenem Zylinder | hinaus auf die Nordsee und ward | nie mehr gesehn.

> [a century ago Edward FitzGerald, | the translator of Omar Khayyam, | vanished out there. At an advanced age | one day he boarded his boat, | sailed off, with his top hat | tied on, into the German Ocean | and was never seen again.] (*NdN*, 93; *AN*, 106)

By *Die Ringe des Saturn*, such a disappearance is no longer possible, and the place, time, and manner of FitzGerald's death on land are instead meticulously noted. Still, FitzGerald takes the *Scandal* to the sea as a move against oppression, to escape the 'mit immer fragwürdiger werdenden Mitteln verfolgte Vermehrung des

Privateigentums' [obsession with private property, which was pursued by means increasingly dubious] (*RS*, 241; *RSe*, 203). He seeks a utopian space 'where no friends are buried nor Pathways stopt up', but also seeking a queer love among the crews he hired for the boats from the herring fishermen in Lowestoft, where he searches for a face that reminds him of William Browne (*RS*, 241; *RSe*, 203).

Relatedly, the aeroplane twice serves as an analogous queer heterotopia in Sebald's work. Sebald twice revisits the figure of a young man called Gerald (or, in an early version, Douglas) who studies science. Both men become dear companions of Sebaldian melancholics in his later fictions: Gerald Fitzpatrick in *Austerlitz* and his precursor Gerald Ashman in the posthumously published, unfinished 'Aufzeichnungen aus Korsika' [Notes from Corsica].[60] Both young men are astrophysicists, but they are also pilots, which allows them to achieve, both mentally and physically, soaring moments of levitation, key moments of escape from melancholia.[61] Both share a tender intimacy with the protagonist — Jacques Austerlitz in *Austerlitz*, the Sebaldian narrator in 'Aufzeichnungen aus Korsika'. Gerald Fitzpatrick is Austerlitz's adoptive younger brother or, indeed, romantic friend; after all, Gerald is Austerlitz's fag and Austerlitz tells the narrator that he 'ging mir in der Dunkelkammer gerne zur Hand' ('happily lent a hand in the darkroom'); he stands in a privileged relationship to the older Austerlitz, whom he idolizes: he, too, is another figure on the border between friendship and homosocial attraction (*A*, 117; *Ae*, 109). Gerald not only manages to soar over the heaviness of earthly existence with Austerlitz in his plane, but he also is clear-sighted enough to develop an astronomical theory about the ever-expanding nature of the universe under the influence of gravity. Despite his devotion to the little dog Toby — a well-recognized symbol of melancholy in Sebald's work — Gerald manages both to elude gravity and to transform it, through his intellectual work, into a nursery of new stars. These are signs, perhaps, of another universe where entropy and decay do not reign. Gerald Ashman/Douglas's early history matches Gerald Fitzpatrick's, but instead of dying in a crash, he lives on to meet the Sebaldian narrator in 1995. At this point, he is in his retirement, which means that he spends most of his time in the air.[62] Gerald Ashman/Douglas offers to fly him to Corsica, even making him the offer of being his co-pilot on the flight, a suggestion that the narrator eagerly accepts.[63] Thus, the plane to Corsica becomes a queer heterotopia in its own right, a space of intimacy for the narrator and Gerald/Douglas, and one that allows the true experience of flight that never lets a man go.[64] Gerald/Douglas distinguishes clearly between the mechanized, simulation-like aviation undertaken by commercial airliners, and the lightness enabled by the plane: 'Inzwischen flogen wir freilich ganz anders dahin, so als seien wir noch in einer früheren Zeit' [Meanwhile we flew there in a completely different fashion, as though we were still in an earlier time].[65] This flight back in time, in the opposite direction to the crushing progress of modernity, also allows Gerald/Douglas to formulate, more explicitly than in most of Sebald's published writing, the credo of the Sebaldian bachelor, which is worth quoting at length:

> Einen sogenannten Hausstand zu gründen, zu heiraten oder gar Kinder in die Welt zu setzen, habe ich auch nur im entferntesten niemals erwogen. Die

einzige wirkliche Freiheit, die wir, vom Selbstmord abgesehen, vor anderen Tieren haben, ist ja die, uns nicht fortzupflanzen, & es wundert mich ständig, wie wenig sie wahrgenommen wird. Die Regungen des Sympathicus sind anscheinend unkontrollierbar. Mir selber sind Liebesgeschichten, bis auf wenige, beinahe metaphysische Ausnahmen, grundsätzlich absurd vorgekommen & Ehepaare mit ihrer meistens nur schlecht verhohlenen gegenseitigen Abneigungen geradezu grotesk. Was mich begrifft, so lebe ich nur, um von der Erde abheben zu können.[66]

[I never even remotely considered founding a so-called household, marrying or bringing children into the world. The only true freedom that we have above the animals, apart from suicide, is that not to reproduce ourselves, and I am constantly amazed how little it is realised. The stirrings of the sympathicus appear to be uncontrollable. For myself, love stories, apart from a few almost metaphysical exceptions, have always appeared absurd, and married couples with their generally only poorly concealed mutual antipathies downright grotesque. As for me, I only live to levitate from the earth.]

The cases of Farrar, Swinburne, Le Strange, FitzGerald, and Gerald/Duncan show the limits of bachelorhood and hybrid textual production as systems of resistance. Silence, withdrawal, and heterotopic idylls lead to a tragic crumbling of the physical and mental faculties of the bachelor, which is more akin to the 'bent head' that the line of flight seeks to escape than to concerted resistance. Comic camp performances of self, fleeting moments of queer association, and affinities with animals reproduce elements of the Deleuzian line of flight, and achieve a production of intensities, but eventually get drawn back into the Thanatic history of destruction. Not all of Sebald's bachelors practise resistance solely by virtue of their saintly withdrawal from the world, however. In the next chapter, I show that avowed queer love, as well as the schizo-poetics of the bachelor, can both form explicit resistance to systems of domination in Sebald, and become embroiled in problematic tropes of Orientalism and colonialism.

Notes to Chapter 2

1. 'Summa Scientiae: System und Systemkritik bei Elias Canetti', in *Die Beschreibung des Unglücks*, pp. 93–102 (p. 98).
2. Christian Moser, 'Peripatetic Liminality: Sebald and the Tradition of the Literary Walk', in *The Undiscover'd Country: W. G. Sebald and the Poetics of Travel*, ed. by Markus Zisselsberger (Rochester, NY: Camden House, 2010), pp. 37–62 (p. 54).
3. Jorge Luis Borges, 'Tlön, Uqbar, Orbis Tertius', in *Collected Fictions*, trans. by Andrew Hurley (New York: Penguin Putnam, 1988), pp. 68–69.
4. John Beck and Gabriele Eckhart have dealt persuasively with the significance of the melancholy aspect of this quote for *Die Ringe des Saturn*. John Beck, 'Reading Room: Erosion and Sedimentation in Sebald's Suffolk', in *W. G. Sebald: A Critical Companion*, ed. by J. J. Long and Anne Whitehead (Edinburgh: Edinburgh University Press, 2004),, pp. 75–88, and Gabriele Eckart, 'Against "Cartesian Rigidity": W. G. Sebald's Reception of Borges', in *W. G. Sebald: Schreiben ex patria/Expatriate Writing*, ed. by Gerhard Fischer (Amsterdam: Rodopi, 2009), pp. 509–22.
5. Borges, 'Tlön, Uqbar, Orbis Tertius', p. 78.
6. 'Unterm Spiegel des Wassers — Peter Handkes Erzählung von der Angst des Tormanns', in *Die Beschreibung des Unglücks*, pp. 115–30.

7. See Mikhail Bakhtin, 'The Bildungsroman and its Significance in the History of Realism (Towards a Historical Typology of the Novel)', in *Speech Genres and Other Late Essays*, trans. by Vern W. McGee, ed. by Caryl Emerson and Michael Holquist (Austin: University of Texas Press, 1986), pp. 10–59; also, Jürgen Jacobs, *Wilhelm Meister und seine Brüder* (Munich: Wilhelm Fink, 1972).

8. Santner, *On Creaturely Life*, p. 178.

9. Deleuze and Guattari, *Kafka*, p. 70.

10. Ibid., p. 71.

11. Judith Ryan, '"Lines of Flight": History and Territory in *The Rings of Saturn*', in *Schreiben ex patria/Expatriate Writing*, pp. 45–60 (p. 52).

12. Deleuze and Guattari, *Kafka*, p. 71.

13. Hutchinson, *Die dialektische Imagination*, p. 160.

14. Deleuze and Guattari, *Kafka*, p. 5.

15. Hutchinson, *Die dialektische Imagination*, pp. 129–31.

16. Deleuze and Guattari, *Anti-Oedipus*, p. 78.

17. Borges, 'Tlön, Uqbar, Orbis Tertius', p. 70.

18. Ibid., p. 71.

19. Adrian Daub, 'Donner à Voir: The Logics of the Caption in W. G. Sebald's *Rings of Saturn* and Alexander Kluge's *Devil's Blind Spot*', in *Searching for Sebald: Photography after W. G. Sebald*, ed. by Lise Patt with Christel Dillbohner (Los Angeles: Institute of Cultural Inquiry, 2007), pp. 306–29 (p. 309).

20. Stuart Jeffries, 'Atlas of the Soul', *The Guardian*, 18 December 1999. See Hutchinson, *Die dialektische Imagination*, p. 24, for a witty analysis of the parody.

21. Hutchinson, *Die dialektische Imagination*, p. 131.

22. Andrew Fippinger, 'Intimations and Imitations of Immortality: Swinburne's "By the North Sea" and "Poeta Loquitur"', *Victorian Poetry*, 47 (2009), 675–90 (p. 678).

23. Oscar Wilde, review of Swinburne's *Poems and Ballads* (Third Series), *Pall Mall Gazette*, 27 June 1889, quoted in Richard Ellmann, *Oscar Wilde* (London: Penguin, 1988), p. 272.

24. Ibid.

25. Thaïs E. Morgan, 'Reimagining Masculinity in Victorian Criticism: Swinburne and Pater', *Victorian Studies*, 36.3: *Victorian Sexualities* (1993), 315–32 (p. 325).

26. Cited in Richard Dellamora, *Masculine Desire: The Sexual Politics of Victorian Aestheticism* (Chapel Hill: University of North Carolina Press, 1990), p. 70.

27. Morgan, 'Reimagining Masculinity', p. 316.

28. Ibid., p. 317.

29. Dellamora, *Masculine Desire*, p. 82.

30. Ibid., p. 83.

31. Ibid., p. 92.

32. Deleuze and Guattari, *Kafka*, p. 78.

33. Ibid., p.79.

34. Ibid., p. 80.

35. The English trade paperback places the words 'liberated the camp at Bergen Belsen on the 14th of April 1945' before the page turn to the photo, which is reproduced across pages 60–61.

36. Daub, 'Donner à Voir', p. 324.

37. Ibid., p. 322.

38. Ibid., p. 324.

39. Deleuze and Guattari, *Kafka*, p. 36.

40. Long, *Image, Archive, Modernity*, p. 42.

41. Hutchinson, *Die dialektische Imagination*, p. 128.

42. Ibid., p. 128.

43. Peter de Polnay, *Into an Old Room: The Paradox of Edward Fitzgerald* (London: Secker & Warburg 1950), p. 10.

44. Ibid., p. 14.

45. Robert Young, *Colonial Desire: Hybridity in Theory, Culture, and Race* (London: Routledge, 1995), p. 23.

46. Ibid., p. 24; Mikhail Bakhtin, *The Dialogic Imagination: Four Essays*, trans. by Caryl Emerson and Michael Holquist (Austin: University of Texas Press, 1981), p. 361, cited in Young, *Colonial Desire*, p. 22.

47. Sheppard, 'Dexter — Sinister', p. 424; Fuchs, *Die Schmerzensspuren der Geschichte*, p. 61.

48. Long, *Image, Archive, Modernity*, p. 170.

49. Ahmed, *Queer Phenomenology*, pp. 80–81.

50. Havelock Ellis, Henry, *Studies in the Psychology of Sex*, II (1927), available in e-book form at <http://www.gutenberg.org/files/13611/13611-h/13611-h.htm> (accessed 15 December 2012).

51. Ibid., ch. 1.

52. Ibid.

53. Mary Cosgrove, 'Sebald for Our Time: The Politics of Melancholy and the Critique of Capitalism in his Work', in *W. G. Sebald and the Writing of History*, pp. 91–110 (p. 99).

54. Citing Gilles Deleuze and Felix Guattari, *Kafka: Für eine kleine Literatur*, (Frankfurt am Main 1976), p. 98 (*Kafka*, p. 71).

55. Michel Foucault, 'Of Other Spaces (1967), Heterotopias', trans. by Jay Miskowiec, available at <http://www.foucault.info/documents/heteroTopia/foucault.heteroTopia.en.html>, accessed 15 December 2012).

56. Öhlschläger, *Beschädigtes Leben*, p. 141.

57. Kevin Hetherington, *The Badlands of Modernity: Heterotopia and Social Ordering* (London and New York: Routledge, 1997), p. 46.

58. Foucault, 'Of Other Spaces'.

59. Ibid.

60. Sebald, 'Aufzeichnungen aus Korsika: Zur Natur- & Menschenkunde', Zweite Fassung, in *Wandernde Schatten*, pp. 159–211 (p. 159).

61. Hutchinson, *Die dialektische Imagination*, p. 146.

62. Sebald, 'Aufzeichnungen aus Korsika', p. 159. Translation mine.

63. Ibid., p. 160.

64. Ibid., p. 167.

65. Ibid., p. 168.

66. Ibid., p. 173.

CHAPTER 3

The Ruins of Sodom and Gomorrah: Queer Orientalism and Colonialism

Sebaldian Orientation and Disorientation

The chastity of the bachelor, as we saw in the last chapter, is a mode of minor resistance to bourgeois masculinity and its relentless drive for oppression and self-reproduction. In this chapter, I show how these fantasies of oppositional queer masculinity are connected to utopian fantasies of queer resistance to racist and colonial structures. In these fantasies, queer desire and queer love become sites of reconciliation between Germans and their racial others, become ways to undermine racist and colonial structures, and enable a transgression of bourgeois categories of gender, race, and nation. Sebald's queer oriental fantasies thus provide access to the Sebaldian utopias of transgression, reconciliation, and the suspension of time. As we have seen in the previous chapter, Edward FitzGerald's verse is, for Sebald, a place where the mediaeval Orient and the dwindling Occident can meet and reconcile in a way never allowed by the calamitous course of history (*RS*, 238; *RSe*, 200). FitzGerald's homosexuality facilitates a break with the repressive reproductive tradition of his aristocratic family and allows for a tender, poetic transgression of the border between his colonial and oppressive West and the oriental other. As so much of the rest of *Die Ringe des Saturn* chronicles the cataclysm of Western colonial expansion, including the misery that ensued when imperial Britain attempted to gain hegemony over nineteenth-century China, and the horrors of Belgian colonialism in the Congo, FitzGerald's poetic reconciliation achieves the rare status of a moment of redemption, underlined by its heterotopic presentation. In this chapter, I show that the orientation of Sebald's queer characters is frequently expressed by travel to, engagement with, or mimicry of the Orient. This is most clearly shown in Sebald's hagiography of Roger Casement in *Die Ringe des Saturn*, whom he canonizes for his political resistance to empire.[1] In *Nach der Natur*, Grünewald is caught between a Jewish wife and a male lover. In *Die Ausgewanderten*, Sebald also devotes the only narrative about a non-Jewish figure to his homosexual uncle, Ambros Adelwarth, who serves as a reconciliatory figure by having a love relationship with his Jewish employer, Cosmo. In these three narratives, Sebald can be viewed in a rich tradition of German queer Orientalist fantasy. The term 'Orientalism' was defined by Edward Said as a Western academic practice that dominated, restructured, and had authority over the Orient.[2] It has since been more broadly used as a term to describe a set of Western practices and fantasies about geographical locations and populations who are imagined as the other of the West. While Said excluded Germany from his initial study of Orientalism, subsequent research has demonstrated that not only did Germany have its own tradition of academic Orientalism, but that it has a long history of peculiarly German Orientalist fantasies, which, as Todd Kontje has shown, stretch back at least to the Middle Ages. These contain racist and violent elements, the most toxic and murderous of which were codified in National Socialist ideology.

Sebald's project certainly is in opposition to such racist and violent fantasies. However, other, more benign, and queerer fantasies are also part of German Orientalist traditions, such as a nineteenth-century fantasy of 'utopian cosmopolitanism'.[3] The vision of the FitzGerald minarets thus can be viewed as a part of this more reconciliatory fantasy. Moreover, fantasies about the Orient are necessarily also fantasies of gender, as the construction of the modern masculine self required a hegemonic relationship to feminized and racialized others. As we saw in the first chapter, Sebald's critical work problematizes the reciprocal construction of German and Jewish masculinities via the mid-nineteenth-century move away from the ghetto. In his fiction, Sebald both dismantles and parodies racialized constructs of gender. In the three characters studied in this chapter, Sebald delineates masculinities that hover between categories of gender and race, blurring and transgressing binary distinctions. Grünewald, Casement, and Adelwarth disrupt three constitutive moments in the history of German and European intersections of gender and race. This history moves from Grünewald's unhappy embroilment in the German inner colonization of Jews in the early modern period, to Casement's political resistance against European colonialism, which Sebald attributes to his queer sensibility, to Adelwarth's queer love affair and Greek journey with the Jewish Cosmo.[4] The queer moments in Grünewald's story occur in relation to fellow-Germans, whereas Casement and Adelwarth both engage in homoerotic practices which verge between oriental and Orientalist. While queer love between white Europeans and Jewish or non-white others carries within it the potential to overthrow categories of race, the danger of reinscribing those very categories is still present. Joseph A. Boone suggests that an examination of Orientalist homoerotics can undo fixed colonial categories, generating ambiguity and collision rather than reasserting 'an unproblematic intellectual domination over a mythic East as an object of desire'.[5] Jesse Matz sceptically asks whether it can really be proven, when examining individual practice rather than the rhetoric of queer advocacy, that Orientalist homoerotics really open up 'fissures in imperial discourse'.[6] As I will show, Sebald's Casement and Adelwarth are both located on an uneasy line between utopian transgression and ethically questionable reinscription of racial categories, both of which have long prehistories in German culture and letters. The disruptive potential of the Adelwarth figure, however, lies not only in his queer transgression of racial categories, but also in his status as the narrator's uncle. Thus, he opens up a space for alternative genealogies and family constellations within the narrator's familial imaginary that disrupt German patriarchy. Ahmed argues that sexual orientation can be thought together with race, because whiteness can be viewed as a 'straightening device' that is linked to compulsory heterosexuality and the generation of individuality. 'The prohibition of miscegenation and homosexuality belong, as it were, in the same register', Ahmed argues, and links the heterosexual reproduction of the family line to the reproduction of whiteness.[7] Ahmed's arguments shed light on Sebald's treatment of the entwined literary tropes of queer desire and colonialism. Part of the disorientation of Sebald's characters can be viewed as precisely an attempt to go astray, to resist compulsory heterosexuality and to transgress the borders of Germany and Europe in search of a queer affinity that might provide a source of resistance to the straightening and oppressive orientation of bourgeois society and family.

A brief passage in *Die Ringe des Saturn* demonstrates how the Sebaldian narrator links queer encounters and oriental travels. In Section IV, the Sebaldian narrator recalls a trip to The Hague. Here, he stays in the heterotopic zone next to the station, a zone which he describes as 'exterritorial', populated as it is by both businesses and people operating on the fringe of society (*RS*, 101; *RSe*, 81). The narrator walks past Bristol Bar, Yuksels Café, Videoboetik, Aran Turk's pizza shop, a Euro-Sex-Shop, an Islamic butchers, and a carpet shop, above which a fresco shows a caravan crossing the desert (*RS*, 100; *RSe*, 80). In this marginal quarter, characterized by immigration, sexual commerce, and migration, the narrator has two distinct but linked queer encounters. In a questionable hotel near the station, the reception is staffed by two men whom he characterizes as a queer couple: 'zwei nicht mehr ganz junge, offenbar miteinander seit langem vermählte Herren und zwischen ihnen, an Kindes Statt sozusagen, ein aprikosenfarbener Pudel' [two gentlemen, no longer in their first youth, who must have been partners for a long time; and between them, in the stead of a child, as it were, was an apricot-coloured poodle] (*RS*, 99; *RSe*, 80). The narrator then leaves the hotel to travel around the exterritorial area, and while staring at the fresco of the caravan, a dark, bearded man slips so close to him that their elbows touch (*RS*, 100; *RSe*, 81). The brief but intimate touch opens up a view for the narrator through the door into the building, where he sees hundreds of pairs of shoes piled on top of each other, for an 'unvergeßlichen, ganz aus der Zeit gelösten Moment' [unforgettable moment that seemed to exist outside time] (*RS*, 101; *RSe*, 81). Further, he sees a minaret soaring from the dealership into the azure Dutch evening sky, echoing the minarets that are visible from FitzGerald's park at Boulge. This intimate touch between Occident and Orient is doubled by the fleeting touch between narrator and dark, bearded man, and enables the suspension of time that characterizes Sebaldian utopias. The queer pair of elderly gentlemen, by contrast, is a camp phenomenon more akin to FitzGerald on his yacht in a feather boa. While their poodle 'in the stead of a child' calls to mind at once their refusal to reproduce and the melancholy dog that is governed by the text's ruling planet of Saturn, with its apricot colouring, it remains a comic rather than an illuminating image. The bachelors act as gatekeepers to the exterritorial zone, which contains not only the transgressive possibility of an encounter between Orient and Occident, but other more grotesque and sinister sexual deviations from the bourgeois order. These include a pimp in a white suit, cruising in a limousine, and a man, whom Sebald describes as 'dark-skinned', pursued by another dark-skinned man wielding a knife, eyes gleaming with rage. Terrified by these violent and sexually perverse sights, the Sebaldian narrator repairs to bed, where he imagines that he feels the knife pass through his own ribs, a clear fantasy of homosexual penetration.

In The Hague, queer oriental visions and fantasies mobilize two elements of the Sebaldian utopia, the suspension of time and a reconciliation between East and West. As well as the promise of visions of oriental secrets and dangerous encounters with dark-skinned men, the exterritorial zone carries with it threats to the narrator's bodily integrity and bourgeois security. Further, just as the touch by the dark-skinned man enables a vision of the Orient for the narrator, Moser suggests that the near-stabbing enables a liminal and compassionate form of vision for the narrator, which leads to his empathetic experience when viewing Rembrandt's *The Anatomy Lesson* the next day.[8] Sebald develops a similar queer combination of paranoid *jouissance* and liminal vision yet more strongly in *Schwindel. Gefühle.*, as we will see in the next chapter. In The Hague, racist and old-fashioned gay clichés jostle with queer desire and terror.

German–Jewish Affinities at the Dawn of Modernity: Matthias Grünewald

European colonialism, which Sebald always links to its criminal nadir in Nazism and the subsequent resonance of Nazi crimes throughout contemporary times and spaces, is a key concern particularly of *Die Ringe des Saturn*, but also appears in all of Sebald's poetic texts. As we have seen in the discussion of FitzGerald, for Sebald, the history of colonialism is not restricted to the nineteenth and twentieth centuries.[9] While one manifestation of early modern colonialism in Sebald's work is the rapacious Anglo-Norman FitzGerald family, the oppressive and exploitative relationship of Gentile to Jew in early modern Europe is fundamental to Sebald's understanding of the dialectic of Enlightenment, and can be seen as the constitutive moment of racialized and gendered injustice in his work. In *Nach der Natur*, the vicissitudes of this exploitation are explored in the relationship between the painter Matthias Grünewald and his Jewish convert wife. In the first section of the poem, Grünewald is a martyr to the prison of bourgeois masculinity being constructed in Germany in the late sixteenth century. In Sebald's poem, he attempts to escape this by treading a perilous line between sanctioned, sometimes doomed, heterosexual love, and forbidden homosocial or homosexual identification. Grünewald is thus not only a *Wahlverwandtschaft* of Sebald's, but his *Isenheim Altarpiece* forms a key image of creatureliness throughout Sebald's work, in particular in the 'Max Aurach' narrative of *Die Ausgewanderten*. Öhlschläger shows how Grünewald's vision of the crucifixion, in Sebald's ekphrasis, links the level of personal suffering with the objective progress of history.[10] Further, she notes how this pain, in Grünewald's picture, is articulated through the gestures of the body. This painting acts as a gateway to painful memory for Max Aurach, for whom viewing the paroxysm of pain in the altarpiece reminds him of the painful bent position he took while learning to write as a child (*DA*, 256; *E*, 171). The memory is accompanied by a photo that shows a writing boy with precisely the *panischer Halsknick* [panic-stricken kink in the neck] diagnosed by Eric Santner as 'the trace of creaturely life registered in the limbs', the bodily attitude that reveals the utter fallenness of nature and human history.[11] Here,

Sebald's programmatic statement 'Die Beschreibung des Unglücks schließt in sich die Möglichkeit zu seiner Überwindung ein' [the description of calamity includes the possibility of overcoming it] shows its full force (*BU*, 12). Hence, Grünewald's exemplary depiction of unhappiness enables Aurach's painful work of memory to begin. Aurach begins to remember his painful childhood memories in Colmar, and this process of remembrance holds out a hope for escape from his unhappy burden of human history and personal suffering.

The *Isenheim Altarpiece* does not only trigger *mémoire involuntaire* as a form of resistance to the course of history, just as memory is not the only route to healing the *panischer Halsknick*, which can be unbent by a Deleuzian line of flight, as we have seen. The *Isenheim Altarpiece* is one in a series of images in the poem that invokes the averted, disoriented, or liminal gaze, which is awakened by queer oriental encounters in *Die Ringe des Saturn*. Corkhill demonstrates that Grünewald's repeatedly averted gaze has a series of meanings, among them 'Grünewald's own self-doubts and existential angst', empathy, and a fear of the future.[12] For Corkhill, Grünewald depicts the opposite of 'the oozing self-confidence of the Renaissance self-made man', thereby eschewing the humanism and positivism of the Renaissance, which with the hindsight of the twentieth century appears a precursor of Enlightenment hubris.[13] Grünewald's paintings instead become a site of resistance to the developing constraints of modern masculinity. In place of the individualist self-aggrandisement of the Renaissance portrait, Grünewald favours *Wahlverwandtschaften* with brother painters such as Holbein, who paints him into one of his pictures:

> Ja, es scheine, als hätten im Kunstwerk
> die Männer einander verehrt wie Brüder,
> einander dort oft ein Denkmal gesetzt,
> wo ihre Wege sich kreuzten.

> [Indeed, it seemed as though in such works of art
> men had revered each other like brothers, and
> often made monuments in each other's
> image where their paths had crossed.] (*NdN*, 8; *AN*, 6)

The politically resistant implications of this brotherly affinity emerge when the Sebaldian narrator tells us that the author of this affinity theory is the art critic Fraenger, whose books were burned by the fascists. He thus sets up a direct opposition between affinity and Nazi cultural persecution. Grünewald's affiliation with brother artists is at once an aesthetically productive relationship, not dissimilar to Edward FitzGerald's literary *Wahlverwandtschaften*, and a resistance to the strictures of bourgeois masculinity. Just as Grünewald's averted gaze is a refusal of the hubristic direct gaze of Renaissance man, his queered sexual orientation is a side-step away from the heterosexual norms of the times. The affection of German men for each other, in the section set in the sixteenth century, is framed by the narrator as a response firstly to the terrible separation of the genders enforced by the church, but also to the burden of gender itself: 'Auch das Unglück der Heiligen | ist ihr Geschlecht' [The misfortune of saints | is their sex] (*NdN*, 9; *AN*, 7). Indeed, the narrator claims that the transition to modernity around 1490 is marked by the replacement of the mediaeval disease of St Antony's Fire with new so-called plagues of lust, which have been widely believed (though this is nowhere explicitly suggested) to have come to Europe as a consequence of the colonization of the New World (*NdN*, 20; *AN*, 23).[14] The dawn of European modernity is marked by this plague of sexual disease, which seems to link the suffering caused by sexuality to a divine punishment for the crimes of colonialism. The 'panischer Halsknick' endemic to Grünewald's work indicates, for Sebald, that reproduction itself is a blind experiment, created by a nature that is 'wie ein unsinniger Bastler' [like a senseless botcher] (*NdN*, 24; *AN*, 27).

Transgressing the painful boundary between male and female is Grünewald's St Georgius Miles, whom Albes correctly deems a 'hermaphrodite', and who, the Sebaldian narrator suggests, is a representation of Grünewald himself. The narrator describes St Georgius Miles as displaying a combination of male and female traits, as a 'Mann mit eisernem Rumpf, erzen geründeter | Brust, rotgoldnem Haupthaar und silbernen | weiblichen Zügen' [man with the iron torso, rounded chest | of ore, red-golden hair and silver | feminine features] who is about to transgress the threshold of the painting (*NdN*, 7; *AN*, 5). Grünewald also, like St Georgius Miles, transgresses a boundary, here to overcome the sexual segregation of Jews and Christians, which in mediaeval times was effected by sumptuary laws intended to prevent all carnal intercourse between them on pain of death (*NdN*, 12; *AN*, 13). Sebald emphasizes the continuation of anti-Semitic laws from the mediaeval into the early modern period, and by implication also into the twentieth century, as these sumptuary laws are superseded 'im Zuge der bürgerlichen | Ordnungswaltung' [in the train | of civic reform] by the erection of a ghetto to enclose the Jews, a punitive structure that foreshadows his Foucauldian critique of 'pre-modern methods of exercising power' in *Schwindel. Gefühle.*, *Die Ringe des Saturn*, and *Austerlitz* (*NdN*, 12; *AN*, 13).[15] Grünewald transgresses these ghetto boundaries to marry a Jewish woman, Enchin, who is baptized Anna shortly before their marriage. However, this is not a utopian transgression leading to a German–Jewish reconciliation: although the Sebaldian narrator insists that her conversion does not take place at Grünewald's insistence, the marriage is unhappy. Grünewald marries her because of his desire to set up a household and take up an apprentice, aspirations that are couched in terms of Grünewald's desire to complete the *Isenheim Altarpiece*, but which also entail the construction of a bourgeois household. Thus, the foundered marriage of German artist and beautiful Jewess is grounded in embourgeoisement and conversion, and cannot provide any founding genealogy for any idealized German–Jewish symbiosis. Instead, Anna's unhappy marriage exposes the cruelty of early German anti-Semitism, and demonstrates that the nascent modern German state, consecrated in the institution of the Christian bourgeois family, merely perpetuated rather than dissolved the mediaeval clerical oppression of Jews by Germans. At the end of the poem, Grünewald tries to pass on his artistic legacy to their son, but the child dies inexplicably at the age of fourteen, marking the end of any hope to create a German–Jewish line of heterosexual reproduction and artistic inheritance.

If German–Jewish reconciliation via bourgeois marriage fails to redeem Grünewald from the straitjacket of modernity, Sebald infers that Grünewald's queer desires provide a more radical source of community. This community undermines

the strictures of bourgeois manhood by brotherly affinity and artistic blurring of
the boundaries of masculine individuality. However, this gender transgression also
leads to gendered victimization of women. The poet claims that it is because of
Grünewald's 'better eye for men', which lovingly paints the faces and 'ganze Körper-
lichkeit' of men, that Grünewald's Anna becomes 'ein Opfer der bösen Vernunft'
[a victim of perverse reason] (NdN, 15; AN, 16). Grünewald's queered artistic gaze
makes victims of women, who feature as malicious gossips engaged in a conspiracy
against men in Grünewald's Lindenhardt Altarpiece. Grünewald's 'eye for men',
which culpably ignores his wife, is both an attempt to subvert the restrictiveness of
bourgeois masculinity and a demonstration of the limits of queer utopian strategies.
Eve Kosofsky Sedgwick suggests that homoerotic triangles are constitutive of queer
identity in nineteenth-century British literature, as the rivalry between two men
over a woman proves a stronger bond than the purported heterosexual desire for
her.[16] Here, the pretext of heterosexual desire is quickly abandoned, and the woman
becomes the victim of the victorious homoerotic bond between Grünewald and his
chosen male brethren; Grünewald repeats the intertwined logic of anti-Semitism
and misogyny.

The political-sexual significance of the Grünewald figure lies not in heterosexual
German–Jewish reconciliation, but rather in his resistance to the heroic individualism
of the Renaissance male. Sebald's Grünewald is a doubled figure, thereby putting
into question the boundaries of the unitary self in life and in painting. The text asks
the question whether two painters, Mathis Nithart and Grünewald, hide between
the name of Matthias Grünewald. The narrator, puzzling out this riddle, suggests
that the obscure Nithart may be depicted on the Isenheim Altarpiece, and have
contributed to his own portrait as the homoerotic martyr Saint Sebastian:

> Hier haben zwei Maler in einem Körper,
> dessen verletztes Fleisch ihnen beiden gehörte,
> ihre Natur ausstudiert.
>
> [Here two painters in one body,
> whose hurt flesh belonged to both,
> to the end pursued the study
> of their own nature.] (NdN, 17; AN, 19)]

Like the tortured image of St Sebastian, their male friendship contains both homo-
erotic and abject aspects, a 'Männerfreundschaft | schwankend zwischen Entsetzen
und Treue' [male friendship wavering | between horror and loyalty] (NdN, 18; AN,
19). Like FitzGerald's friendship with Browne, this relationship ends in tragedy
when Nithart dies young of melancholia. Nithart also belongs to the register of camp
Sebaldian bachelors who demonstrate a fondness for gaudy clothes, as evidenced by
the register of Nithart's belongings after his death (NdN, 19; AN, 19). The poem
asserts that these colourful clothes must also have belonged to Grünewald, thereby
underscoring the brotherly line of inheritance between them that undermines the
strict paternal line of heterosexual inheritance. In a similar fashion to FitzGerald's
mournful incorporation of his lost lover Browne, Sebald suggests that Grünewald
carries both his own unhappiness and that of Nithart with him until the end of his
life (NdN, 32; AN, 32).

Male–male solidarity and friendship are also connected to an attempt at more directly political moments of resistance to state oppression in 'Wie der Schnee auf den Alpen' [As the Snow on the Alps]. Significantly, the narrator names one of Grünewald's political sympathizers as his namesake, Sebald Beham, an engraver, heretic, and friend of Grünewald. Sebald Beham is also a precursor of Sebald's later exiles, as he has been banished along with his brother: 'als gottlose Maler | verhaftet und wegen Ketzerei | aus ihrer Heimatstadt ausgewiesen [seized on January 12 as godless painters | and driven out of their native city for heresy] (*NdN*, 29; *AN*, 32). In exile from their home towns, the artists discuss the potential for resistance promised by Thomas Müntzer's peasant uprising of 1525. This mass uprising, however, is cruelly put down, and the news of the defeat reaches Grünewald on 18 May (Sebald's birthday). The oppressing classes put out the eyes of the rebels, and Grünewald covers his own eye — which had been an 'eye for men' — in empathy: 'Er hörte aber das Augenausstechen | das lang noch vorging [...] Wochenweis trug er damals | eine dunkle Binde | vor dem Gesicht [Yet he could hear the gouging out | of eyes that long continued [...] For weeks at that time he wore | a dark bandage over his face] (*NdN*, 31; *AN*, 35).

At the end of the section, Grünewald's optic nerve breaks, signalling the end both of his life and of the potential for the queerly oriented gaze to draw the painter away from the calamities of history. All the elements of the Sebaldian complex of queerness and resistance are present in this early poem: distrust of bourgeois marriage and the domestic sphere, frustrated longing for a German–Jewish symbiosis, aesthetic affinity, scopophilia, political resistance, and martyred male flesh. Further, the repeated doublings and affiliations between Grünewald, Sebald, St Georgius, Nithart, St Sebastian, and others, the redoubling between the Sebaldian narrator and Fraenger, and finally between the mysterious companions M. N. and 'engineer D. in Zürich' in the last, autobiographical part of the triptych, point forward to the uncanny queer doppelgangers of *Schwindel. Gefühle.* These queer doublings will be discussed in more detail in the next chapter; suffice it here to say that the drawing of the Sebaldian narrator himself into this series of doubles indeed suggests that the poem's ekphrasis illuminates, as Albes argues, those elements of Sebald's self that cannot be explained in words.[17] A queer orientation of the eyes allows Grünewald both to see clearly the cruel workings of fallen nature and to gaze aside from the prescriptions of Christian marriage towards forbidden objects of desire: a Jew and a man. However, the suffering caused by Grünewald's melancholic apprehension of the world, his turning away from earthly success, and his cruel treatment of his wife (a species of queer misogyny) mean that such resistant disorientation ends in blindness and tragedy. Grünewald's treatment of Echen/Anna further highlights the dangers of exploitation inherent in attempts to reconcile Germans with their exploited ethnic others by means of sexual union. These dangers become particularly pertinent when considering the narrative of Roger Casement in *Die Ringe des Saturn*.

Queer Martyr: Roger Casement

Grünewald's disorientation from bourgeois masculinity at the outset of modernity carries within it a passive political resistance to the oppressive powers both of the modern German nation and of normative Renaissance masculinity. However, as we have seen, this passive resistance becomes subsumed in the general melancholy that overcomes Grünewald. The Irish human rights defender, republican rebel, and homosexual martyr Roger Casement, by contrast, is a figure in Sebald's work striking both for the success of his political resistance to colonialism and exploitation, and for the unreservedly positive way in which this decidedly un-Saturnine figure is portrayed. Although his narrative is central to *Die Ringe des Saturn*, and draws together many of the concerns that permeate the text, Sebald's Casement shares in none of the eccentricities, poetic practices, traumas, or indeed romantic yearnings that characterize the other melancholy bachelors of *Die Ringe des Saturn*. He forms an ethically heroic counterpart to Joseph Conrad's imperial complicity, as he makes his appearance in *Die Ringe des Saturn* as a figure from Joseph Conrad's Congo diaries. His quixotic commitment to the overthrow of Belgian and British colonial rule mirrors that of Conrad's father, Apollo Korzeniowski, to the overthrow of Russian rule in Poland. In his diaries, as they are represented in Sebald's novel, Conrad describes the rapacious greed and sickening violence that marked the Belgian colonization of the Congo. Conrad becomes marked with colonial guilt for even entering the brutalized territory of the Congo: 'die Mühen, unter denen er zu leiden hat, [befreien] ihn nicht von der Schuld, die er durch seine bloße Anwesenheit im Kongo auf sich lädt' [his own travails did not absolve him from the guilt which he had incurred by his mere presence in the Congo] (*RS*, 147; *RSe*, 120).

Conrad subsequently attempts restitution by producing a work of literature, *Heart of Darkness* (1902), and his hitherto blithe sense of adventure gives way to the characteristically Sebaldian 'immer wieder lang anhaltende, mit seiner schriftstellerischen Arbeit abwechselnde Verzweiflungsanfälle' [protracted bouts of despair [...] alternating with his writing] (*RS*, 147; *RSe*, 121). Margaret Bruzelius argues that the Conrad narrative demonstrates the bankruptcy of the adventure plot in an age of decay and melancholy: 'Tale-telling loses whatever redemptive or integrative function it may once have had'.[18] The textual status of *Heart of Darkness* can be seen, then, as akin to that of the writings of FitzGerald, Swinburne, and of Sebald himself, or the paintings of Grünewald, a politically impotent attempt to make good the catastrophes of history by describing suffering in art. By contrast, Casement's redemption from imperial complicity is achieved by heroic political martyrdom, and his career as a human rights defender in the Congo and Central America is marked by political success. In keeping with Sebald's overriding concern with the active preservation of memory throughout *Die Ringe des Saturn*, Conrad presents Casement as a hero of remembrance: he reports to a London acquaintance that Casement could report things that Conrad had long tried to forget. Casement's clarity of vision is juxtaposed with the inadequacy of the historian's panoramic vision in trying to discern how history really was — 'wir, die Überlebenden, sehen alles von oben herunter, sehen alles zugleich und wissen dennoch nicht, wie es war' [we, the survivors, see everything from above, see everything at once, and still we do not know how it was] (*RS*, 152; *RSe*, 127). By contrast, Casement is described as unusually clear-sighted: 'Wer nicht geblendet ist von der Gier nach dem Geld, so schrieb Casement, vor dessen Augen entfaltet sich die Agonie eines ganzen Volkes' [Anyone [...] who was not blinded by greed for money, wrote Casement, would behold the agony of an entire race in all its heart-rending details] (*RS*, 154; *RSe*, 127). If, in the Matthias Grünewald episode in *Nach der Natur*, the averted gaze is a sign of melancholy resistance, here it is the direct gaze, akin to that of Benjamin's angel of history, that denotes Casement's uncompromising commitment to bear witness to and fight the injustice in the Congo. Although, like Grünewald, who turns away from the recognition of society, Casement is depicted as careless of his reputation, possessed of a 'quixotischer, dem beruflichen Fortkommen des an sich vielversprechenden Envoyés gewiß nicht zuträglicher Eifer' [quixotic zeal incompatible with the professional advancement of otherwise so promising an envoy], he nonetheless is knighted by the British government for his humanitarian efforts, in an attempt to 'deal with' his excess zeal (*RS*, 156; *RSe*, 128). Furthermore, when he becomes involved in the Irish rebellion, he is portrayed as taking an active and also wise role in the turn of events, undertaking a dangerous secret mission to Berlin and then attempting to call the Easter Rising off when it becomes clear that the rebellion is doomed to failure. Sebald's depiction of Casement's ethically responsible actions casts into a sorry light his co-conspirators, characterized as idealists, poets, trades unionists, and teachers, who decide to push on with the Easter Rising nonetheless. Again, this positive representation of his engagement in politically motivated violence is an unusual perspective, given that elsewhere in his writings Sebald's sympathies are repeatedly manifested for precisely such poets and teachers, whose resistance lies in bachelor withdrawal and a literature of restitution. Heroic figures who engage in military adventures are, in Sebald's work, more often exemplars of the dialectic of Enlightenment, rash adventurers whose grandiose plans come to grief and bring historical catastrophe in their wake, such as the 'Corsican comet' Napoleon, or Henri Beyle, whose early military enthusiasm is replaced by doubt and darkened memory in his middle years in *Schwindel. Gefühle*. Fuchs is therefore correct to refer to the Casement section in exalted terms as a 'hagiography', portraying a tragic hero who undertakes a solitary attempt to change the negative course of history.[19] She rightly notes Sebald's overriding concern to stylize Casement as an isolated advocate of oppressed colonial peoples, whether this stylization bears a close relationship to the historical record or not.[20]

Sebald's account goes beyond anti-colonialist approval of Casement's activism, to develop a hybrid image of Casement that contributes to a particularly queer hagiography. In Sebald's account, Casement's isolation is compounded by his hybridity, which affords him a liminal position within Irish history, despite his wholehearted identification with Irish nationalism, as he is the son of a Catholic mother and an Ulster Protestant father. Casement's hybrid nature is emphasized throughout Sebald's account: for instance, the one image of Casement that is retained by the Sebaldian narrator from the BBC television documentary about Casement and the Congo is Conrad's description of seeing Casement 'nur in Begleitung eines Loanda-Jungen und seiner englischen Bulldoggen Biddy und Paddy in die gewaltige Wildnis aufbrechen' [start off into an unspeakable wilderness [...] with two bulldogs: Paddy (white) and Biddy (brindle) at his heels and a Loanda boy carrying a bundle] (*RS*, 126; *RSe*, 104). The hybridity and liminality inherent in the Anglo-Irish position is clear here: Casement is accompanied by English bulldogs with Irish names, is perceived in a state between waking and dream, and is radically deterritorialized, given that he is in the Congolese wilderness, yet appears as though he were returning from an afternoon stroll in Hyde Park. Here, we should attend to how Sebald makes slight changes to the historical record in order to create this view of Casement. Michael Hulse, when translating this section, noted that Sebald's German version contained several changes to Conrad's original description that emphasize this aura of hybridity:

> He added the comment that, in the Congo, the wilderness surrounds every settlement; he added the adjective 'englisch' to the bulldogs, but removed their colours, [...] the park had become not just any park but one iconically recognizable to every German reader, Hyde Park.[21]

The hybrid Casement can bear witness to the horrors of the Congo, whereas the Congolese victims of Belgian atrocities, excluded from the bounds of the regulated public sphere as examples of *homo sacer*, cannot. Equally, Casement's privileged position as an Anglo-Irishman gives him precisely the critical perspective and connections he needs to engage in the Irish cause. Casement's background, Sebald claims, meant that, like FitzGerald, he belonged to the class whose task it was to uphold English rule over Ireland, but Casement instead identifies with the cause of the indigenous 'white Indians of Ireland' (*RS*, 147; *RSe*, 129). Sebald makes it clear that Casement's sympathies are on the side of the group that he calls Catholics in the Easter Rising, and he dismisses Ulster Unionists as merely interested in shoring up their own privilege (*RS*, 147; *RSe*, 129). Such unabashedly partisan accounts of Irish history have been out of favour in Irish historiography for at least two generations, and Sebald's mobilization of them demonstrates his commitment to a hagiography rather than to either history 'as it was' or lived, experienced history.[22] This insistence on Casement's status as exemplary and active freedom fighter is important, as Sebald makes his clearest link between queerness and the politics of resistance when discussing Casement:

> Der einzige Schluß, der daraus gezogen werden kann, ist der, daß es möglicherweise gerade die Homosexualität Casements war, die ihn befähigte, über die Grenzen der gesellschaftlichen Klassen und der Rassen hinweg die andauernde Unterdrückung, Ausbeutung, Versklavung und Verschrottung derjenigen zu erkennen, die am weitesten entfernt waren von den Zentren der Macht.

> [We may draw from this the conclusion that it was precisely Casement's homosexuality that sensitized him to the continuing oppression, exploitation, enslavement and destruction, across the borders of social class and race, of those who were furthest from the centres of power.] (*RS*, 162; *RSe*, 134)

Such an empathetic, indeed affective reading of Casement's political commitment is in keeping with certain lines of queer theorizing current in the early twentieth century. For instance, Havelock Ellis argues that 'among moral leaders, and persons with strong ethical instincts, there is a tendency toward the more elevated forms of homosexual feeling'. Havelock Ellis explains this by saying that a 'person who sees his own sex also bathed in sexual glamour, brings to his work of human service an ardor wholly unknown to the normally constituted individual; morality to him has become one with love'.[23] Freud agrees, writing that homosexual inclinations can join with the ego-drives to help contribute an erotic element to the 'general love of mankind'. 'Manifest homosexuals', Freud claims, 'are marked out by particularly intensive participation in [...] general interests of humanity', though for Freud this only holds true for 'those that resist physical activity'.[24] One account of Casement's trial argues that the historical Casement himself subscribed to these views; his lead council, A. M. Sullivan, claimed in 1954 that Casement argued that his 'filthy practices and the rhapsodical glorification of them were inseparable from genius, and I was to cite a list of all truly great men to prove it'.[25] Sebald's assertion that homosexuality, which doomed Casement to execution, also enabled a politically transgressive vision is one still claimed by queer activists. Here, Colm Tóibín's essay on Casement in *The New York Review of Books*, whose starting point is this moment in *Die Ringe des Saturn*, is particularly relevant: 'we all bring our own concerns to Casement's story: Sebald is interested in the literary connections; Dudgeon is interested in the gay Casement; McCormack entertains the idea of the text as shifting and unstable'.[26] In the period following the publication of Casement's 'Black Diaries' in 1994, during which *Die Ringe des Saturn* was written, ascribing secular sainthood to Casement became fashionable among left-wing Irish historians and critics, after a period during which, as both Sebald and the novelist Colm Tóibín write, Casement's homosexuality was vigorously denied by the Catholic Irish establishment, as being incompatible with his holy status as nationalist martyr. Brian Lewis's essay on 'The Queer Life and Afterlife of Roger Casement' therefore places Sebald in a line with Tóibín of liberal commentators in the 1990s who agreed that 'Casement's sexuality was the key to all the laudable aspects of his life'.[27] Matz's scepticism about the inherent power of queerness to open up fissures in imperial discourse is salutary here. Indeed, Tóibín himself, although he supports Sebald's view by suggesting 'It is possible that his nocturnal activities with the very people he was trying to save gave him tenderness for them', also quotes from Casement's writings, showing unpleasant racist views that Sebald excludes from his hagiography. On the inhabitants of Brazil, for instance, Tóibín cites Casement as follows: 'Heavens! what loathsome people they are! A mixture of Jew and Nigger, and God knows what; altogether the nastiest human black pudding the world has yet cooked in her tropical stew pot.'[28] Barzilai's analysis of Sebaldian masculinity examines the suspicion that Sebald at times uses the politically marginalized other to frame the anxieties of male identity. If, as she argues, and as we have seen in Sebald's critical writings, the Jew represents the repressed colonized other of the German bourgeois self, so the colonized Irishman was constructed, throughout English discourse in the nineteenth century, as feminine, queer, unmanly. However, when such sainthood is ascribed by a German narrator concerned to anatomize the dark corners of Germany's history, rather than by a gay Irish writer such as Tóibín seeking to brush his own country's history against the grain, Sebald appears to be reversing the process of Orientalism to project onto the queer Irish other all of those politically resistant virtues that the Germans lack. In other words, Sebald in part reinstates those boundaries across which Casement is supposed to have wandered. Tóibín also writes that

> As his dislike of England increased, so did [Casement's] admiration of Germany. He admired 'the honesty and integrity of the German mind, the strength of the German intellect, the skill of the German hand and brain, the justice and vigour of German law, the intensity of German culture, science, education and social development.' When the war broke out, he had no difficulty supporting Germany.[29]

Thus Casement, by Tóibín's account, in no way saw any clear historical teleology that already foresaw the roots of National Socialism in nineteenth-century German culture. Moreover, after spending time in Germany, he described the German officer class as 'lower than the Congo savages', once more confusing the boundaries of colonial history.[30] Sebald's hagiography elides such discontinuities and fragmentations in Casement's world-view.

If Sebald's Casement simultaneously reflects fashionable queer discourses of the 1990s and a melancholic view of history, Sebald's uncritical retelling of the Casement hagiography in no way questions Casement's own sexual tourism in the Congo. The Black Diaries mentioned by Sebald document a decade-long series of sexual encounters with underage South American and African boys. We should remember that Casement appears to Sebald in the dream accompanied by a Loanda boy, who does not speak, but who might well, if Casement's Black Diaries are to be believed (as Sebald suggests they should be), be paid by Casement in return for sexual favours. Such dubious paedophile tourism sits ill with Sebald's heroic portrayal of Casement. Fuchs, correctly, writes that Casement's historically verifiable attitudes are not to the point in *Die Ringe des Saturn*, since he is not writing a critical account of the historical Casement, but creating an affective *lieu de mémoire*.[31] Sebald's rewriting of Casement goes beyond that of a *lieu de mémoire*, though, as I have shown. It is also one around which Sebald's connection between historical resistance and queer desire can crystallize. Sebald's hagiography of Casement reveals his investment in discourses that assimilate queer desire to anti-colonial resistance, such as those advocated by Havelock Ellis and Edward Carpenter, while overlooking the historical evidence that demonstrates the profound complicity of gay sexual tourism in the apparatus of colonialism.[32] Thus, Sebald's reproduction of Casement's diary from 24 and 25 March 1903 appears as though Sebald is compulsively adducing documentary evidence to his narrative that testifies to the 'truth' of his homosexuality, and hence to his moral virtue. Both Long and Carol Duttlinger have criticized Sebald's reproduction, arguing that such an archival production of the 'truth' about Casement's sexuality demonstrates the alignment of Sebald's narrator with 'a medical-judicial apparatus that forces the diaries to speak the truth', while at the same time defining homosexuality as the constitutive truth of a life and criminalizing it.[33] Long further shows that the diary extract does not, in fact, demonstrate Casement's queer sexual activity, and Duttlinger argues that this demonstrates the paranoia of the Sebaldian narrator, who must necessarily see persecution at every turn, even if it is unfounded.[34] Yet, just as Sebald's subtle rewording of Conrad's narrative makes of Casement a more culturally hybrid and exiled figure, and, as we will see, the 'Ambros Adelwarth' narrative contains a forged diary, forged textual evidence has in itself a queer charge in Sebald. As Tóibín shows, the discovery of the 'truth' of Casement's diaries in 1994 has led to yet more projection and fantasy being invested both in the historical and in the textual Casement. Far from establishing the 'truth' of a queer martyr, they make Casement a nexus for widespread Irish public discourses surrounding queer rights, homophobia, the validity of the Irish revolution of 1916 and colonialism. Mario Vargas Llosa's 2010 novel *The Dream of the Celt* further explores this phantasmic, forged Casement; although his novel takes a positivist view of the biographical facts of Casement's life, for him, the Black Diaries are in part a self-forgery. They represent Casement's own production of a fictional queer self where he composes fantasmic sexual encounters, few of which actually take place.[35] It is thus not necessarily the case that Sebald aligns himself with a disciplinary and paranoid apparatus that mistakenly scrutinizes Casement's diaries for the 'truth' of his homosexuality. Far more queerly, Sebald, like Vargas Llosa, rewrites his own fantasy of Casement to create his own fantasy of queer anti-colonial resistance which is dependent less on historical textual evidence than on the desire to create alternatives to oppressive masculinities. This desire becomes yet stronger when Sebald writes about a fictionalized family member, as he does in 'Ambros Adelwarth'.

Lure of the Orient: Cosmo and Adelwarth

In *Die Ausgewanderten*, the Sebaldian narrator inserts a family member into the matrix of homosexuality, resistance, and Jewish messianism. This insertion is at once reminiscent of his literary stylization of his grandfather, but also contains the cathexis of homosexual desire present in the figures of Kafka and Casement. In the story 'Ambros Adelwarth', he creates for himself a homosexual great-uncle, Ambros, who becomes the lover of his Jewish master Cosmo Solomon. In interview, Sebald asserted that Ambros was indeed his great-uncle, who just had another name in real life, but that his story had been repressed because of his family's stern Catholicism:[36]

> Now, as soon as I saw that picture, I knew the whole story... In a Catholic family that all gets repressed. It isn't even ignored — it's not seen, it doesn't exist. It doesn't fit in anywhere at all.[37]

Yet this coherent picture of a real existing uncle whose queer history had been repressed by bourgeois and religious orthodoxy is complicated as soon as the interviewer presses Sebald on the authenticity of the documents in *Die Ausgewanderten*. Sebald admits that he wrote them himself. Everything that is important is real, he insists, merely the details are faked, to create *l'effet du réel*. Adelwarth, then, like the other three figures in *Die Ausgewanderten*, and like 'Roger Casement', is a phantasm, composed of certain 'real' elements and those invented elements that the Sebaldian narrator considers more real than the real, because of their persuasive value — the diary entry in English, for instance, but perhaps also the queer desire with which Sebald invests the figure. McCrea considers that this textual creation of an avuncular relationship is key to the modernist creation of queer literary families in narrative. Writing about *Ulysses*, he suggests that the novel addresses the question of conscious will — 'of forging, plotting, and creation' — as part of the queer alternative to automated genealogy.[38] McCrea suggests that the *mémoire involuntaire* aroused by the 'madeleine moment' in Proust is exaggerated; the narrator must create his rich family narrative in imagination once the initial impetus of *mémoire involuntaire* has dissolved. McCrea argues that the queer modernist narrative is far more concerned with an avuncular world — such as the network of aunts, uncles, and chosen affiliates that one finds in Proust — than with the direct family line. The same is true of the Adelwarth narrative; the forgery of the diaries suggests less that the narrator is revealing an archival queer 'truth' about Adelwarth, and more that he is creating — forging — a chosen queer ancestor to replace the biological father. Given the over-cathected and textually uncertain nature of Adelwarth, it is no surprise that Adelwarth is, in the narrator's memory, a literary figure, who impresses the narrator greatly with his ability to speak 'high' German rather than the local dialect redolent of tradition and latent Nazism. Adelwarth's linguistic facility is both cosmopolitan and resistant to interpretation:

> [Ich] entsinne mich doch, zutiefst beeindruckt gewesen zu sein von der Tatsache, daß er anscheinend mühelos nach der Schrift redete und Wörter und Wendungen gebrauchte, von denen ich allenfalls ahnen konnte, was sie bedeuteten.

> [I do recall being deeply impressed by the fact that his apparently effortless German was entirely free of any trace of our home dialect and that he used words and turns of phrase the meanings of which I could only guess at.] (*DA*, 98; *E*, 68)

Adelwarth is introduced to the reader as something of an alternative, queer masculine authority, combining as he does a most distinguished presence and a status as the eldest of the emigrants and their forefather, thereby disorienting the heteronormative line of familial inheritance. He is also another of Sebald's hybrid, liminal figures by reason of his titular status as an exile and wanderer, and, in his position as manservant — only in the finest households of New York, of course — shares something of the subaltern status of Moravian and Bohemian Jewish immigrants to Vienna and Berlin in the mid-nineteenth century.

   The setting where the narrator encounters him for the only time, when the narrator is a child in 1951, is reminiscent of the family portrait. Long writes of the disciplinarity inherent in the family photograph, which 'continued its ideological work within the bourgeois home, establishing "the normative 'scene' of the family with its appropriately gendered subjects, its self-evident hierarchy, and passive children on display"'.[39] The photographs that accompany the start of the Adelwarth narrative bear out this reading. Adelwarth's story begins in the context of three family photographs depicting the next generation of emigrants, Fini, Theres, and Kasimir, variously in exile in America and as children in their home German village. These photographs display all of the disciplinary bourgeois tropes suggested by Long above, as well as additional elements reinforcing the ethnic and national orientation of the subjects. The hierarchically ordered photo taken in the Bronx depicts Kasimir and Lini at the head of a table beneath which are gathered the younger members of the family, and above it hangs a sentimental picture of the family *Heimat* of W. The studio photograph of Theres, Kasimir, and Fini as children, on page 108 [74], shows them in German folk costumes in front of a backdrop of mountains. Finally, on page 109 [75], the photograph taken in Falkenstein showing Fini and the narrator's mother Rosa includes the representation of the Alpine landscape in the previous photographs, and also includes, in Fini's ekphrasis of the photo, their teacher Fuchsluger, who had been one of the first National Socialists. All three photographs clearly orient the subjects as German, rural, and members of an extended and patriarchal bourgeois family, even in exile. However, the expectation of the reader that the figure of Adelwarth, who has been introduced in such striking terms on the first page of the narrative, will appear in these photographs is frustrated. Adelwarth is not depicted within such national and familial frames, and the photographs following the three family snaps instead depict buildings on the stations of the emigrants' wanderings. The narrator explains the lack of photos of Adelwarth with 'wahrscheinlich, weil er, [...] trotz seiner Weltgewandtheit ausgesprochen leutscheu gewesen ist' [probably because [...] he was very shy, despite his familiarity with the ways of the world] (*DA*, 135; *E*, 92). The two photographs provided of Ambros suggest a second explanation. The first photo of Adelwarth presented in the narrative shows him entirely outside the familial context; it is a tourist photograph of Adelwarth in Arab costume from the 'Jerusalem time', gazing directly into the camera with his hand laid on a hookah. Only once the readers have made the acquaintance of this photo depicting Adelwarth in sexually confident oriental drag do they encounter the second photograph, which finally depicts Adelwarth in the contest of family disciplinarity (*DA*, 147; *E*, 101). It depicts, as Fini tells the narrator, Fini, Theo, and Adelwarth's sister Balbina, on her first visit to America. At this point, Adelwarth has already embarked on his *Trauerlaufbahn* [*via dolorosa*], and in marked contrast to Fini, Theo, and Balbina, each of whom smiles directly or indirectly at the camera, Adelwarth's head is slightly sunken, his eyes slightly obscured by a shadow, and his face unsmiling. In place of the flamboyant oriental drag of his youth, he wears the dapper clothes of the superior servant. As Ahmed suggests, the family photo pressures the child towards a heterosexual line of inheritance, by depicting the family as happy, and by putting aside 'what does not follow this line, those feelings that do not cohere as a smile'.[40] The two photographs of Adelwarth suggest a narrative of decline, not only from hopeful young emigrant to despairing sufferer from 'Korsakov syndrome', but also from confident queer traveller directed towards the Orient to constrained family member, whose feelings cannot 'cohere as a smile' within the disciplinary context of the family photo.

In his essay on Robert Walser, Sebald suggests an alternative family orientation for Adelwarth; he writes that the Adelwarth figure is connected both to Walser and to his own grandfather.[41] Sebald suggests that episodes from the Adelwarth narrative echo those from Robert Walser's *Der Räuber* [*The Robber*]. Sebald claims that he had not read *Der Räuber* at the point of composing the narrative, and moreover that the textual echo in *Die Ausgewanderten*, where a young Ambros sails by moonlight over Lake Constance, cannot possibly have been true in reality.[42] At the beginning of the 'Trauerlaufbahn' of both Ambros and Walser is the figure of a mysterious woman dressed in brown. Sebald concludes that these textual coincidences cause the irresistible feeling that one is being waved to 'from the other side', the reverse practice to Sebald's more usual poetic habit of paying homage to his own favourite writers in his texts.[43] This has two implications. On the one hand the term *Trauerlaufbahn*, and its link to the figure of a *femme fatale*, suggests not only the irresistible and linear progress of sorrow and mourning in the biographies of Walser and Adelwarth, but also a heterosexual genesis for this misery. However, on the other hand, the reversed chronology of the intertextuality, as claimed by Sebald, suggests a queered, non-linear, possibly uncanny influence. Just as Ambros Adelwarth was 'of the other persuasion', so Walser waves at the Sebaldian author 'from the other side'. In the same essay, Sebald links Walser to his maternal grandfather Egelhofer, suggesting that they are related by dress, habitus, and their dates of death. As we saw in the introduction, Egelhofer functioned as an alternative father in Sebald's imaginary biography. There is an uncanny family resemblance, here, between the three alternative fathers: Sebald's grandfather, to Walser, and Adelwarth. Thus, Öhlschläger is right when she suggests that Walser, like Adelwarth, is an allegory for the key function of the word *Trauerlaufbahn*, and that the Adelwarth text is an exemplar of *Nachträglichkeit* in narrative, a form of narrative that is at once memory and mourning.[44] Further than this, though, the links to Sebald's grandfather and to 'the other side' — indicating both Adelwarth's sexuality and the hereafter or realm of the spirits — suggest an extra element to the Adelwarth narrative, at once an alternative queer or bachelor lineage for the Sebaldian narrator, and an uncanny reversal of the sorrowful progress of history through the power of neighbourly or queer love.

The family disruptions of the Adelwarth figure do not end, though, with his queer status as an alternative, avuncular male or uncanny doppelganger of Walser. Adelwarth becomes the servant and lover of the Jewish Cosmo Solomon, thereby creating a queer bond of love, or alternative family, between Aryan and Jew that succeeds where Matthias Grünewald's bourgeois marriage to a Jewish convert to Christianity failed. In one passage, Adelwarth has the task of watching over Cosmo at the roulette table as if he were a sleeping child, an image of great tenderness and intimacy (*DA*, 133; *E*, 91). Adelwarth's queer relationship to Cosmo cannot easily be defined by terms such as 'homosexual' or 'gay'; it is one suspended between friend and leader (the name *Adelwarth*, as Gary Schmidt notes, 'emphasizes that he is the servant of that which is noble'[45]). Cosmo, for his part, treats Adelwarth as a companion and equal, and is never far from his side. Taberner describes this relationship as an 'idyllic co-dependency', exemplary of the 'German–Jewish symbiosis' that he detects in *Die Ausgewanderten*.[46] Certainly, such a social co-dependency is shown in Uncle Kasimir's statement that the re-roofing of the local synagogue provided the only employment for him in Germany in the Weimar years, suggesting that the local Jews, who had donated the original roof patriotically for the First World War effort, function as selfless supporters of impoverished Germans. By adding an idyllic queer relationship to his family tree, he gestures towards the possibility of disorienting his narrator's petit-bourgeois German family tree in favour of a queer German–Jewish genealogy. As we have seen, the 'inner colonization' of Jews by Germans in modernity and the assimilation of Jews to nineteenth-century German ideals of masculinity are key staging posts in Sebald's conception of the catastrophic line of German history. The figure of the Jew can be viewed as a challenge to the straight line of patriarchal inheritance: McCrea argues, for instance, that in *Ulysses* as in *Oliver Twist*, the Jew is associated with twisted rather than straight paths, possibilities of transformation, and 'a world where the future is not always already directly mapped out in advance'.[47] If, as Rohde argues, Jews occupied a 'threatening' third position between nationalities and genders, appearing as effeminate homosexuals to German observers in the late nineteenth and early twentieth centuries, Cosmo and Adelwarth's liaison occupies a utopian repurposing of that destabilizing 'third space'.[48] The idyllic relationship between Adelwarth and Cosmo is not merely one that stands metonymically for an idealized pre-war German–Jewish symbiosis, as exemplified in the childhood reminiscences of Luisa Lanzberg, contained in the 'Max Aurach' narrative. It also stands in for an impossible orientation of the Sebaldian narrator's family tree, a hybrid, non-reproductive one that subverts the heterosexual logic of German national reproduction. (The same seems to be true of Cosmo Solomon; his father describes Cosmo's life, in a foreshadowing of Edelman, as 'without future', denying the familial future-oriented narrative of reproduction [*DA*, 132; *E*, 90]). In this sense, Adelwarth is literally *ausgewandert*, has wandered out and away from the prescribed orientation of the family line. Although the Adelwarth character appears under the rubric of the *Trauerlaufbahn*, and thus the narrative describes a tragedy, the figure contains a reserve of utopian potential.

Adelwarth's disorientation leads to a corresponding disorientation in the Sebaldian narrator during his childhood. The narrator tells us that he responds to the summer visits of the emigrants with the internal notion that he would one day emigrate to America. The narrator links this idea of emigration with the allure of the occupying American forces in his village, who overturn the normative categories of gender and race expected in his small Alpine village: 'die Weiber gingen in Hosen herum [...] und was man von den Negern halten sollte, das wußte sowieso kein Mensch' [The women folk went about in trousers [...] and as for those negroes, no one knew what to make of them] (*DA*, 102; *E*, 70). This transnational unsettling of categories leads the narrator to mimic a form of American hypermasculinity — 'die Geistes- und Körperhaltung eines Hemingway-Helden' [the mental and physical attitudes of a Hemingway hero] — mimicry which he describes as a failed venture (*DA*, 103; *E*, 70). The narrator's disorientation from his inherited nationality then moves on to the traditional student anti-Americanism of the 1960s. The melancholy attached to the idea of emigration throughout the text here is replaced by a series of libido-driven disorientations that are at once performative and liberating, even if they are described with a tinge of narrative irony. This disorientation is marked by the non-domestic spaces in which Adelwarth leads his life, a series of heterotopias.

Adelwarth's career is spent in hotels, casinos, boats (recalling the bachelor boats of *Die Ringe des Saturn*), and in various other queer liminal spaces such as the swimming, almost empty house that belongs to the counsellor from the Japanese legation with whom Adelwarth lives for two years (*DA*, 115; *E*, 79). These places, in Foucauldian fashion, at times mark out the limits of disciplinary bourgeois society. At the casino in Deauville in 1913, it seems as though the entire world has gathered to join the carnivalesque celebrations on the eve of the destruction of the bourgeois world. At other times, however, they facilitate a utopian form of love. Again and again, the tender togetherness of the couple is emphasized, perhaps most explicitly in Greece en route to Jerusalem, where the couple spend a night sleeping together under the stars. Adelwarth writes in his diary,

> Über uns die Milchstraße (where the Gods pass on their way, says Cosmo) so hell, daß ich in ihrem Licht dieses aufschreiben kann [...] Kaum glaube ich, daß ich derselbe Mensch und in Griechenland bin. Aber ab und zu weht der Geruch der Wacholderbäume zu uns herüber, und also ist es wohl wahr.

> [Above us the Milky Way (where the Gods pass, says Cosmo), so resplendent that I can write this by its light [...] I can scarcely believe I am the same person, and in Greece. But now and then the fragrance of juniper wafts across to us, so it is surely so.] (*DA*, 191; *E*, 129)

This moment of tender bliss is worth citing at length because of the rare sensual and subjective integrity it conveys: an unclouded relationship between the lovers, a Romantic one-ness with nature and with the gods, ease of writing, and an untroubled continuity between past and present selves. That this scene takes place in Greece, celebrated in queer culture as the birthplace of 'Greek love', underlines the queer nature of the utopian moment.[49] It is also a moment of sensuous immanence, not requiring the messianic hope held out by 'Jerusalem', but a completed line of escape in itself.

Of what, then, does Adelwarth's *Trauerlaufbahn* consist? Sebald's description of Adelwarth's tragic decline and death in the wake of Cosmo's death suggests, like the death of Roger Casement, the Sebaldian narrator's mourning for the loss of a utopian queer potential, the potential of a selfless queer heroism in Casement's case and of an idyllic German–Jewish queer symbiosis in Adelwarth's. Adelwarth suffers a patient, silent death, fading away in a sanatorium in Ithaca with an attack of melancholy brought on by the death of his lover. Just as his absence from family photographs is pathologized by his shyness, his eventual death is ascribed to the electroconvulsive therapy that he undergoes to cure his melancholy, an exemplar of those technological innovations of the industrial age, omnipresent in Sebald's work, that dialectically destroy humanity as they aim to perfect it. His attempt to escape the European dialectic of Enlightenment fails. Indeed, the doctor who performs the treatment on Adelwarth, Dr Abramsky, a man originally from Lemberg, is only persuaded to do so by the Austrian accent of his boss, Fahnstock, who is eager to try out the new therapy. Abramsky implicitly trusts Fahnstock because he reminds him of his own father, who had emigrated from Galicia to the West after the collapse of the Habsburg empire. By the time he realizes the cruel and catastrophic nature of the inherited tradition of electroshock therapy, it is too late for him to save Adelwarth from it. Although Adelwarth has emigrated to the United States and disoriented himself from his German, patriarchal family, his dying years are spent as an experimental subject of European doctors, bound into a European line of paternal influence and medical paternalism. Thus, Barzilai's queer reading of the Adelwarth narrative notes the link between Adelwarth's *Trauerlaufbahn* and familial homophobia, suggesting that the narrative 'reveals the force of familial and societal homophobia' that erases Adelwarth's homosexuality from the family narrative. Such an interpretation of Adelwarth's life is given implicitly by the narrator's uncle Kasimir:

> Er ist natürlich, wie jeder leicht sehen konnte, von der anderen Partei gewesen, sagte der Onkel Kasimir, auch wenn die Verwandtschaft das immer ignoriert beziehungsweise verbrämt oder zum Teil vielleicht wirklich nicht begriffen hat. Je älter der Adelwarth-Onkel geworden ist, desto hohler ist er vorgekommen, und wie ich ihn das letzte Mal gesehen habe [...] war es, als werde er bloß noch von seinen Kleidern zusammengehalten.

> [Of course, said Uncle Kasimir, he was of the other persuasion, as anyone could see, even if the family always ignored or glossed over the fact. Perhaps some of them never realized. The older Uncle Adelwarth grew, the more hollowed-out he seemed to me, and the last time I saw him [...] it was as if his clothes were holding him together.] (*DA*, 129; *E*, 88)

Kasimir is the only person explicitly to suggest that Adelwarth is 'of the other persuasion', and he immediately follows this up with a pitiful account of Adelwarth's decline. Other critics view Adelwarth's *Trauerlaufbahn* as variously symptomatic of the 'experience of dislocation' that is a 'function of modernity', as Long argues, or *Heimat* as a dream of loss, or a burden of memories that lead him to a desire for amnesia.[50] Certainly, all of these complexes are present in the Adelwarth narrative, which carries through it the themes of modernity, exile, and amnesia present in the other three stories of *Die Ausgewanderten*. Adelwarth's desire for self-dissolution can also be read as a romantic self-immolation, pining away for love of Cosmo, and thereby as an indirect consequence of the Holocaust, for Cosmo's final decline is caused by the terrible news that arrives from Europe after 1939, and his tormented body therefore functions as a site of conflict where outer historical catastrophes mingle with inner emotional ones.[51] Moving to a queer reading of his attachment to Cosmo, Santner suggests that Adelwarth is a 'textbook case of what Judith Butler has analyzed as the *melancholy of gender*', produced, in Butler's theory, by the prohibition of homosexual pleasures and desires.[52] This would then, Santner argues, explain Adelwarth's physical composure and stiffness towards the end of his life; both his loss of his lover Cosmo and the gender melancholy attendant on societally imposed compulsory heterosexuality work themselves out in his body. His *Trauerlaufbahn* certainly begins with Cosmo's death and with the enforced move to a domesticated sphere that follows on the dissolution of the Solomon household. In this context of queer melancholy — mourning both the possibility of a queer life, and the loss of his lover — Aunt Fini, the representative of his German bourgeois family, feels that he wishes he could speak to her but cannot do so. His queer narrative is so unassimilable to her bourgeois understanding of family narrative, which is concerned rather with the capitalist trappings of family life such as her twins or the new Oldsmobile with white-walled tyres, that she assumes that he must be suffering from Korsakoff's Syndrome. His narrative of a queer cosmopolitan life is fantastic to her, incomprehensible. Lisa Diedrich indicates his radical queerness when she describes Adelwarth's relationship to Cosmo as follows: 'Master and man, two friends, relatives, or brothers? In Sebald's text, Ambros and Cosmo's relationship doesn't quite fit any of these categories; it queers the categories and causes people to look but without being able to see'.[53] Adelwarth is in a sense, like Cosmo as queer Jew, also a doubled figure, crossing the border between the fictive and the historical, as well as between the Old and New World. Thus, while the Adelwarth narrative evokes the possibility of a queer German–Jewish utopia that resists the destructive pull of history, but is ultimately destroyed by it, there are constant hints of something yet queerer about Cosmo and Adelwarth's relationship. The Sebaldian narrator imagines that he sees them seated together at the gaming table and hears the rumours going around about the couple: 'sie seien Herr und Diener, ein Freundespaar, einander Anverwandte oder gar Brüder. Zu jeder dieser Thesen gab es ein endloses Für und Wider' [whom I heard variously described as master and man, two friends, relatives, or even brothers. Endlessly the pros and cons of all of these theories were advanced] (DA, 184; E, 125). Their relationship resists the dialectical resolution of these theses, and thus cannot be entirely interpreted by the dialectic of Enlightenment. Instead, there are several references to the ambiguity of their relationship and indeed of their ontological status. 'Wir sitzen auf einem offenen Altan etwas überhöht und ausgestellt wie zwei Heilige' [We are sitting on an open balcony at some height, on show like two saints], writes Adelwarth, suggesting that they are poised somewhere between the human and the divine (DA, 197; E, 133). The queer potential inherent in the Cosmo–Adelwarth relationship transgresses the boundaries of unitary, bourgeois subjectivity and masculinity itself. Adelwarth himself thus appears as a figure of infinite mystery, 'legendary', says Kasimir, and the Sebaldian narrator suggests that he is possibly a trickster, possibly crossing the boundaries of gender when compared to a *femme au passé obscur*, or possibly possessed of the occult powers of a magnetist (DA, 185; E, 125). This dizzying array of queer potentiality entirely bursts the line of family inheritance suggested by the discipline of the family photograph.

Adelwarth approaches a queer site of resistance to interpretation itself, particularly psychoanalytic interpretation. Martin Klebes argues that spa travel in Sebald's texts — Austerlitz's trip to Marienbad, Dr K's journey to Riva — 'calls into question the very notion of self-identity', and rather than curing its protagonists, the Sebaldian spa visit renews his protagonists via 'intertextual references that reveal the split within each of them not as a feature of their psychological constitution but rather as a division visible on the textual surface itself'.[54] The trip to the fashionable resort or heterotopia ('vacation village', in Foucault's term) of Deauville fulfils just such a textual function, acting as a textual counterweight to the narrative's attempts to diagnose the mental illnesses suffered by the two men. Cosmo's descent into mental ill-health is ascribed variously to his gambling mania, to an early film or the search for his brother — a brother he never had; Adelwarth's mental decline has been discussed above, and he is eventually killed by the psychiatric help he sought. Both men are anti-psychiatric subjects, who resist psychic integration and, in Adelwarth's case, the spa cure. In this light, the seemingly pathetic statements that Adelwarth had never had anything like a childhood and ends his life in a 'hollowed out condition', often advanced as evidence that Adelwarth personifies the tragedies of the twentieth century or of modernity, can also be seen to demonstrate that the Adelwarth figure resists constitution into an autonomous bourgeois subject, complete with childhood narrative, inner life, and reintegration into the family line. Instead, he represents a radically queer counter-subject, representing a textual rather than a psychic reality held together only by his clothes because he refuses interiority. We have already noted his literary facility with language; in another place, the narrator's aunt Fini recalls that Adelwarth could learn any foreign language solely through certain adjustments that he claims to make to his inner person (*DA*, 114; *E*, 78). Santner suggests that this facility implies that Adelwarth can 'adapt or assimilate to various symbolic systems without becoming libidinally implicated in them', an interpretation that links Klebes's suggestion that the 'spa cure' demonstrates nothing more than the radical textuality of Sebald's figures with Adelwarth's lack of psychic integrity or subjective interiority.[55] Adelwarth's linguistic faculty and profound textuality also demonstrates his resistance to libidinal implication in such symbolic systems as the familial one. Despite the Sebaldian narrator's attempts at an affective identification with him via a visionary conjuration of Adelwarth and Cosmo at Deauville, he resists such attempts to bind him into the narrator's family line, or the master-narrative of loss in *Die Ausgewanderten*. Inherent to Klebes's argument about the functions of the spa cure in Sebald is its theatrical nature. We have seen above how Adelwarth and Cosmo take up staged positions in the theatre of the world that is Deauville, placed on display like two saints, seated on a table that is just for them and separated from all others, or conspicuously intimate at the roulette table. Further underlining the performative nature of Adelwarth's identity, and in keeping with the conspicuous elegance of Sebald's numerous queer dandies, Adelwarth is remarkable for his fine wardrobe as well as for his habitus of composure. Klebes argues that this theatricality creates the split in the self that then seeks to be cured by the subsequent journey on from the spa, a 'mnemonic journey' intended to 'enable a more thorough awareness of self'.[56] As we have seen above, Adelwarth's fragmented *Trauerlaufbahn* leads to no such awareness, any more than, Klebes argues, Austerlitz's journey on from Marienbad or Dr K's journey from Riva leads to an understanding of self.

Like Casement's journeys to Africa, Adelwarth and Cosmo's disorientation is spatial as well as ontological, and also like Casement's sexual tourism in the Congo and Amazon, it contains elements of dubious Orientalist paedophilia. Adelwarth and Cosmo journey on from Deauville to Greece and Jerusalem. Jerusalem itself, in contradistinction to the Holy City of Jewish theology and messianic hope, is represented as a uniformly grim ruin. Although the journey to Jerusalem can be read as an attempted return to a happier Jewish past, and to a site of reconciliation between Jew and Gentile, little remains of Jerusalem's former glories. Equally ominously, Cosmo points out to Adelwarth the ruins of Sodom and Gomorrah, among other cities, noting that although they were once full of flowers, now only the 'shadowy outlines of the cities of the plain remain. The reminder of the divine punishment of the sin of Sodom, and hence of the outlawed and doomed nature of homosexual love, is clear. Zilcosky correctly notes that this attempted and failed return to Jerusalem is properly 'unheimlich', because it orients Adelwarth back only to precisely that home village which he had tried to escape by emigration; in a dream of the Jordan valley, Adelwarth realizes that the 'gouty beggars and lepers' he encounters there are actually from Gopprechts, his home town in Allgäu (*DA*, 210; *E*, 142).[57] While this touristic disillusionment in part is a demonstration of Sebald's poetics, whereby only writing, not earthly places or relationships, can carry the metaphysical burden of hope, in part it also replays cultural clichés that associate homosexuality with unhappiness, sickness, and death. In this light, the only idyll that Adelwarth discovers in Jerusalem is represented, in particularly questionable fashion, by the photo of a twelve-year-old dervish. Cosmo and Ambros make a particular point of returning to take a photo of the 'extraordinarily beautiful' boy, and the ensuing photo brings to mind the spectre of sexual tourism, not dissimilar to Oscar Wilde and André Gide's infamous sexual adventures in the Maghreb, or indeed to Roger Casement's sexual exploitation of young men in the Congo and Panama, and repeats the modernist cliché that equates homosexuality and paedophilia (*DA*, 200; *E*, 135). Long suggests that the act of appropriation represented by the photograph is ameliorated by its status within the economy of the family album, which 'marginalizes their erotic or political import and constitutes the images as evidence of a familiar ritual: tourism'.[58] However, the domestication and trivialization of acts of colonial appropriation are precisely one of the mechanisms through which Orientalism functions. The picture of the small sexualized boy, pressed between the elaborate covers of a family picture album, is surely the very pattern of the post-colonial uncanny. Returning to FitzGerald, here, De Polnay invokes such clichés when discussing whether FitzGerald was aware of his own homosexuality: 'Omar Khayyám must have led with eastern ease a pretty active pederast existence if and when he felt so disposed. And that, one way or another, proves my point'.[59] Schmidt here sees an echo of *Der Tod in Venedig*, arguing that 'youth becomes a moment of melancholic desire, figured homoerotically as the narrator and protagonist's desire for a fantasmic former self'.[60] This seems to me to ignore the disruptive potential of the Adelwarth figure as much as does Barzilai when she argues, quoting Boyarin's work, that Sebald's protagonists are unable fully to 'escape from Jewish queerdom into gentile, phallic heterosexuality'.[61] Adelwarth and Cosmo's utopian potential lies both in their love and, beyond that, precisely in their resistance to such psychic integration of the bourgeois self that could be found in discovering a 'fantasmic former self' or achieving 'gentile, phallic heterosexuality'.

This is not to say, however, that their resistance is universal. As noted above, the touristic appropriation of the photograph of the young dervish suggests precisely that blind spot for paedophilia and Orientalism demonstrated by the Roger Casement narrative. Equally, the photograph of Adelwarth in oriental garb demonstrates a cognate blind spot in Sebald's empathy with the victims of colonization.[62] Posing for the performative photograph in Arab garb is at once a theatrical liberation from bourgeois German identity — the creation of a counter-image to the discipline of the Adelwarth family photographs of children in German *Tracht* — and what Ahmed calls an 'exercise of power' in creating 'the Orient'. She argues that 'the Orient' 'seems to point to another way of being in the world — to a world of romance, sexuality, and sensuality', an argument consistent with Adelwarth's project of *Auswanderung* from the national and heterosexual confines of Gopprechts.[63] Nonetheless, the ethical problems of such a pose, as Long argues, cannot be ignored. Adelwarth's queer orientation, then, although it holds utopian potential, carries with it a residual normative Orientalism. It is also important to note that neither Roger Casement's Congolese lovers nor the Arab boy photographed by Adelwarth speak; in this sense, both narratives participate in a German 'monologic discourse about race, desire and authority'.[64] In the next chapter, I address the complex involvement of the Sebaldian narrator in this 'sublime melancholy' in *Schwindel. Gefühle*.

Notes to Chapter 3

1. Fuchs, 'Von der Bio- zur Hagiografie: Roger Casement', in *Die Schmerzensspuren der Geschichte*, pp. 200–05.
2. See Todd Kontje, *German Orientalism* (Ann Arbor: University of Michigan Press, 2004), p. 2.
3. Ibid., p. 101.
4. Achim Rohde, 'Der Innere Orient: Orientalismus, Antisemitismus und Geschlecht im Deutschland des 18. bis 20. Jahrhunderts', *Die Welt des Islams*, 45 (2005), 370–411 (p. 378).
5. Joseph A. Boone, 'Vacation Cruises; or, the Homoerotics of Orientalism', *PMLA*, 110 (1995), 89–107 (p. 91).
6. Jesse Matz, 'Masculinity Amalgamated: Colonialism, Homosexuality, and Forster's Kipling', *Journal of Modern Literature*, 30 (2007), 31–51 (p. 33).
7. Ahmed, *Queer Phenomenology*, pp. 127–28.
8. Moser, 'Peripatetic Liminality', p. 52.
9. Öhlschläger, *Beschädigtes Leben*, p. 132.
10. Ibid., p. 97.
11. Santner, *On Creaturely Life*, p. 99.
12. Alan Corkhill, 'Angles of Vision in Sebald's *After Nature* and *Unrecounted*', in *W. G. Sebald: Schreiben ex patria/Expatriate Writing*, pp. 347–68 (p. 352).
13. Ibid., p. 350.
14. The science behind this claim is still under debate. Bruce Thomas Boehrer shows that, as early as 1496, the German author Joseph Grünpeck attributed it not to the discovery of the New World, but to an astrological conjunction that occurred in the year 1484. Bruce Thomas Boehrer, 'Early Modern Syphilis', *Journal of the History of Sexuality*, 1 (1990), 197–214 (p. 201). However, in 2005 Bruce M. Rothschild confidently argued for a New World origin for the disease. Bruce M. Rothschild, 'History of Syphilis', *Clinical Infectious Diseases*, 40 (2005), 1454–63.
15. Long, *Image, Archive, Modernity*, p. 71.
16. Eve Kosofsky Sedgwick, *Between Men: English Literature and Male Homosocial Desire* (New York: Columbia University Press, 1985), p. 21.
17. Claudia Albes, 'Porträt ohne Modell: Bildbeschreibung und autobiographische Reflexion in W. G. Sebalds "Elementargedicht" *Nach der Natur*', in *W. G. Sebald: Politische Archäologie und melancholische Bastelei*, ed. by Michael Niehaus and Claudia Öhlschläger (Berlin: Schmidt, 2006), pp. 47–75 (p. 75).
18. Margaret Bruzelius, 'Adventure, Imprisonment, and Melancholy: *Heart of Darkness* and *Die Ringe des Saturn/The Rings of Saturn*', in *The Undiscover'd Country: W. G. Sebald and the Poetics of Travel*, ed. by Markus Zisselsberger (Rochester, NY: Camden House, 2010), pp. 247–73 (p. 248).
19. Fuchs, *Die Schmerzensspuren der Geschichte*, p. 200.
20. Ibid., p. 202.

21. Michael Hulse, 'Englishing Max', in *Saturn's Moons: A W. G. Sebald Handbook*, ed. by Jo Catling and Richard Hibbitt (Oxford: Legenda, 2011), pp. 192–205 (p. 200).

22. See, for instance, *The Making of Modern Irish History: Revisionism and the Revisionist Controversy*, ed. by David George Boyce and Alan O'Day (London: Routledge, 1996).

23. Havelock Ellis, *Studies in the Psychology of Sex*, ch. 1.

24. Sigmund Freud, *The Schreber Case*, trans. by Andrew Webber (London: Penguin, 2002), p. 52.

25. Cited in Brian Lewis, 'The Queer Life and Afterlife of Roger Casement', *Journal of the History of Sexuality*, 14 (2005), 363–82 (p. 374).

26. Colm Tóibín, 'The Tragedy of Roger Casement', *The New York Review of Books*, 51(27 May 2004) <http://www.nybooks.com/articles/17136>, accessed 17 December 2012.

27. Lewis, 'The Queer Life and Afterlife of Roger Casement', p. 380.

28. Tóibín, 'The Tragedy of Roger Casement'.

29. Ibid.

30. Ibid.

31. Fuchs, *Die Schmerzensspuren der Geschichte*, p. 200. Fuchs herself is interested, in keeping with Tóibín's remark that Casement provides a space to which analysts bring their own concerns, with establishing Casement as one of Sebald's many *lieux de mémoire*.

32. Matz, 'Masculinity Amalgamated', p. 31.

33. Long, *Image, Archive, Modernity*, p. 75.

34. Carol Duttlinger, '"A Wrong Turn of the Wheel": Sebald's Journeys of (In)Attention', in *The Undiscover'd Country: W. G. Sebald and the Poetics of Travel*, ed. by Markus Zisselsberger (Rochester, NY: Camden House, 2010), pp. 92–122 (p. 109).

35. Mario Vargas Llosa, *The Dream of the Celt*, trans. by Edith Grossmann (London: Faber and Faber, 2012).

36. According to Sebald's biographer, Mark M. Anderson, Adelwarth is 'loosely based on his aunt Fanny's brother-in-law'. Mark M. Anderson, 'Fathers and Son: W. G. Sebald', *Bookforum* (Jan./Feb. 2007), <http://www.bookforum.com/>, accessed 16 December 2012.

37. 'Who is W. G. Sebald?', p. 71.

38. McCrea, *In the Company of Strangers*, p. 188.

39. Long, *Image, Archive, Modernity*, p. 112.

40. Ahmed, *Queer Phenomenology*, p. 90

41. 'Le promeneur solitaire', in Sebald, *Logis in einem Landhaus* (Frankfurt a. M.: Fischer, 2000), pp. 127–68.

42. Ibid., p. 138.

43. Ibid., p. 139.

44. Öhlschläger, *Beschädigtes Leben*, p. 80.

45. Schmidt, 'Sublime Melancholy', p. 313.

46. Taberner, 'German Nostalgia?', p. 195.

47. McCrea, *The Company of Strangers*, p. 117.

48. Rohde, 'Der Innere Orient', p. 408.

49. See, for instance, David M. Halperin, *One Hundred Years of Homosexuality: And Other Essays on Greek Love. The New Ancient World* (New York: Routledge, 1990).

50. Long, *Image, Archive, Modernity*, p. 110; Fuchs, *Die Schmerzensspuren der Geschichte*, p. 127; Iris Denneler, *Von Namen und Dingen: Erkundungen zur Rolle des Ich in der Literatur am Beispiel von Ingeborg Bachmann, Peter Bichsel, Max Frisch, Gottfried Keller, Heinrich von Kleist, Arthur Schnitzler, Franz Wedekind, Vladimir Nabokov und W. G. Sebald* (Würzburg: Königshausen & Neumann, 2001), p. 149.

51. Öhlschläger, *Beschädigtes Leben*, p. 85.

52. Santner, *On Creaturely Life*, p. 172.

53. Lisa Diedrich, 'Gathering Evidence of Ghosts: W. G. Sebald's Practices of Witnessing', in *Searching for Sebald: Photography after W. G. Sebald*, ed. by Lisa Patt with Christel Dillbohner (Los Angeles: Institute of Cultural Inquiry, 2007), pp. 256–79 (p. 271).

54. Martin Klebes, 'If You Come to a Spa: Displacing the Cure in *Schwindel. Gefühle.* and *Austerlitz*', in *The Undiscover'd Country: W. G. Sebald and the Poetics of Travel*, ed. by Markus Zisselsberger (Rochester, NY: Camden House, 2010), pp. 123–41 (p. 126).

55. Santner, *On Creaturely Life*, p. 173.
56. Klebes, 'If you Come to a Spa', p. 134.
57. Zilcosky, 'Sebald's Uncanny Travels', p. 113.
58. J. J. Long, 'History, Narrative, and Photography in W. G. Sebald's *Die Ausgewanderten*', *MLR*, 98 (2003), 117–37 (p. 131).
59. De Polnay, *Into an Old Room*, p. 98.
60. Schmidt, 'Sublime Melancholy', p. 301.
61. Barzilai, 'Facing the Past and the Female Spectre', p. 214.
62. Long, *Image, Archive, Modernity*, p. 55.
63. Ahmed, *Queer Phenomenology*, p. 114.
64. Katrin Sieg, *Ethnic Drag: Performing Race, Nation, Sexuality in West Germany* (Ann Arbor: University of Michigan Press, 2002), p. 190.

CHAPTER 4

Eros in Venice:
The Strange Case of Dr S. and Dr K.

Schwindel. Gefühle. is possibly the queerest of Sebald's texts. The disorientation of the masculine German subject in 'Ambros Adelwarth', and the hopes contained in it for a redemption from the catastrophic path of German-Jewish history, are found everywhere in the first three sections of *Schwindel. Gefühle.* This is a text that is queer on the level of subject matter, as the Sebaldian narrator and the shade of Franz Kafka haunt each other in scenarios infused with homoerotic longing. It is also queer on the level of textual coherence. Perhaps more than any other of Sebald's texts, it dissolves the direct lines of heterosexual narrative, in particular the inherited patriarchal structures of the *Bildungsroman*, the *Odyssey*, and the detective novel, to create an associative, rhizomatic text informed by a queer textual erotics. 'Beyle oder das merckwürdige Factum der Liebe' [A Madness Most Discreet] bids farewell to masculine, Enlightenment structures of the self and structures of narrative, while 'All'estero' and 'Dr. K.s Badereise nach Riva' are associative textual structures that combine queer desire, messianic longing, and paranoia. This chapter explores both the queer sexuality and the radically queer textuality of these narratives.

In the 'All'estero' section of *Schwindel. Gefühle.*, the narrator's flies from his homeland, and moves away from linear narrative structures towards a dissociative textual constellation in Italy. Hence, as he pursues the shade of Kafka in Italy, he is on a line of flight away from Oedipal structures analogous to the line of flight in Kafka's work. The queer paranoia of the narrator further suggests an intertextual connection to Dr Schreber in Freud's 1911 study of paranoia and homosexuality. Freud's study glosses the memoirs of a respected judge who records his paranoid breakdown in middle years, characterized by a conviction that he has become feminized, and that God is thereby persecuting him. In *Schwindel. Gefühle.*, Sebald's queer poetics oscillate between Freud's Oedipal interpretation of Schreber's paranoid homosexuality, which attributes Schreber's breakdown to his unresolved Oedipus complex and failure to become a father himself, and Deleuze and Guattari's more liberating, schizo interpretation, which resists the colonization of the psyche by the Oedipal model. The associative order of the two inner sections of the text closely resembles a Deleuzian rhizome, without Oedipal origins or future-oriented direction. If Sebald's queer figures elsewhere resist interpretation, here the whole text refuses textual coherence, becoming instead a schizo text or 'desiring machine' governed by the associative order of 'either ... or ... or ...' rather than the normative structures of 'and then' or 'either/or' prescribed by a patriarchal Law.[1] The text further incorporates messianic hope, embodied in the Dr K. figure: as Ambros Adelwarth consummates a queer German–Jewish symbiosis with Cosmo, so the Sebaldian narrator pursues a close affinity with Kafka. This is no straightforward path of escape, as the queer potential of Kafka becomes over-freighted with political redemption, messianism, and a hope for the victory of Eros over Thanatos.

For several critics of this text, Thanatos, either in the form of historical catastrophe or 'a search for subjective dissolution', is victorious.[2] While the messianic overdetermination of the Kafka figure, and the calamitous course of history, may in part explain the apocalyptic overtones of the text, they may also be attributed to the paranoid disposition of the narrator. The tension in the first three sections of *Schwindel. Gefühle.* is, more precisely, between what Deleuze and Guattari term 'a schizo Eros and an Oedipal Thanatos', here a queer erotics that resists the Oedipal process, as opposed to the straight lines of history and family that lead to catastrophe.[3] It further demonstrates what Laura Penny has usefully diagnosed as a tension between Benjaminian and Deleuzoguattarian readings of Kafka, between 'Benjamin's modernist mourning and Deleuze's schizoid affirmation'. Deleuze's affirmation of forgetting as liberating dispenses with Benjamin's commandment to remember; hence, whereas a Benjaminian reading of Kafka is saturated with mourning, Deleuze and Guattari see multiple lines of escape in Kafka's texts.[4] In both cases, the Kafka figure is linked to a form of redemption or escape, as it is in *Schwindel. Gefühle.* This question of redemption and, connected to it, messianism, is symbolized by the figure of Kafka's hunter Gracchus who sails through the text, suspended between life and death. He signals both the possibility of escape from Thanatos via Eros, and the failure of theological redemption. *Schwindel. Gefühle.* describes a complex set of movements between a messianic redemption and an immanent line of flight. If the first three chapters of the text are a queer narrative of resistance to genealogical closure, and go astray along queer lines of desire, the final section, 'Il ritorno in Patria', returns to a genealogical plot, heterosexual themes, and the German homeland, in part undoing the queer potential that came before.

Theaterdamen and the Heterosexual *Bildungsreise*

Although *Schwindel. Gefühle.* is the queerest of Sebald's fictions, it opens with the robustly heterosexual memoirs of Henri Beyle alias Stendhal, author of *De l'amour*, containing elaborate descriptions of heterosexual love affairs. Öhlschläger suggests that Sebald's rewriting of Stendhal's memoirs, with its emphasis on 'crystallization' and memory, can be read as an allegory or discussion of a false way of constructing reality.[5] Within the four-part structure of *Schwindel. Gefühle.*, however, 'Beyle oder das merckwürdige Faktum der Liebe' also functions as an ironic heterosexual counterpart to the Sebaldian narrator's and Kafka's queer disorientations in Italy. If, as we will see below, the Sebaldian narrator and K. both go astray once they cross the Alps, Henri Beyle's journeys to Italy function as an ironic model of heterosexual formation, or *Bildung*—a 'comedy of sexual fulfilment', as David Kaufmann terms it.[6] An echo of this narrative structure can be found in Hofmannsthal's fragmentary novel *Andreas*, which Sebald anatomizes in an essay in *Die Beschreibung des Unglücks*, 'Venezianisches Kryptogramm: Hofmannsthals *Andreas*' [Venetian Cryptogram: Hofmannsthal's *Andreas*].[7] Sebald's analysis of *Andreas* is worth discussing at some length, as the 'Venetian cryptogram', as Sebald terms the novel, can also be read as a cryptic clue to the three journeys over the Alps in *Schwindel. Gefühle*. In *Andreas*, a young Austrian man crosses the Alps to Venice, where he becomes initiated into a series of mysterious and sexually ambiguous scenarios. In keeping with the attack on bourgeois identity that runs throughout *Die Beschreibung des Unglücks*, Sebald reads the novel as an intended but failed *Bildungsroman*. In Sebald's reading, Hofmannsthal distorts the integrative or normative intention of the classic *Bildungsroman* into a 'Venetian cryptogram', an exploration of the centrifugal powers of our lives which tend not to 'eine schöne Bildung' [a beautiful education or formation], but to deformation and destruction (*BU*, 63). Bourgeois mores, he writes, repress the erotic and cruel lusts that in fact constitute the psyches both of Andreas and of Hofmannsthal. Instead of cementing a solid male identity by undertaking a *Bildungsreise*, Andreas enters into a state of gender confusion in Venice, where he cannot tell male from female or heterosexual from homosexual desire, and undergoes a disintegration of self. For Sebald, erotomania drives the novel's centrifugal powers, which place *Andreas* in opposition to the *Bildungsroman*. Further, the concluding heterosexual marriage with which Hofmannsthal planned to end *Andreas* could never have been written, because of Hofmannsthal's *horreur des femmes* (*BU*, 65). Instead of presenting a perfected narrative of *Bildung*, *Andreas* is suspended, Sebald argues, between two equal horrors: on the one hand consumption by a woman, on the other homosexual rape. For Sebald, the mysterious and romantic figure of the 'Maltese', who draws Andreas into adventures in Venice, is a composite of the homosexual poet Stefan George and of Hofmannsthal himself, who is yearning for a younger version of himself, personified by the youth Andreas. In Sebald's Freudian reading, the novel thus throws up both a homosexual and a narcissistic complex. We can thus deduce that the transalpine journeys of three male protagonists in *Schwindel. Gefühle*. — Henri Beyle, the Sebaldian narrator, and Dr K. — are instances of the centrifugal powers at work in *Andreas* that overtake the European bourgeois male once he crosses the boundary to Italy. The outlines of Beyle's narrative certainly seem like a 'comic' *Bildungsroman*. Beyle recalls crossing the Alps as an adolescent soldier in the army of Napoleon, in the historical period when Napoleon still seems an undefeatable icon of heroic manhood. Beyle hopes to use the military tour to overcome the deficits of his bourgeois education that has left him with the constitution of a fourteen-year-old girl, in order to attain instead a Napoleonic model of heroic masculinity and come of age. In keeping with this masculine model, Beyle is determined not only to come of age by acts of military violence, but also to be rid of his tiresome virginity with an Italian *donna cattiva*, or prostitute. Once rid of his innocence, he moves on to courtly love for a woman named Angela Pietragrua, whom he later adds to his sexual conquests. Clad in the costume first of a Napoleonic soldier and then of a dandy, he considers his entry to heterosexual manhood accomplished. Beyle's, then, appears to be the *Bildungsreise* that Andreas fails to complete.

Yet this heroic narrative of masculinity is ironized within the text on many levels. Beyle confesses that heterosexual fulfilment is a dead end; despite his most arduous efforts, he knows he will never be able to find a woman who corresponds to his imagination. Further, 'Beyle oder das merckwürdige Faktum der Liebe' is shot through with reflections on the inconsistency, unreliability, and irretrievability of memory, including the memory of the name and face of the prostitute who relieves him of his virginity. Thus, the very narrative of heterosexual initiation is also informed, if not quite by *Andreas*'s *horreur des femmes*, then certainly by implied misogynist power relations, as demonstrated by the barely consensual sexual act by which Beyle 'conquers' Angela Pietragrua, who sees herself 'forced to capitulate' (*SG*, 17; *V*, 13). While this is doubtless an ironic pastiche of Stendhal's own robustly misogynist language, it also suggests that Sebald's own reluctance to write empathetically or politically about women is at play here. Sexual and military conquest thus functions as a seamless system, just as Sebald bracketed them together in his book on Carl Sternheim. This systematic association of heterosexual masculinity with military violence is made explicit when, that summer of 1800, Beyle feels as though his life is finally assimilated into 'ein vollendetes oder doch der Vollendung zustrebendes System, in dem Schönheit und Schrecken in einer exakten Relation zueinander standen' [a perfect system, or at least one that was aspiring to perfection, and in which beauty and terror bore an exact relation to each other] (*SG*, 18; *V*, 14). Sebald's horror of such perfect systems is expressed most explicitly in his essay on Elias Canetti, 'System und Systemkritik bei Elias Canetti' [System and the Critique of Systems in Elias Canetti], where he draws on Foucault to demonstrate that any system generates power and authority. In this essay, he describes power as a self-enclosed system that constantly requires the sacrifice of outsiders for its preservation (*BU*, 93). Within 'Beyle oder das merckwürdige Faktum der Liebe', no sooner has Beyle felt this access of systemic euphoria than the dog days enter and with them not only melancholy, but also syphilitic symptoms, the dialectical consequence of his sexual initiation. Heterosexual initiation, for him as much as for Andreas, introduces him to a world of 'hazard', a term implying both physical and mental decay. Furthermore, Napoleonic masculinity is itself a contradictory and politically dubious construct. Napoleon is a figure that stands for a rich complex of poetic associations in Sebald's textual universe as a whole. Napoleon's early victories led Enlightenment intellectuals across Europe to hope for the spread of liberalism through his political conquests, and also proved to be the catalyst for the ensuing Prussian educational reforms, which were intended to put into political praxis the philosophical theory of *Bildung*. In Sebald's melancholy metaphysics, the Enlightenment connotations of the figure become dialectically transformed into oppressive ones. The same complex arises in *Austerlitz*, where Jacques Austerlitz, like Beyle, initially finds in the association with Napoleon a means to secure his shaky masculine identity. With the aid of his history teacher, he manages to build an illusory identification with the Napoleonic victory at Austerlitz, an act that transforms his unusual name, for him, from a shameful flaw into a guiding light — hence giving him the illusion of a heroic masculine identity (*A*, 111; *Ae*, 102). In an interview, Sebald said that the figure of Napoleon informed all of his writings because his conquests foreshadowed the even more brutal attempts at hegemony by the Germans.[8] Sebald expands on this connection between the defeat of Napoleon and the catastrophic progress of German history in his essay on Hebel:

> Möglicherweise ahnte Hebel um 1812/1813, daß mit dem Fall Napoleons und der Erhebung der Deutschen eine abschüssige Bahn begann, auf der man nicht leicht würde einhalten können, und daß die Geschichte, wie sie von da ab sich anließ, im Grunde nichts als das Martyrologium der Menschheit sei.[9]

> [Possibly Hebel sensed, around 1812/13, that with the fall of Napoleon and the elevation of the Germans, a downward trajectory began, which it would not be easy to halt, and that history, as it would proceed from then on, would be in essence nothing but the martyrology of humanity.]

As the defeat of Napoleon is followed by the rise of a militaristic Prussia, so the significance of Beyle's achievement of heroic masculinity and of the name 'Austerlitz' is dialectically transformed, both within the diegeses of *Schwindel. Gefühle.* and *Austerlitz*, and within Sebald's overall metaphysics. The summer of 1800 could in a sense be seen to be the origin of the negative dialectic of Enlightenment. Beyle makes this very connection when reflecting on this summer in retrospect, when he feels as though he had foreseen the coming fall and exile of Napoleon, and decides, instead of seeking his fortune in the army, to become the greatest writer of all time. Such a turn to literature denotes in Sebald's ethics a commitment to a painful but morally necessary task of restitution. Although Sebald's Beyle retains traces of Napoleonic grandstanding in his initial ambition, by the end of his narrative he is evincing the familiar suffering and doggedness of the Sebaldian melancholy writer.

The ironic undermining of the heroic *Bildungsreise* found in *Schwindel. Gefühle.* does not stop with the melancholy results of Beyle's performance of military and heterosexual masculinity. That this is a performance is underlined by Sebald's attention to his chosen outfits — first, a fetishistic and minute description of the precise accoutrements of his officer's uniform, describing the chamois-leather trousers, the helmet fitted with horse's hair, and so forth, and subsequently the clothes he wears to court Mathilde, a *Wertherfrack* in reverse (*SG*, 24; *V*, 20). Heterosexual masculinity appears in the guise of a theatrical masquerade, just as the site where Beyle learns about heterosexual love is La Scala, where he watches the opera *Il matrimonio segreto* by Domenico Cimarosa. Not only is Beyle warned against the dubious morals of the ladies of the theatre, Sebald himself warns in his essay on *Andreas* that a theatrical company is a milieu 'in dem die Identitäten, und selbst diejenigen des Geschlechts, gewechselt werden je nach der Szene' [in which identities, even those of gender, are exchanged according to the scene] (*BU*, 63). Viewed in this light, the discussion on crystallization between Beyle and Mme Gherardi takes on an additional level of allegorical meaning, beyond that of the question of representation and 'fidelity to nature'.[10] When Mme Gherardi describes love as a 'chimera', the word exposes the theatricality of *Il Matrimonio Segreto*, of Beyle's studied performance of hypermasculinity, and of the elaborate rituals of heterosexual courtships summarized in 'Beyle oder das merckwurdige Faktum der Liebe' and discussed at length in *De l'amour*. Equally Beyle describes 'crystallization', or the creation of an imaginary and perfect version of the beloved, as an allegory for the growth of love in the salt mines of the soul (*SG*, 31; *V*, 26). 'Crystallization' becomes here a betrayal of *natura naturans*, as Öhlschläger says, an attempt to fix nature artificially. The heterosexual love that Beyle ostensibly desires is, like fixed gender roles, heroic masculinity, or military success, an idealist chimera, which may have disastrous consequences for the identity of the writer. Thus, although Beyle does not fall victim to the rich seam of perversions that Sebald suspects are lying in wait for the hapless Andreas in Venice, including incest, male rape, sadism, and masochism, his *Bildungsreise* is no less a voyage of subjective disintegration. Yet, although Beyle becomes a melancholic and falls victim to syphilis (or more precisely, his attempts to cure it via quack method), his story is still, and importantly, entitled 'Das merckwurdige Faktum der Liebe' in German, literally 'The peculiar fact of love'. This is a title that should be heeded, Rovagnati argues, suggesting that love is the *Leitfaden* of the whole of *Schwindel. Gefühle*.[11] Beyle's pantomime of heterosexual love still denaturalizes and disrupts the line of heterosexual love, pointing towards the queerer forms of love lying in wait for the Sebaldian narrator and Dr K on their own journeys to Venice.

Dr S. crosses the Alps

If Beyle's *Bildungsreise* exposes at once the fallacies of heterosexual love and the origins of the negative dialectic of Enlightenment, the narrator of 'All'estero', a man in middle years, is past the age of *Bildung*, and his journey to Venice is from the start one of disorientation. Instead, like Dr Schreber, he is a man 'at a time of life which is sexually of critical importance', when previously repressed homosexual fantasies tend to return.[12] My reading of 'All'estero' takes as a point of departure John Zilcosky's claim that the Sebaldian narrator's journey is one of compulsory reorientation, when the narrator, driven by a fear of heterosexuality, repeatedly attempts to escape the logic of heterosexual orientation but instead is incapable of getting lost. Zilcosky argues that the narrator instead 'returns to the beaten path of his heterosexuality and, what is more, to the equally uncanny track of historical repetition'.[13] I argue that the text as a whole follows no straight trajectory of attempted loss and compulsory return to heterosexuality, despite its dispiriting *Ritorno in Patria* at the end. *Schwindel. Gefühle.*, as we have already seen, subverts the *Bildungsreise*, which for Andreas as much as for Goethe's Wilhelm Meister is perfectly capable of incorporating sexual deviation in its middle period of wandering as long as the final heterosexual resolution reorientates the protagonist to bourgeois masculinity. Instead, within 'All'estero', the Sebaldian narrator undertakes wanderings which, although they are bound by the possibility of catastrophe and death, also contain an element of wonder that proves a moment of resistance to such catastrophe.[14] Moreover, what is at stake here is not the narrator's engagement in gay sex, but rather his embroilment in queer textuality (we think again, here, of the queer textuality and afterlife of Roger Casement or Algernon Swinburne). Although the whole text of *Schwindel. Gefühle.* contains within it a return, or indeed two returns, to the *Heimat*, it preserves, within its two central sections, associative texts that refuse linear plot.

Crucially, the narrator's journey through northern Italy refuses the coherence or legibility of a linear *Bildungsreise*; instead, his travels are constantly determined by chance, coincidence, affect, and material encounters with artefacts. Although he starts his travels in Vienna, the city of psychoanalysis, which might seem to promise a journey of subjective reintegration, he soon begins to lose his reason. Throughout 'All'estero', his condition fluctuates between catatonic paralysis and compulsive wandering, suggesting that he oscillates between Deleuze and Guattari's 'neurotic on the analyst's couch' and the freer, less colonized 'schizophrenic out for a walk'.[15] Indeed, the narrator's disintegration of self in Vienna, marked by hallucinations and compulsive walking, in part mirrors that of Schreber's descent into schizophrenic paranoia. Freud suggests that such paranoia can be triggered when the subject's social relations break down, which occurs here when the narrator tries and fails to contact his friends in Vienna by telephone. The breakdown takes place, Freud continues, when the subject's homosexual desires cease to be sublimated into their social drive and instead become sexualized, just as the narrator substitutes paranoid homosexual lusts for the social networks of *Heimat* when he crosses the Alps. Such homosexual desires, Freud argues, necessarily have an Oedipal origin: although the paranoid Schreber invests first his therapist Flechsig and then God with libido, Freud argues that this necessarily must be the return of libido that was originally invested in the father.[16] While Freud thereby imposes an Oedipal logic upon his conception of homosexuality, he also suggests that the cause of the paranoia is not homosexual desire *per se*, but its repression. Deleuze and Guattari, by contrast, reject Freud's demand that homosexual desires (or any other desires) should be subordinated to Oedipal logic, instead of allowing the schizo dissolution of the self and its production of desiring machines. 'All'estero' is just such a schizo desiring machine as they describe. When the now paranoid Sebaldian narrator travels across the Alps, he experiences a dissolution of the self in a sexually indeterminate territory, and conventional narrative logic evaporates along with the structures of the self, in a similar fashion to one of Herbeck's schizoid poems. 'All'estero', notes Long, is a narrative 'whose cohesion is greatly attenuated'.[17] Such refusal of narrative cohesion is in itself a queer moment. If irony is 'the queerest of rhetorical devices', as Edelman argues, then it works in the textual machine and 'threatens, like a guillotine, to sever the genealogy that narrative syntax labors to affirm'.[18] The reader seeks in vain for narrative orientation in the text of *Schwindel. Gefühle.*, which generates an alternative sexual-textual order. When, at the midpoint of the second trip to Italy, the Sebaldian narrator is asked which the text he is writing, he can give no coherent answer. He can only reply that the narrative takes place in northern Italy, that it concerns a series of unsolved crimes and the reappearance of a person who has been lost for a long while (*SG*, 108; *V*, 95). This confused and non-linear description itself resembles, but does not correspond exactly to, the narratives 'All'estero' and 'Dr. K.s Badereise nach Riva'. While the two outer narratives — 'Beyle oder das merckwurdige Faktum der Liebe' and 'Il ritorno in patria' — draw on patriarchal narrative structures inherited from works of major European literatures, the *Bildungsreise* and the *Odyssey*, the two inner narratives, and most particularly 'All'estero', depart from this nod to European narrative convention.[19] Instead, like *Die Ringe des Saturn*, they conform to several of Deleuze and Guattari's descriptions of the rhizomatic or schizo text, which exists not to reproduce a fixed social structure but to produce desire or a line of flight. This is shown, for instance, in the use of *bricolage* in 'All'estero'. In Sebald's other texts, such as *Austerlitz, bricolage* is celebrated for its ability to encode memory.[20] In 'All'estero', the random images and objects assembled, for instance, from the newspaper archive and reproduced on pages 134 to 135 [pages 118 to 119], are playful rather than melancholy, and thus resemble the 'production of production' that is characteristic of Deleuze and Guattari's desiring machine.[21] Instead of providing the reader with psychoanalytic, political, or narrative orientation, 'All'estero' offers a series of half-terrifying, half-magical episodes linked by the associative and playful logic of dreams. Time itself is repeatedly suspended, following the logic of the unconscious which, as Freud tells us, is not ordered by linear time, is not changed by time, and has no relationship at all to time. These episodes explore, among other literary complexes, the sexual possibilities offered to the disoriented self once it has left behind it the restrictive structures of German major literature. As the schizophrenic bachelor-poet Ernst Herbeck is the catalyst for the Sebaldian narrator's journey, it is no surprise that 'All'estero' breaks with the normative forms of major literature. Instead, it corresponds in several ways with Deleuze and Guattari's concept of minor literature: 'A major, or established, literature follows a vector that goes from content to expression [...] a minor, or revolutionary literature begins by expressing itself and doesn't conceptualize until afterward'.[22] In keeping with this concept, *Schwindel. Gefühle.* is structured, like *Die Ringe des Saturn*, as an assemblage of series. Nonetheless, the political element of collective enunciation that is so prominent in Deleuze and Guattari's analysis, and the anti-colonial resistance of the bachelors in *Die Ringe des Saturn*, is here confined to a personal longing for redemption from inherited guilt. However, the queer desire of the narrator informs a politicization of textuality itself, and a resistance to colonizing Oedipal formations.

Thus, 'All'estero' defies generic categorization in its heterogeneous expression, while parodying inherited narrative structures. Just as 'Beyle oder das merckwürdige Faktum der Liebe' echoes the form of the *Bildungsreise*, 'All'estero' flirts with the structure of a detective novel, with its promise of a soluble riddle and the figure of the outsider detective who imposes patriarchal order on lawlessness. The plot of this detective novel might run as follows. In 1980, while visiting northern Italy, the narrator is pursued by two young men, whom he associates with a terrorist organization called the Organizzazione Ludwig. Seven years later, when the narrator has returned to Italy in an ostensible attempt to document and reconstruct the narrative of the crime, his friend Salvatore tells the narrator that the Organizzazione's mission is the death of those who have betrayed God (*SG*, 147; *V*, 130). Salvatore tells the narrator a linear story with which he declares the narrator must already be familiar: the Organizzazione has for years directed violence against perpetrators of sexual transgressions, among them a prostitute and the patrons of a pornographic cinema in Milan. The group call their arson attack on the cinema a 'Scheiterhaufen der Schwänze' [blazing pyre of pricks], the remarkably un-Sebaldian sexual crudity of the language emphasizing the fanatically puritanical nature of their mission (*SG*, 147; *V*, 130). This conclusion might seem to impose the coherent narrative resolution of a detective novel on 'All'estero', and indeed Salvatore tells the narrator that 'diese Geschichte ist, um es gleich vorwegzunehmen, inzwischen fast schon an ihrem Ende angelangt. Der Prozeß ist gemacht' [that story, to tell you the end of it first, has now almost reached its conclusion. The trial has been heard] (*SG*, 146; *V*, 129). It might appear, then, that the paranoia of the narrator has a logical cause: he fears being pursued for his homosexual deviance by the zealots of the Organizzazione. In the end, just as at the end of Kafka's *Der Proceß* [*The Trial*] (hinted at in Salvatore's wording), the law is imposed on the lawless Organizzazione and the narrator can flee the disorienting site of homosexual temptation back to the order of his Germanic *patria*.

But *Schwindel. Gefühle.* baffles narrative resolution of the detective plot just as it mocks that of the *Bildungsreise*. If 'All'estero' were a detective story, in light of the narrator's disorientation it might be more true to say that the text flirted with the structure of a postmodern or metaphysical detective novel, where 'the mystery is a maze without an exit. The armchair detective confronts a labyrinthine literary text; the private eye, a convoluted entanglement of streets'.[23] The rhizomatic structure of 'All'estero' resists the extraction of a linear or even a self-reflexive detective story from amidst its densely packed images. Moreover, if an attempt were made to extract the chronology of the Organizzazione plotline from the incoherent images in 'All'estero', the Sebaldian narrator then would show himself complicit in the pursuit of the two men, and the pursuit itself would reveal a sexual tone, contaminating the sexually puritanical manifesto of the Organizzazione. On the Sebaldian narrator's first trip to Venice in 1980, he recalls that the two men seem to have been in the bar where he meets a Jewish man named Malacchio. We may presume this is a gay bar, and will discuss the sexual and theological significance of the narrator's pick-up below. The sexual charge surrounding the men is evident from the beginning, as he becomes aware of their eyes on him at the station bar, another heterotopic location. The narrator flees their gaze for Verona, but feels sure that the men have followed him there to the amphitheatre, where he is paralysed with fear by their appearance and finds it almost impossible to leave. As the narrator forces himself to move to the exit of the amphitheatre, a compulsive image of penetration comes to him:

> das Bild auf von einem den grauen Luftraum sausend durchfliegenden Pfeil, der jeden Augenblick mein linkes Schulterblatt durchschlagen und mit einem eigenartig satten Geräusch mitten in meinem Herzen sich festsetzen würde.

> [a compulsive vision of an arrow whistling through the grey air, about to pierce my left shoulderblade and, with a distinctive, sickening sound, penetrate my heart.] (*SG*, 84; *V*, 72)

The fantasy of phallic penetration, which as Santner rightly comments is associated with *jouissance* (*satt* meaning 'satisfied', 'replete' as well as 'full'), foreshadows the narrator's fantasy of being penetrated by a knife wielded by an 'oriental' in *Die Ringe des Saturn*.[24] If in *Die Ringe des Saturn* this fantasy of homosexual penetration is bound up in Orientalist transgressions, here it also calls to mind the martyrdom of St Sebastian, which is at once a homoerotic icon, the subject of a painting by

Grünewald in *Nach der Natur,* and a key image for *Der Tod in Venedig.*[25] The sexual allure of the two men is also mentioned by Salvatore at the end of 'All'estero', who recalls seeing one of them playing the guitar on the television as an adolescent. Salvatore ends his story by saying he was 'sehr bewegt [...] von seiner Erscheinung und seinem wundervollen Spiel' [his whole appearance and his wonderful playing affected me deeply], suggesting that the two younger men have an allure akin to that of the adolescent Tadzio (*SG*, 148; *V*, 132). Further disrupting the detective story plot, the sexual aura surrounding the two men is established long before the narrator discovers the existence of the Organizzazione Ludwig. It is only after he has escaped the amphitheatre that he reads a newspaper report about the Organizzazione, which has been perpetrating a series of unsolved murders of young men living on the edge of society — a Gypsy, a waiter, and a heroin addict — killed by fire and stabbing. The narrator is filled with fear while reading this account. Ostensibly, this fear may be a fear of being pursued by the terrorists, as the narrator realizes that, thanks to his queer desires, he also now belongs to this series of marginalized and rootless males. However, as we know from Freud, paranoid homosexuality produces a 'wishful fantasy' in which 'he who had been longed for' is transformed in the mind of the paranoiac into a persecutor.[26] The narrator's paranoia is shown to be phantasmic rather than grounded in any real threat, as far from pursuing the narrator with the same vigour that the Organizzazione Ludwig accords to other sexual and moral deviants, the two treat him with a strange courtesy. In Verona, they keep watch over him as he visits the Arena, and bow to each other before leaving him (*SG*, 83; *V*, 72).

The theatrical scene in the Arena draws the narrator and his two pursuers into the realm of the theological. With this bow, the two men are associated with the two pallbearers in dark coats from Kafka's 'Gracchus' story, making them mediators between life and death as well as objects of queer desire. It is to be remembered that the narrator met them under the eyes of a scornful barmaid similar to those in Kafka's novels, a topos where the barmaid presides over an inn that belongs to death and the devil (*BU*, 90). The two men thus hover between a mourning Thanatos and a queer Eros. The Organizzazione theme also disrupts the authoritative structures of the detective plot, where the restoration of order is simultaneously a disciplinary restoration of meaning. The Foucauldian procedure of the police investigation could not provide any explanation of their series of crimes (*SG*, 148; *V*, 131). In keeping with the psychological fragmentations of the entire narrative, Salvatore says that the psychiatric evaluation of the two by the police could not afford any insights into their inner world, suggesting that, like Ambros Adelwarth, they have none. Instead, their relationship with each other carries an enigmatic affect between brotherhood and angelic innocence. Salvatore tells the narrator: 'Ich glaube, sie waren zueinander wie Brüder und wußten nicht, wie sie herauskommen sollten aus ihrer Unschuld' [I think they were like brothers to each other and had no idea how to free themselves from their innocence] (*SG*, 148; *V*, 131). The term 'innocence' opens up a theological dimension to the two that far exceeds the narrow puritanical mission of the Organizzazione Ludwig. If they are avenging figures sent to punish those who have betrayed God, such as the hunter Gracchus from Kafka's story, the sexual overtones of their encounters with the narrator opens up far more Prager's 'eroto-salvific' dimension. They are caught between theological violence and queer transgression, far exceeding any single interpretation that can be placed upon them.

As the uncanny pursuit of the Organizzazione shows, the homosexual panic and paranoia of the narrator in 'All'estero' are of a qualitatively different order from the homosexual melancholy and love that characterize the queer bachelors of *Nach der Natur*, *Die Ringe des Saturn*, and *Die Ausgewanderten*. These bachelors all experience, in one form or another, a species of homosexual love. The narrator in 'All'estero', by contrast, is constantly tempted by homosexual love and desire, but is afflicted with paranoia and the fear of dissolution far more than with a historical melancholy or romantic loss. The dissociative journey of the narrator moves away from the Oedipal model that posits that desire must necessarily be associated with lack or loss. Instead it moves towards the schizo model that understands it as a desiring machine that lacks not an object, but a subject, the normative Freudian subject that is fixed by repression.[27] The tutelary geniuses of the voyage, if such a term can be used, are the figures of Ernst Herbeck, Casanova, and Kafka, all of whom exhibit symptoms of schizo desire. All three figures resist being bound in a conjugal model of love, and, as Deleuze and Guattari suggest when discussing Kafka, 'it doesn't matter whether the conjugality is official or unofficial, heterosexual or homosexual'.[28] In 'Dr. K.s Badereise nach Riva', Sebald spins a fantasy about Kafka at a crucial moment in his bachelor existence, a trip taken to northern Italy in 1913 shortly after he tried to break off his relationship with Felice, pleading that his devotion to literature rendered him incapable of conjugal love.[29] 'All'estero' repeats and echoes this journey, and similar conjugal anxieties also plague the Sebaldian narrator. Like Kafka in his engagement to Felice, the Sebaldian narrator is attracted by the chimera of a stable heterosexual marriage, fantasies that centre around Luciana, the proprietor of the hotel in Limone. As his head is bent over his work, he fantasizes that Luciana touches him on the shoulder. Although he has been exchanging smiles and glances with her, the narrator makes it clear that he is not used to cruising for women:

> es ist mir gewesen, als spürte ich ihre Hand auf meiner Schulter. Selten genug ist es vorgekommen in meinem Leben, habe ich mir dabei gedacht, daß ich von einer mir an sich fremden Frau angerührt worden bin, aber immer hatte dieses unvermutete Angerührtwerden etwas Gewichtloses, Geisterhaftes.

> [I thought I felt her hand on my shoulder. It occurred to me then how few and far between in my life were the moments when I had been touched in this way by a woman with whom I was barely acquainted, and, thinking back, it seemed to me that about such unwonted gestures there had always been something disembodied and ghoulish.] (*SG*, 111; *V*, 97)

The Sebaldian subjunctive 'it seemed to me' and the words 'disembodied' and 'ghoulish' cast both the reality and the pleasure of the spectral touch into doubt. Nonetheless, the episode has a sequel. As he leaves the hotel the next day, after a visit to stamp his identity document, the narrator tells us that the official ceremony, restoring to him his German bourgeois identity, also opens up a chimera of marriage. He comments, once again in the subjunctive,

> [es] war mir, als seien wir von dem Brigadiere getraut worden und könnten nun miteinander hinfahren, wo wir wollten. Die mit einem Gefühl der Glückseligkeit erfüllende Vorstellung hielt allerdings nicht lange an.

> [I felt as if we had just been married by the *brigadiere* and might now drive off together wherever we desired. But this notion, which filled me with intense pleasure, was shortlived.] (*SG*, 117; *V*, 103)

Here, the fantasy of happy heterosexual marriage carries with it the associated fantasy of freedom of movement, which has earlier been repeatedly frustrated by the narrator's disorientation. Yet the narrator himself confesses that the giddy moment of heterosexual happiness with Luciana, whose name is derived from the patron saint of the blind, is a false vision: in that moment of supposed marital bliss, he sees everything as though through a pair of glasses that do not belong to him (*SG*, 112; *V*, 98). Instead of leading towards the conventional orientation of marriage with Luciana, the homosexual temptations in 'All'estero' mirror its rhizomatic narrative structure. They lure the narrator towards a queer line of flight away from bourgeois heterosexuality that also disrupts any idea of narrative closure on the lines promised by the marriage plot. 'Marriage', McCrea reminds us, 'is the narrative goal par excellence, the redeeming moment toward which we expect stories [...] to tend'.[30] The queer stranger often disrupts such redemption in the modernist novel, proving a threat to the narrative coherence of the marriage plot. The narrator's queer eye and ekphrasis disorients the heteronormative marriage plot. This queer disorientation is also shown in the narrator's reading and reproductions of Pisanello's painting of *St George and the Princess* in Verona. The narrator tells us

> Zum Erstaunen ist es, wie es Pisanello verstanden hat, den jäh heraustretenden, seitwärts schon auf die schwere blutige Arbeit abschweifenden männlichen Blick des Ritters abzusetzen von der nur durch die geringfügigste Senkung der unteren Lidgrenze angedeuteten Beschlossenheit des weiblichen Auges.

> [It is astounding how Pisanello contrived to set the wide open eyes of the knight, already wandering sideways to the hard and bloody battle ahead, against the self-contained expression of the woman indicated by little more than a slight lowering of her gaze.] (*SG*, 87; *V*, 76)

The ekphrastic narrative focuses on the way in which the expected orientation of the gazes of the heterosexual couple is baffled by the painting; instead of gazing at his female counterpart, the gaze of St George drifts sideways, and although the narrator tells us that he is gazing on the 'bloody work' to come, the painting is cropped so severely that all the reader sees is two close-ups of the eyes of St George and the princess, with no evidence of 'bloody work' anywhere. Öhlschläger suggests that his melancholy gaze may be turning towards the princess, hence mirroring Stendhal's melancholy history of heterosexual love. But rather than appearing with Stendhal's conspicuous props of masculinity St George appears feminized, his soft features surrounded by waving hair, which makes the reader initially identify the 'masculine eye' with the princess.[31] Thus, the reader can perceive St George's slantwise gaze in Ahmed's queer sense of 'slantwise'; St George, whose wavy blonde hair recalls that of Tadzio, is a queerly enigmatic object of desire.[32] Both reader and narrator are disorientated by the straying eye of St George and by his ambiguous gender presentation; the shattered image therefore functions as an index of the narrator's general sexual disorientation in northern Italy.

The Doppelganger: The Strange Case of Dr K. and Dr Sebald

The Organizzazione Ludwig is just one in a series of doubles and doppelgangers that the Sebaldian narrator encounters in the course of the narrative, further destabilizing his sense of self. Like the voyage over the Alps to Italy, the doppelganger has a long history in post-Romantic German literature; indeed, the doppelganger narrative is in many ways the jeering uncanny other of the *Bildungsroman*. In *Schwindel. Gefühle.*, doppelgangers also represent an upsetting of the linear course of history, a spectre, in Derrida's terms, that attempts to make the dead present, and demands justice, thereby calling forth both the work of mourning and a hope for redemption.[33] Hence, Sebald's doppelgangers demonstrate Andrew Webber's description of their doubled movement: 'Like all ghosts, it is at once an historical figure, re-presenting past times, and a profoundly anti-historical phenomenon, resisting temporal change by stepping out of time and then stepping back in as revenant'.[34] In 'All'estero', the doppelgangers who haunt the narrator are symbols of the uncanny, which is the conflict between the desire to return home and the fear of the return of the repressed in that homely space. The narrator is not only haunted by the doppelganger, but also by more concrete evidence of home in the form of tourists from southern Germany who mortify the narrator when they speak in the dialect of his *Heimat* (SG, 107; V, 93). (We are reminded of the opposition between Adelwarth's queer cosmopolitan facility in High German and the local, historically suspect dialect in W.) Despite this, the doubled terrorists are enough to drive the Sebaldian narrator back over the Alps at the end of his first visit to northern Italy. Dr K. is similarly tormented by splittings, which are 'absolutely characteristic of paranoia. As hysteria condenses, so paranoia splits', Freud says of Schreber.[35] Dr K. constantly encounters uncannily doubled men in his travels, and his days are plagued by a phenomenon of split vision: 'eine Verzweifachung, wie sie ihm aus seinen Träumen bekannt war, in denen auf eine furchterregende Weise alles beständig sich weiter und weiter aufspaltete' [a mirroring effect he was familiar with from his dreams, in which everything was forever splitting and multiplying, over and again, in the most terrifying manner] (SG, 165; V, 149). The narrator claims that Dr K. would have recognized his doppelganger in Balduin, the hero of *The Student of Prague*, who is haunted by his own mirror image. Eventually, Balduin attempts to shoot his other self, but in doing so, penetrates his own heart. According to Otto Rank's 1914 study, Balduin's murderous shadow is the personification of an atavistic fear of death that finds expression in an infantile narcissism.[36] This narcissism disrupts the bachelor student's ability to form love relationships with women and may be caused by a homosexual disorder, just as literary doppelgangers frequently disrupt love scenes between the protagonist and his female beloved, representing the stern parental law.[37] In Rank's reading, the doppelganger in the *Student of Prague* presents a seemingly homoerotic moment that only appears to offer the chimera of love for another person, but which is in fact an auto-erotic moment that can instead prove lethal.[38] The doppelganger appears as a return of past experience, and is hence inherently backward-turned.[39] Rank's analysis and Balduin's death suggest that the queer moments in 'Dr. K.s Badereise nach Riva' are imperilled by the overall Thanatic threat hanging over Dr K.'s journey.

The complex relationship between guilt and desire figured by the doppelganger becomes apparent in the intense desire and shame felt by the narrator when he returns to Italy in 1987 and encounters twin adolescent boys on the bus to Riva, who 'auf die unheimlichste Weise, die man sich denken kann, den Bildern glich, die Kafka als heranwachsenden Schüler zeigt' [bore the most uncanny resemblance imaginable to pictures of Franz Kafka as an adolescent schoolboy] (SG, 101; V, 88). Like the twin pallbearers, the twin Kafkas represent at once a possibility of desire beyond the Oedipal, but they also signal the danger of an Aschenbach-like fall into abjection and sexual disgrace.[40] The narrator longs to take a photograph of them, but is prevented by their outraged parents, who assume he is a paedophile on tour. Shortly after this unsettling encounter, the narrator checks into a hotel, and hands his passport over to the hotel owners to be locked into a drawer. When he comes to check it out, however, it is discovered that the friendly son of the house, Mauro, has mistakenly given his passport to a German traveller called Herr Doll, and the narrator must travel home on a hastily typewritten substitute. This document is reproduced in the novel with a thick line bisecting the identifying photograph, in a way that negates the supposed authenticity of the photograph, and indeed the integrity of the person depicted at all.[41] After receiving it, the narrator feels no more grounded in his identity than before: when he next needs to check into a hotel, he gives his name as 'Jakob Philipp Fallmerayer', a historian from the Tyrol (SG, 132; V, 117). Thanks to the disruptive intervention of Mauro (who is also linked to the heterotopia of the boat) the Sebaldian narrator's heterosexuality and his officially certified German identity are at once under question. Moreover, the episode is interwoven with his chimerical fantasies of heterosexual marriage with Luciana: when his temporary passport is issued to him, the narrator feels as though the official stamp has married him to her. Yet the combination of the bifurcated photograph and the narrator's realization that the glasses through which he sees Luciana are 'not meant for him' demonstrate how the uncanny twin Kafkas disrupt any fantasies of a heterosexual trajectory. Equally, the fuss about the narrator's missing passport becomes 'ein regelrechtes Familiendrama' [a family drama], but it is left unclear which role the narrator plays here: comic outsider, spouse to Luciana, errant son to the Padrone, lover of Mauro, who is in the ambivalent territory between boy and man (SG, 113; V, 99)? The attempt to photograph the twin Kafkas also has overtones of the episode in 'Ambros Adelwarth', where Adelwarth and Cosmo take a photograph of a young dervish while in Jerusalem. Yet, in keeping with the more radically fragmented style of 'All'estero', the attempt at a photographic act of appropriation or verification is here frustrated by the boys' parents, foiling the narrator's attempt at touristic scopophilia and cementing his status as an outsider to the self-defensive fortress of the nuclear family. The disruptive influence of the Sebaldian narrator on the heterosexual dyad is repeated when he returns to Verona and demands that a young man from Erlangen on honeymoon take a photograph for him. The narrator succeeds in wringing one photograph from him, but when he asks for a second photograph, the photographer's bride frustrates him, looking at him with mistrust or enmity (SG, 143; V, 127). Once more, an appeal that the narrator presents as motivated by a desire to archive an image with personal significance is interpreted as a sexually predatory one. The queer disorientation informing the seemingly hapless narrator's conduct becomes ironically apparent to the reader, and indeed the narrator even begins to doubt his own narrative. Rather than an example of successful sexual tourism, the sequence with the twin Kafkas reflects and queers elements of the doppelganger tradition, including the association of doubling with repressed queer sexual desire, the splintering of identity, or indeed the fact that the narrator's unseen doppelganger Herr Doll appears to have successfully purloined his identity, leaving 'W. G. Sebald' as the dubious copy of himself. Herr Doll's very name is a punning reference to two key elements of Hoffmann's *Sandman* story: the uncanny doll or puppet Olimpia, and through the German meaning of *doll* as mad, the unhappy fate of madness that befalls Nathaniel, the protagonist, when he looks through glasses that distort his vision.[42] This paranoid moment of madness inspired by the image of a boy in North Italy returns us again to the echoes of *Der Tod in Venedig*, yet, as Prager rightly comments, in keeping with the influence of Gracchus over the text, Sebald refuses his narrator 'the easy way out that was given to Mann's Aschenbach'.[43] The taut opposition between Apollo and Dionysos that structures *Der Tod in Venedig* is replaced by the dreamlike, uncanny, and rhizomatic structure of 'All'estero'.

However, as the Organizzazione shows, the political complex of doubling in *Schwindel. Gefühle.* exceeds Freudian readings of doppelgangers and their psycho-analytic mechanisms of return, Oedipal punishment, and death. For Rank, heterosexual love and marriage are the moral destiny of the bourgeois subject, which the homoerotic narcissism represented by the doppelganger threatens to destroy.[44] Both Rank and Freud insist on Oedipal structures to uphold bourgeois society: for them, 'Oedipus is a requirement or a consequence of social reproduction, insofar as this latter aims at domesticating a genealogical form and content that are in every way intractable'.[45] By contrast, Sebald analyses this romantic fiction of self-fulfilment in love as one of the nineteenth-century literary myths that binds the bourgeois individual into the framework of society and utilitarian progress. The doppelgangers of *Schwindel. Gefühle.* carry with them a more intractably queer and political freight than Rank or Freud allow. Analysing the proliferation of doubles in Kafka's work, Deleuze and Guattari diagnose an anti-Oedipal 'homosexuality of doubles, of brothers or of bureaucrats', which function as an element in the series of the 'line of flight' along which Kafka's novels tend.[46] The doubles correspond to the schizo-incest that resists Oedipus, instead manifesting a 'sort of homosexual effusion'.[47] The doppelgangers in *Schwindel. Gefühle.* have a further political meaning. In his essay 'Kafka im Kino' [Kafka goes to the Movies], Sebald tells us that, beyond pastiche, the modernist doppelganger figure expresses the chronic alienation of the individual and the disassociation of the bourgeois subject in the machine age, and thereby functions as a historical index.[48] The doppelganger is proliferated by photography, something that, Sebald tells us, Kafka felt to be uncanny. Sebald further elaborates that Kafka's works show a horror at 'den mit dem beginnenden Zeitalter der technischen Reproduktion sich anbahnenden Mutationen der Menschheit, mit denen er wohl das Ende des von der bürgerlichen Kultur ausgebildeten autonomen Individuums heraufkommen sah' [the impending mutations of mankind as the age of technical reproduction opened, mutations in which he probably saw the imminent end of the autonomous individuality formed by bourgeois culture] (*CS*, 200; *CSe*, 163). For Sebald, the figures in Kafka's works who are called into life according to an 'undurchsichtige[s] Seriengesetz' [obscure serial law] are harbingers of this machine age. In his essay on 'Kafkas Evolutionsgeschichten', Sebald refers to duplicated beings in Kafka's work as 'Zwillinge, Drillinge und all die einander zum Verwechseln ähnlich Androiden' [twins, triplets, and all the androids who are similar to the point of confusion].[49] This essay echoes, if it does not directly draw on, Deleuze and Guattari's analysis of Kafka's doubles as harbingers of the next, mechanical stage of evolution into which the misguided human belief in technological reproduction has precipitated itself. In keeping with his melancholic view of history, Sebald's version of a technological post-humanity is no liberating cyborg vision, such as those proposed by Donna Haraway, but a vision of technocratic horror.[50]

Deleuze and Guattari read the 'series' of doubles and triplets in Kafka's work — such as the three lodgers who move in with the Samsa family in *Die Verwandlung* — as examples of a movement away from the Oedipal tripartite structure of the bourgeois family — mother, father, son — and towards the great bureaucratic machines of the twentieth century. The 'bureaucratic doubles' are an apocalyptic harbinger showing how, in the coming century, desire will be expressed through the machines of power.[51] 'Capitalist America, bureaucratic Russia, Nazi Germany — in fact, all the "diabolical powers of the future" — are knocking at the door of Kafka's moment with segmental and contiguous blows'.[52] In 'Kafka im Kino', Sebald remains with the bureaucratic doubles of the earlier stage of Deleuze and Guattari's line of flight, tending towards a Benjaminian analysis of photographs. Thus, he assigns an apocalyptic function to the doppelganger, warning 'war der Doppelgänger in der Zeit der Romantik, in der erstmals die Furcht vor den Apparaten sich rührte, noch eine spukhafte Ausnahmeerscheinung, so ist er jetzt überall' [In the Romantic period the doppelganger which first aroused a fear of mechanical appliances was still a haunting and exceptional phenomenon; now it is everywhere] (*CS*, 200; *CSe*, 164). Sebald here alludes to the proliferation of mechanical reproductions in the twentieth century, which seem to hollow out the originals of which they are the copy Sebald also reminds us that the apparition of the doppelganger also leads to the uncanny result 'daß einer, der seinem Doppelgänger begegnet, sich selber vernichtet fühlt' [a man meeting his doppelganger is said to feel his real self destroyed] (*CS*, 201; *CSe*, 164). The use of the word 'annihilate' is far more absolute than the mortal death of which the traditional Romantic doppelganger warns. Kafka's recurring doppelgangers do not only represent the destruction of the bourgeois self in the coming machine age, but they also presage the annihilation of European Jewry barely fifteen years after Kafka's death. Although, as we have seen, the central sections of *Schwindel. Gefühle.* break down the narrative logic of traditional teleological plot in favour of an associative textual strategy, they also contain an apocalyptic threat.[53] This is seen most clearly in the repeated references to the year and number 1913, the year before the outbreak of the First World War, but there are also oblique references to the Shoah.[54] Dr K. is in Riva, as the very first sentence of the story tells us, en route to Vienna to take part in a congress on rescue services and hygiene (*SG*, 157; *V*, 141). These two words suggest the two extreme poles of Jewish experience that resonate through Sebald's work: the messianic rescue that is made more explicit in Sebald's essay on the *Schloß*, and the murderous 'racial hygiene' of the Nazis that destroyed Kafka's family and culture. In several interviews, Sebald betrays a sense that Kafka is in some sense his own double, bound to him because he was born in the same month as Kafka's sister Ottla was deported: 'It's the chronological contiguity that makes you think it is something to do with you'.[55] Thus, Sebald's invocation of Kafkan doppelgangers takes on some of the political import that drives Deleuze and Guattari's reading of Kafka's work, as well as being emblems of his own personal guilt.

But what of the queer undertone of the doppelgangers, and their role as a segment along a Deleuzian line of escape, amidst these undertones of catastrophe? In *Schwindel. Gefühle.*, the ironic intertextual relationship to the Schreber case suggests that the apocalyptic fantasies of the text — which ends, in the German edition, with an apocalyptic vision of fire over London in the year 2013, twenty years after the book was published — may themselves be part of the narrative paranoia. Schreber develops the conviction of a great catastrophe at the peak of his illness, which Freud diagnoses as the projection of an internal catastrophe, the end of love, or libidinal investment in the world outside the schizo self.[56] The apocalyptic fantasies in the text are in tension with its queer Eros, which is why the doubles retain their queer character, and cannot be fully assimilated to an apocalyptic narrative, nor to one of guilt. To distinguish between apocalyptic doubles and queer doubles, we should recall Deleuze and Guattari's definition of three kinds of homosexuality in Kafka's lines of flight: firstly, Oedipal homosexuality, then, the 'homosexuality of doubles, of brothers or of bureaucrats' that is linked to schizo-incest, but function as indices only, as do the doubles in the Organizzazione or the twin Kafkas.[57] At the end of the segments of the Deleuzian line of flight, as we saw in our discussion of Ernst Herbeck, lies the figure of the manifestly homosexual artist, who stands at the end of the series and is a figure of escape.[58] When considering the power of sexual desire in a 'line of flight', we should bear in mind Penny's distinction between Benjamin's modernist mourning and Deleuze's schizoid affirmation. As we have seen in Chapter 3, Sebald's work often mourns a lost and utopian queer relationship between German and Jew. In 'All'estero', in keeping with the wondrous tone of the section, the mourning is suspended and a 'schizo-effusion' can take place when the Sebaldian narrator himself is able, briefly, to enter a queer relationship with a Jewish man. This relationship appears linked to Casanova's miraculous transcendence of oppressive operation of the Law, which is in itself a successful line of flight. The narrator tells us that Casanova is imprisoned in the Doge's Palace, ostensibly for treason but, the narrator argues, also to discipline his libidinal drives. In support of his theory, the narrator tells us that in the Doge's Palace, Casanova discovers an archive consisting of the records of the trials of sexual transgressors, paedophile schoolmasters, or seducers of virgins in orphanages. Long's reading of Casanova's imprisonment as Foucauldian is useful here: Casanova's imprisonment exemplifies the disciplinary formation of the subject through the mode of confession.[59] His imprisonment, without trial or legal rights, also recalls the arbitrariness of justice in *Der Proceß*. Casanova's imprisonment demonstrates both the subjection of the sexually unruly subject, and also with its concomitant reduction to bare or creaturely life, 'life that has been delivered over to the space of [...] sovereign jouissance'.[60] Casanova represents a form of non-bourgeois, libidinous sexuality that is associated with resistance to oppressive and arbitrary legal structures.[61] Yet, in contrast to the fate of Roger Casement, this disciplinary subjection does not lead to martyrdom and death. Instead, Casanova successfully achieves a flight from the 'crocodile-like' fortress. The Deleuzian 'line of flight', which in Kafka cannot achieve transcendence of the law, here succeeds, thanks to the miraculous workings of a magical system of numbers devised by Casanova.[62] The wonderful and libidinous exceed the confines imposed by the Law.

Again, this libidinous escape is associated with queer desire. Although Casanova, like Beyle, is heterosexual, the narrator discovers that Casanova's escape happened on 31 October, the date on which the narrator returns to the gay bar on the Riva where he also saw the pursuing doubles of the Organizazzione. Whereas the law of coincidence implicates the biographical Sebald in guilt for Kafka's death, here the law of coincidence propels the narrator along the line of flight. On his return to the bar, the narrator meets a man called Malachio who had studied astrophysics in Cambridge, and who can thus be viewed as a distant cousin of the companionable astrophysicists Gerald Fitzpatrick in *Austerlitz* and his precursor Gerald Ashman. Like them, Malachio possesses the liberating art of mental levitation, as he sees everything 'aus der größten Entfernung, nicht nur die Sterne' [from a great distance, not only the stars] (*SG*, 70; *V*, 61). Malachio takes the narrator on a midnight boat journey out of the Grand Canal into the open water. His boat becomes a queer heterotopia that also, linked as it is by coincidence to Casanova's escape from the dungeon of sexual discipline, is a queer line of escape from the dark visions and paranoia that have been besetting the narrator in Venice. Malachio silences the motor, and the narrator sits beside him in an idyllic moment reminiscent of the desert idyll shared by Cosmo and Adelwarth on the route to Jerusalem.

> Das Boot hob und senkte sich mit den Wellen, und es verging, wie mir schien, eine lange Zeit. Vor uns lag der verglimmende Glanz unserer Welt, an dem wir, wie an einer Himmelsstadt, uns nicht sattschauen können.

> [The boat rose and fell with the waves, and it seemed to me that a long time passed. Before us lay the fading lustre of our world, at which we never tire of looking, as though it were a celestial city.] (*SG*, 70; *V*, 61)

Once more, queer desire achieves the Sebaldian utopia of suspension of time. In keeping with this theme of transcendence, Malachio tells the narrator that he has been considering the theme of resurrection, and wonders about the meaning of the text 'demzufolge unsere Gebeine und Leiber von den Engeln dereinst übertragen werden in das Gesichtsfeld Ezechiels. Antworten habe er keine gefunden, aber es genügten ihm eigentlich auch schon die Fragen' [saying that our bones and flesh would be carried into the domain of the prophet. He had no answers, but believed the questions were quite sufficient for him] (*SG*, 71; *V*, 62). Malachio articulates an immanent state of grace in which the drive for interpretation and meaning is stilled, the condition of the text of 'All'estero' as a whole. He bids the narrator goodbye with the Jewish promise 'Next year in Jerusalem!' (*SG*, 72; *V*, 62). In his barque, the Sebaldian narrator experiences a moment of escape and reconciliation: not only the Jewish messianic dream of reunion in the lost *Heimat* of Jerusalem, but an implicit reconciliation between German narrator and the Jewish boatman. 'Next year in Jerusalem' exists in a messianic future, beyond history, and is less despairing than Gracchus's hopeless voyage between death and life.

The queer encounter with Malachio on All Soul's Eve, while bringing the Sebaldian narrator close to Jewish messianic promise, also acts as the gateway to a Christlike re-enactment of death, purgatory, and resurrection, adding a further theological aspect to the eroto-salvific dimension of 'All'estero'. After Malachio leaves him at his hotel, the narrator lies on his bed for three days, immobilized by his constantly circling thoughts, and lies on his hotel bed 'wie ein Bestatteter oder doch zumindest wie ein Aufgebahrter' [as if I had already been interred or laid out for burial] following an imaginary line of flight over the Venetian lagoon and dreaming of Christian saints (*SG*, 75; *V*, 65). He awakens on the third day, in a curious condition of weightlessness, and restores his animal spirits with bread and red wine (*SG*, 76; *V*, 66). The clear overtones of the Christian resurrection narrative suggest that the queer encounter with Malachio has enabled the narrator to transcend the weight of history that is immobilizing him, and restore himself to mobility, possibly opening up a route of escape. Moreover, Venice itself has held out possibilities to him of redemption during his time in his hotel room. On waking the next day, the narrator is struck by the Venetian absence of the traffic noises, which elsewhere lead him to conclude 'daß aus diesem Getöse jetzt das Leben entsteht, das nach uns kommt und das uns langsam zugrunde richten wird' [that it is out of this din that the life is being born which will come after us and will spell our gradual destruction] (*SG*, 73; *V*, 63). Just as Malachio's boat appears as a queer heterotopia, far removed from the narrator's paranoia, so the Venetian stillness provides a respite from the natural history of destruction that is driven on by the machine age. The stillness enables the narrator to recall the rituals of All Souls and All Saints Days in his childhood village of W., in which the dead were commemorated and bread rolls called 'Seelenwecken' — either 'soul rolls' or 'soul awaken' in English — eaten. Nonetheless, in keeping with the segmented structure of the narrative, the time spent between death and life and subsequent resurrection do not form a completed line of flight. The narrator considers whether to return to the bar on the Riva, but his immobility returns, rendering him incapable of doing so. Likewise, for Cosmo and Adelwarth, the messianic promise of Jerusalem is continually deferred, and with it the promise of queer love — a repeated meeting with Malachio. This complex sequence demonstrates the interplay between mourning messianism and schizo Eros; two kinds of promise for transcendence arise in the sequence, the first a queer one, which carries in it the promise of messianic futurity and a line of escape, and the second a Benjaminian 'weak' messianism, that of attempting to commemorate and redeem the dead, through the rituals of 'Seelenwecken'.[63] A similarly Christian redemptive force of homoerotics appears in Sebald's posthumously published work, 'Die Alpen im Meer', along with a further manifestation of the tormented hunter, like Gracchus.[64] Here, the Sebaldian narrator reads Flaubert's *Legende de Saint-Julien*, fascinated and revolted by the lust for killing that drives the young Prince Julian. Julian attempts to overcome his murderous lusts, but is persecuted both by images of his endless animal victims, and by fantasies of killing ever more. In the end, Julian can only find redemption in the house of a ferryman, on top of whom he must lie, pressing his body into the ferryman's dirty, stinking flesh, in order to make the final crossing between life and death.

> Drüben auf der anderen Seite muß Julian das Lager des Fährmanns teilen, und dann, indem er das von Schrunden und Schwären bedeckte, teils knotig verhärtete, teils schmierige Fleisch umarmt und Brust an Brust und Mund an Mund mit diesem ekelhaftesten aller Menschen die Nacht verbringt, wird er aus seiner Qual erlöst und darf aufsteigen in die blaue Weite des Firmaments.[65]

> [On the opposite bank Julian must share the ferryman's bed, and then, as he embraces the man's fissured and ulcerated flesh, partly hard and gnarled, partly deliquescent, spending the night breast to breast and mouth to mouth with that most repellent of all human beings, he is released from his torment and may rise into the blue expanses of the firmament.] (*CS*, 48; *CSe*, 46)

This motif has a precedent in Goethe's *Wilhelm Meisters Wanderjahre*, albeit here without the abject element of revulsion, where Wilhelm Meister revives a drowned fisher boy by lying on top of him.[66] Hartmut Böhme notes the strong homoerotic undertones to this moment, suggesting that the body of the fisher boy, reanimated, is itself a godly text, suggesting an intimate link between the homosexual moment of contact and the revelation of the Gnostic cipher-language of nature.[67] The Sebaldian narrator, too, undergoes a process of suffering and redemption by reading the text of St Julian's fall and act of contrition:

> Nicht ein einziges Mal während des Lesens hatte ich meinen Blick heben können von der mit jeder Zeile tiefer in das Grauen eindringenden, von Grund auf perversen Erzählung über die Verruchtheit der Menschengewalt. Erst der Gnadenakt der Transfiguration auf der letzten Seite ließ mich wieder aufschauen.

> [Not once as I read could I take my eyes off this utterly perverse tale of the despicable nature of human violence, a story that probes horror further with every line. Only the act of grace when the saint is transfigured on the last page let me look up again.] (*CS*, 48; *CSe*, 46)

In these complex intertextual images, an abject transition through perverse physical contact paradoxically redeems the sinner from his human perversity, and awakens the lost, alienated language of pre-modern nature. The rejection of futurity that Gracchus represents then not only is a refusal of reproduction, but also a possible way backwards from the nightmarish technological future represented by the apocalyptic doppelganger.

The Truth about Dr Kafka

All of these themes — the apocalyptic double, the homosexual artist, the queer moment of reconciliation with a Jewish man, the line of escape from reproductive heterosexuality, dissociation of narrative, and hopes for theological redemption — cross in the enigmatic figure of Kafka. In 'All'estero', the narrator consciously retraces Kafka's travels in August of 1913, driven by homotextual desire for queer contact with the dead writer. In the railway station at Desenzano, he conscientiously follows Kafka's traces right into the twilight zone of the bathroom, notoriously a space where men feel their heterosexuality threatened by the gaze of other men — or cross the boundary of heteronormativity into homosexual encounters. While washing his hands, the narrator tells us, he looks in the mirror

> und fragte mich, ob Dr. Kafka, der, von Verona herüberkommend, gleichfalls an diesem Bahnhof ausgestiegen sein mußte, nicht auch in diesem Spiegelglas sein Gesicht betrachtet hatte. Es wäre eigentlich kein Wunder gewesen.[68]

> [and wondered whether Dr K., travelling from Verona, had also been at this station and found himself contemplating his face in this mirror. It would not have been surprising.] (*SG*, 99; *V*, 86)

In the queer heterotopia of the railway toilet, through the ritual of repetition, the narrator attempts to move backwards in time through the mirror, indeed possibly to go through the mirror into the reversed world of homosexuality. The sight of graffiti by the mirror reinforces his conviction that Kafka's reflection must once have looked out of the same mirror: '*Il cacciatore*, stand da in einer ungelenken Schrift' [*Il cacciatore*, it read, in awkwardly formed letters] (*SG*, 99; *V*, 87). The narrator here inscribes himself not only into Kafka's biography, but also into his literary work, by adding the words *nella selva nera* to the inscription, turning the fragmentary scrawl into a deliberate reference to Gracchus, the hunter from the Black Forest. Returning to the case of Schreber, if Schreber is afraid that he is turning into a feminized Jew, thereby suffering an attack on his Aryan masculinity, this paranoid phantasy is one that the Sebaldian narrator here comes close to welcoming.[69]

Sebald's paranoid and queer reinscription of himself into Kafka's biography is also to be found in his critical work. The essay 'Via Schweiz ins Bordell: Zu den Reisetagebüchern Kafkas' [To the Brothel by Way of Switzerland: On Kafka's Travel Diaries] can be read as a continuation of Sebald's attempt to follow the Kafkan line of flight.[70] Here, Sebald writes that Kafka's diaries of his trip from Prague via Switzerland to Paris seem to him to be about himself, not just because Max is mentioned so frequently. As a child, Sebald writes here, he travelled the very same journey through Switzerland as Kafka did before the Second World War, and, Sebald claims, his reactions to the ultra-modern, clean-scrubbed Switzerland match Kafka's own. Max and Franz, Sebald says, in the only time he refers to Dr K by his first name in 'Via Schweiz ins Bordell', almost seem like a pair invented by Franz himself. Sebald's attachment to the pair suggests that Max and Franz have an imaginary relationship in another sense, too: earlier in their journey, they had been exclaiming about their joy over discovering that their bedrooms were linked via a double door, one side of which can be opened from each room — an arrangement, Max remarks, that is suitable for a married pair.[71] In Paris, Sebald reports, Max and Franz seek to escape their depressed mood in a 'rationally ordered' brothel, where the proceedings are so mechanized that one is out on the street again before one knows it, and where, Kafka writes, it is difficult to get a close look at the girls. If Sebald inserts himself into Kafka's diary narrative via the coincidence of repetition of his chosen name, Max, he also inserts himself into the homoerotic negotiations of Max and Franz. These mediate their desire for each other through the joint visit to the heterosexual brothel that leaves so few traces on their memory. Rational modernity has dissolved the immediate sensuality of traditional brothels, but has also cut loose the bonds of traditional family, allowing the two bachelors to travel as a half-separated, half-connected pair that mirrors, if it does not match, a married couple. Further, not only can the brothel be viewed as a heterotopia, but Deleuze and Guattari also place the whore along the line of escape, in a series with sisters and maids. If in Kafka's work sisters help the familial machine take flight, whores are 'at the intersection of all the machines — familial, conjugal, bureaucratic — that they are all the more able to make take flight'.[72] With whores, they argue, 'one penetrates deeper along a line of escape' from Oedipal structures.[73] Sebald links the queer sexuality of Max and Franz to the events of *Schwindel. Gefühle.*, by mentioning that they were in 'Mailand, wo ich vor fünfzehn Jahren einige seltsame Abenteuer erlebte' [Milan, where I had some strange adventures fifteen years ago] (*CS*, 181; *CSe*, 142). The essay also connects Max and Franz's journey to Sebald's own childhood travels from ruinous post-war Germany into a 'ganz andere[s], quasi utopische[s] Land' [entirely foreign, quasi-utopian country], another line of escape from Oedipal domination into a world of wonder (*CS*, 181; *CSe*, 142). Once more, the queer journey provides a line of escape from the catastrophes of German history. In this brief essay, Sebald styles Kafka as a bachelor who performs perfunctory heterosexual rituals, but whose more significant relationships are with other bachelors, among them, like a ghost, the unborn Max Sebald. Max and Franz go to the brothel, Sebald states, in a search for happiness in love (*CS*, 182; *CSe*, 144). This queer and lovelorn portrayal of Kafka becomes more evident in Sebald's fictional reworking of Kafka's autobiographical material in 'Dr. K.s Badereise nach Riva'.

Dr K.'s journey to take the waters at Riva — which is officially no such 'Badereise', but a business trip, as Sebald tells us in the first paragraph of the narrative — is the third journey in *Schwindel. Gefühle.* over the border from the German-speaking lands to Italy, a journey over the bounds of bourgeois identity and away from the trap of heterosexual marriage. Like 'All'estero', and unlike conventionally melancholic readings of *Schwindel. Gefühle.*, 'Dr. K.s Badereise' is a highly playful text, where a schizo, queer Kafka enables both the suspension of time and a Sebaldian notion of messianism. Dr K.'s travels are, the narrator tells us, overshadowed by his inability to marry (on the doubly ill-fated date of 13 August 1913, Kafka had broken off his engagement to Felice Bauer, only to resume it days later).[74] They are also haunted by his desire to cross the border to homosexuality, a border that is policed by the violent threat of the Law.

> Es sei unmöglich, notiert er tags darauf, das einzig mögliche Leben zu führen [...] den einzig möglichen Schritt über die Männerfreundschaft hinaus zu tun, denn dort, unmittelbar jenseits der gesetzten Grenze, richte sich schon der Fuß auf, der ihn zertreten werde.

> [It is impossible, he notes the following day, to lead the only possible life [...] to take the only possible step beyond a friendship with men — for there, on the other side of the prescribed boundary, the boot is already upraised that will crush you under its heel.] (SG, 158; V, 143)

For Sebald's Dr K., the voyage to Italy becomes a wandering along this forbidden queer border. Although Dr K. is putatively attending the spa to banish the spectre of his broken engagement with Felice, Sebald illustrates the hygienic ritual prescribed at the Riva baths by images impishly chosen, it seems, to demonstrate the highest degree of homoeroticism possible. In a series of three pictures on page 170 [155], a stern bearded doctor wields a water hose so close to a half-naked male patient's groin that the picture resembles a masturbation scenario as much as it does hydrotherapeutic treatment. The heterosexual bourgeois culture in which Kafka lived and wrote carries within it its own uncanny repressed sexual other. If Sebald makes this point in a critical spirit over and over again in the essays in *Unheimliche Heimat*, here, in keeping with the spirit of wonder informing *Schwindel. Gefühle.*, the point is more playful, and we are reminded by Deleuze and Guattari that the seeming depression of a melancholy text (Dr K. lying paralysed in the grass) and its protestations of guilt may be the cover-up for a joke.[75] The homoerotic images also suggest that the spa cure is highly unlikely to reinforce Dr K.'s heterosexuality or to return him to an Oedipal order. Indeed, it may instead lead to the production of a schizo 'body without organs', which is 'unproductive, sterile, unengendered, unconsumable', for Deleuze and Guattari tell us that 'the catatonic body is produced in the water of the hydrotherapy tub'.[76] Far from recuperating physical and subjective integrity, Dr K.'s spa travels take place in a theatrical space of literary intertextuality. These plunge him into a *mise-en-abyme* that renders 'Dr. K.s Badereise' far from 'a portrait of a split personality potentially amenable to the spa cure'.[77] Klebes argues that the theatricality of *Schwindel. Gefühle.* moves the figure of Dr K. away from any form of psychic coherence to an entirely textual construct, enabling an associative order. Hence, 'Dr. K.s Badereise' is an associative textual game that, like 'All'estero', plays with the idea of a legible set of psychical symptoms, but refuses interpretation. It is here useful to add Prager's argument that although the spa will not cure Dr K., the two poles of Eros and Thanatos form a key tension in the narrative nonetheless.[78] This is, more precisely, a distinction between Oedipal Thanatos and schizo Eros. Like Dr K., Kafka's creation Gracchus the huntsman is cursed to wander between heaven and hell in order to expiate a nameless guilt. The narrator of *Schwindel. Gefühle.* tells us that it seems to him 'als bestünde der Sinn der unablässigen Fahrten des Jägers Gracchus in der Abbuße einer Sehnsucht nach Liebe' [that the meaning of Gracchus the huntsman's ceaseless journey lies in a penitence for a longing for love] (SG, 180; V, 165). Once more, as in 'Kafka im Kino', love is at once a sinful temptation and a means of evading death and the relentless progress of time.[79] Gracchus thus functions as a way to negotiate the Thanatic drive that Sebald otherwise detects all through Kafka's work. In Deleuze and Guattari's terms, Thanatos is linked to Oedipus, and the imperative to reproduce and continue bourgeois family life, as personified by Felice. The 'schizo Eros' that promises a line of escape from this subjection is traced in Dr K.'s moments of queer desire.

In *Schwindel. Gefühle.*, like Balduin's doppelganger, Gracchus represents Dr K.'s guilt and illegitimate desire. Dr K.'s sin is to be caught between the desire to love queerly, and the desire to enter the bourgeois order of heterosexual love and marriage at all. Hence, Sebald claims that Balduin's struggle with his doppelganger is analogous to Kafka's short story, 'Beschreibung eines Kampfes' [Description of a Struggle]. The male narrator has a series of hallucinogenic, homoerotic encounters with a nameless stranger who at once attracts and repels him.[80] The narrator is finally forced into a corner by his companion and must confess that he is engaged.[81] In an echo of Sedgwick's homosocial love triangles, two men's desire for each other alternates with an ostensible attraction to the phantasmagorical figure of a girl in a white dress, whom they both profess to desire.[82] These same elements of homosexual longing, mediated via a virginal young woman, whose chastity conveniently places any corporeal sexual intercourse out of the question, are echoed in 'Dr. K.s Badereise'. Dr K. meets a young woman at dinner who has a masculine voice is, like Dr K. himself, in frail health, and who, they later learn from a fortune teller, will never marry. Dr K. takes the uncanny mermaid, as he dubs her, out one night on a boat, and, in this heterotopia, he spins her a fantasy of incorporeal love, where the bourgeois division between subject and nature is overcome by the dissolution of the body back into nature. Indeed, Dr K.'s presence in the novel is ghostly throughout, and Sebald mentions him on his deathbed, weighing only forty-five kilogrammes, suspended between life and death. This body recalls the schizo 'body without organs' rather than a body that achieves genital fulfilment. Thus, queer desire is encoded in the text of *Schwindel. Gefühle.*, not a desire that is to be corporeally realized.

The messianic aura that surrounds the figure of Dr K. suggests that the sin of love may represent a betrayal of a divine mission. In 'Das Gesetz der Schande — Macht, Messianismus und Exil in Kafkas *Schloß*' [The Law of Shame — Power, Messianism and Exile in Kafka's *Castle*] Sebald explores the idea that K. in *Das Schloß* — to some extent another double of Kafka's — represents a messiah in the Jewish tradition of messianism, whose mission is, according to Sebald, redemption from the exile of history.[83] Kafka's messianism is, for Sebald, the point where dialectics break down, where power and powerlessness have become almost mythical categories that make revolution impossible, and hope mandatory. Sebald focuses on the messianic elements of *Das Schloß*, in particular, in this essay, but the Gracchus thematic complex in *Schwindel. Gefühle.* also contains messianic threads that suggest redemption from the tragic progress of history. Thus, a Benjaminian theology of messianism informs Sebald's discussion of Dr K, a messianism that, according to Gershom Scholem, is in itself a catastrophic theory, one which breaks the logic of history but which is also dependent upon it to unleash the disaster that will bring forth the messiah.[84] This extreme catastrophism, Sebald writes, is intrinsically inimical to the bourgeois spirit, which is committed to progress and the extension of order (*Döblin*, 61). Sebald's version of messianism, then, provides a political or theological form of resistance to the oppressive logic of bourgeois society. Like a nascent messiah, Dr K. almost experiences an annunciation in Trieste himself, without the need for a mediating virgin mother:

> Also wahrhaftig ein Engel, dachte Dr. K., als er wieder Atem schöpfen konnte, den ganzen Tag fliegt er auf mich zu, und ich in meinem Unglauben weiß es nicht. Jetzt wird er gleich zu mir sprechen, dachte er und senkte den Blick.
>
> [A veritable angel, thought Dr K. when he could breathe again, all day long it has flown towards me and I of little faith knew nothing of it. Now he will speak to me, he thought, and lowered his gaze.] (*SG*, 161; *V*, 146)

When Dr K. looks again, this angel, which the Sebaldian narrator has also been seeking out on his journey, turns out not to be the avenging clay angel who murders visitors from the North that he knows stalks Trieste, but only a wooden figurehead, part of the hotel furnishings. In Sebald's essay on *Das Schloß*, he writes that mutability is inherent to the figure of the Jewish messiah, as it is to that of the doppelganger. He refers to the messiah as a tradition in continual metamorphosis (*UH*, 91), whose only stable feature is an ahistorical, timeless hope for redemption. The Kafkan messianic angel, he writes, has nothing to do with metaphysics, but is rather an ontological apparition (*UH*, 103). Ten years after he wrote the original English version of this essay, this wavering, spectral figure of the messiah in Kafka's work — 'Irisierend schwankt es zwischen dem des Königs und dem des Bettlers' (*UH*, 91) has retreated yet further from the physical world, indeed has all but evaporated, in the essay that Sebald wrote on 'Tiere, Menschen, Maschinen: Zu Kafkas Evolutionsgeschichten' [Animals, Humans, Machines: On Kafka's Evolutionary Stories]. Here, he writes, 'dort, wo in Kafkas Texten ihrer inneren Logik nach der Messias erscheinen müßte, finden sich nur Leerstellen oder Vexierbilder' [there, where according to the inner logic of Kafka's texts the messiah should appear, there are only empty spaces or puzzling images].[85] In *Schwindel. Gefühle.*, Gracchus is a failed messiah because of his sin of bourgeois love. He arrives in Riva expecting a festive reception, but is not expected by the townspeople or by its sceptical mayor. Dr K., by contrast, is awaited in Trieste as a messianic figure: 'Die Leute, kommt ihm vor, bleiben auf der Straße stehen und blicken ihm nach, als wollten sie sagen, da ist er ja endlich' [It seems to him that people are stopping in the street, following him with their eyes, as if to say: there he is at last] (*SG*, 160; *V*, 145).

Nonetheless, Dr K. ignores the festive reception organized for him by the townspeople of Desenzano, and they wait for him in vain. Gracchus and Dr K. are doubled aspects of the Sebaldian messiah, who suffers from 'seiner Inkongruenz mit sich selbst' [his incongruity with himself] (*UH*, 99). Taken in the context of Sebald's reading of Jewish messianism, Dr K.'s sin, in being betrothed, would be to bind himself into the historical structures of German bourgeois society, rather than to the traditional Jewish principle and metaphysical homeland of hope.[86] As we saw in Chapter 1, this anti-historical version of messianism emerged with the second generation of Jewish immigrants from the ghetto into the Western metropolis, that of Kafka. These Jews ceased optimistically to believe in the power of the light of bourgeois reason to drive out the shadows of ghetto superstition from the Jewish soul, and ceased to believe that such a metamorphosis would be a transformation for the better. It is this very particular tension between repressed Jewish tradition and assimilation within the German tradition of bourgeois letters, explored in 'Westwärts — Ostwärts. Aporien deutscher Ghettogeschichten' and discussed in Chapter 1, that arises in the opposing pair of Dr K. and Gracchus. At the end of his trip to take the waters at Riga Dr K. writes a letter to Felice, describing how he followed the son of a Jewish bookseller around Prague, an

> armseliger Mensch, der sich, wie Dr. K. weiß, als Deutscher fühlt und darum jeden Abend, nachdem er genachtmahlt hat, ins Deutsche Haus, um dort als Mitglied des Clubs Deutsches Casino die letzten Stunden des Tages seiner Illusion zu frönen

> [wretched creature, who feels himself (as Dr K. knows) to be German and for that reason goes to the Deutsches Haus every evening after supper to nurture his delusion of grandeur as a member of the German Casino Club] (SG, 181; V, 166)

Dr K. writes that he follows this man, veritably lusting after him, and that he watched him enter into the gates of the Deutsches Haus with a feeling of utter pleasure. At this point, the narrator comments, 'es hätte wohl nicht viel gefehlt, und Dr K. hätte an dieser Stelle ein Bekenntnis einer, wie angenommen werden muß, unerfüllt gebliebenen Sehnsucht abgelegt' [at this point Dr K. surely came within an inch of admitting to a desire which we must assume remained unstilled] (SG, 182; V, 167). Dr K.'s queer desire for the son of the bookseller in this anecdote is self-evident, as is its connection to anti-bourgeois and schizo tropes of hazard and illusion. After comparing this passage to Kafka's original text, Medin deems this passage a 'blatant misreading' of Kafka's diary; we might call it rather a deliberately queer reading.[87] For Medin, whose argument is informed by Harold Bloom's *The Anxiety of Influence*, such procedures bear a resemblance to Oedipal struggles, in which Sebald seeks to overcome his predecessor; but the Oedipal struggle in this passage is located in a different place.[88] If we recall the suggestions that Dr K. is a bearer of the Jewish messianic tradition, and is in Italy on a messianic mission, Dr K's illegitimate, unstilled desire also refers to his father's desire to abandon that tradition and assimilate into German culture, as represented by the 'Deutsches Haus'. In a further dialectical twist, this institution represents the tradition of *Bildung* and bourgeois individualism that is already crumbling under the pressures of modernity. The figure of the queer Kafka in *Schwindel. Gefühle.* thus appears as another doubly determined *Zwitterwesen*, one who wanders along the bounds of homosexuality, and also attempts to transgress the racial and social distinctions enforced by the mechanisms of power. Indeed, rather than seeking to overcome or incorporate Kafka, in 'Kafka im Kino', Sebald positions himself as, in some ways, a redeemer of Kafka, for he suggests that Kafka's work has fallen prey to literary theoreticians who are testing their supposedly higher intelligence on Kafka's difficulty, who are happy to erase Kafka's Jewish identity in the interests of bolstering their own intellectual identities (CS, 195; CSe, 158). Earlier, in 'Tiere, Menschen, Maschinen:

Zu Kafkas Evolutionsgeschichten', he had formulated these attacks on the German Kafka industry in the terms of a dialectic of *Bildung*, castigating his colleagues for having erected a 'panoptical tower' on the 'aus eigenen Ausgezehrtheit schon leidende Werk' [work which is already suffering from its own emaciation] of Kafka.[89] Kafka scholarship, here, becomes just one more example of the punitive *Bildungsideal* enforced upon the unhappy migrants from the Jewish ghetto into enlightened German bourgeois society, a panopticon trained on the suffering body of Kafka's prose. The figure of Dr K. does not resolve these conflicting discourses, but remains a painful space where they all cross, conflict, and disturb each other.

Thus, while the Malachio encounter carries within it a certain German yearning for German–Jewish symbiosis, at the same time Kafka functions as the suffering symbol of the negative aspects of that historical symbiosis for Judaism. Kafka, Sebald reminds us, despite his mistrust of utopias, became a supporter of the nascent Zionist movement, which promised a redemptive utopia for militant Judaism on earth through physical training:

> nicht anders als in der seit dem Beginn des 19. Jahrhunderts sich formierenden deutschnationalen Ideologie, an der der Zionismus von Anfang an sich ausrichtete. In dem Selbstbild, das sie von sich projizieren, gleichen die beiden aus langer Unterdrückung beziehungsweise aus vermeintlicher Hintansetzung erwachenden Völker einander beinahe zum Verwechseln.
>
> [as indeed they had been since the early nineteenth century in the emergent nationalist German ideology from which Zionism always took its cue. In the image of themselves that they projected, the two peoples, awakening from long oppression or rousing themselves from alleged neglect, were almost exactly the same.] (*CS*, 205; *CSe*, 169)

This is the German–Jewish symbiosis in dystopian form, where Zionism preaches a quasi-Nazi ideal of physiological regeneration, a superhuman physical ideal which Sebald juxtaposes, without needing to make the contrast explicit, to his own ghostly physical idea of Kafka, weightless, boneless, bodiless — the body without organs. Kafka remains exiled from both peoples, Sebald emphasizes, but these passages make it clear that the negative side of the German–Jewish symbiosis is at all times present to Sebald. If Kafka had to suffer the coexistence of two salvatory fantasies in his own body, so Sebald's narrators suffer a mirrored doubling of their vision, and Kafka suffers inexplicable headaches. Sebald and Kafka discover in their own flesh the wound where the Jewish half of the symbiosis once dwelled. The kind of reconciliation that Sebald's narrators tend towards is defined against these vast dystopian or racist ideals, as a far more queer, erotic one, which nonetheless carries within it the echo of the politics of post-war Germany. What Sebald says of Kafka in this essay reflects his own poetics in *Schwindel. Gefühle.*, that the fantastic elements in Kafka's work obscure the fact that his work mirrors the political concerns of his time.

In Sebald's work, too, sexualized fantasies of queer desire are a political strategy, overt, occluded, or forbidden, to combat the Oedipal imperative of bourgeois society to assimilate by entering the Deutsches Haus. It attempts to resist the pressures of the bourgeois age and to suspend the individual from the progress of history, rather than to bring history to an apocalyptic end. We have seen how 'Das merckwürdige Faktum der Liebe' demolished narratives of heterosexual manhood as the agent of European history, and 'All'estero' substitutes queer fantasies of paranoia, penetration, and messianic redemption for the linear narrative of the *Bildungsreise*; it twice starts, even if it does not finish, a Deleuzoguattarian line of escape. 'Dr. K.s Badereise' contains similar elements of queer desire, queer flight, and messianism. However, the potential for resistance of the Kafka figure is, in Sebald's critical essays, also combined with apocalyptic visions and personal guilt. *Schwindel. Gefühle.* is thus very much an associative Deleuzoguattarian burrow, exceeding its own narrative bounds to combine with Sebald's essays in one textual machine. This associative and miraculous structure baffles any clearly legible interpretation, even a directly queer or liberating one. The text of 'Dr. K.s Badereise nach Riva' ends with Dr K. abandoning the fantasy of the bookseller's son for a fantasy of a queer touch. The narrator asks how one can escape a similar fate:

> daß man nicht zuletzt, unfähig, aus dem Leben zu gehen, vor dem Podestà liegt mit einer Krankheit, die nur im Bett geheilt werden kann, und daß man nicht auch noch diesem, der einen schließlich doch erlösen soll, in einem Augenblick der Selbstvergessenheit lächelnd die Hand aufs Knie legt, so wie der Jäger Gracchus es tut.

> [of being unable to depart this life, lying before the *podestà*, confined to a bed in our sickness, and, as Gracchus the huntsman does, touching, in a moment of distraction, the knee of the man who was to have been our salvation] (SG, 183; *V*, 167)

Dr K.'s journey to Riva ends where it began, suspended between Thanatos — the desire to die — and fantasies of queer desire that baffle the death drive. The German version of the text is more explicitly erotic, as here the sickness mentioned in the passage above 'can only be cured in bed' — whether this is the bed rest suggested by the English translation, or sexual contact, is here deliberately ambivalent. Does queer desire here baffle salvation, or is it a hope for a cure for the unnamed sickness? The text does not answer this riddle.

Notes to Chapter 4

1. Deleuze and Guattari, *Anti-Oedipus*, pp. 34, 52.
2. Prager, 'Sebald's Kafka', p. 119.
3. Deleuze and Guattari, *Kafka*, p. 36.
4. Penny, 'Parables and Politics'.
5. Öhlschläger, *Beschädigtes Leben*, pp. 68–69.
6. David Kaufmann, 'Angels Visit the Scene of Disgrace: Melancholy and Trauma from Sebald to Benjamin and Back', *Cultural Critique*, 70 (2008), 94–119 (p. 99).
7. *Die Beschreibung des Unglücks*, pp. 61–77.
8. 'Ich fürchte das Melodramatische', Sebald in interview with Martin Doerry and Volker Hage, *Der Spiegel* (Hamburg), 11, 12 March 2001, pp. 228, 230, and 232–34.
9. W. G. Sebald, 'Es steht ein Komet am Himmel', in *Logis in einem Landhaus*, pp. 5–42 (p. 34).
10. Öhlschläger, *Beschädigtes Leben*, p. 62.
11. Gabriella Rovagnati, 'Das unrettbare Venedig des W. G. Sebald', in *Sebald: Lektüren*, ed. by Marcel Atze and Franz Loquai (Eggingen: Edition Isele, 2005), pp. 143–56 (p. 148).
12. Sigmund Freud, *The Schreber Case*, trans. by Andrew Webber (London: Penguin, 2002), p. 36.

13. Zilcosky, 'Sebald's Uncanny Travels', p. 108.

14. Long, *Image, Archive, Modernity*, p. 99.

15. Deleuze and Guattari, *Anti-Oedipus*, p. 2.

16. Freud, *Schreber*, p. 39.

17. Long, *Image, Archive, Modernity*, p. 100.

18. Edelman, *No Future*, p. 24.

19. The *Odyssey* provides the title for the last section, drawing on Monteverdi's opera *Il ritorno d'Ulisse in patria*. The opera was first performed in Venice at the carnival season of 1639, thus providing a further connection to the Venetian themes of sexual performativity, paranoia, and hazard that inform the first three narratives of *Schwindel. Gefühle*.

20. Fuchs, *Die Schmerzensspuren der Geschichte*, p. 171.

21. Deleuze and Guattari, *Anti-Oedipus*, p. 8.

22. Deleuze and Guattari, *Kafka*, p. 28.

23. Patricia Merivale and Susan Elizabeth Sweeney, 'The Game's Afoot: On the Trail of the Metaphysical Detective Story', in *Detecting Texts: The Metaphysical Detective Story from Poe to Postmodernism*, ed. by Patricia Merivale (Philadelphia: University of Pennsylvania Press, 1999), pp. 1–26 (p. 9).

24. Santner, *On Creaturely Life*, p. 169.

25. Thomas Mann, *Death in Venice*, trans. by Michael Henry Heim (New York: HarperCollins, 2004), p. 17.

26. Freud, *Schreber*, p. 37.

27. Deleuze and Guattari, *Anti-Oedipus*, p. 28.

28. Deleuze and Guattari, *Kafka*, p. 34.

29. Franz Kafka, *Briefe an Felice und andere Korrespondenz aus der Verlobungszeit*, ed. by Erich Heller and Jürgen Born (Frankfurt a. M.: Fischer, 1976), pp. 456ff.

30. McCrea, *Company of Strangers*, p. 8.

31. Öhlschläger, *Beschädigtes Leben*, pp. 149–50. Öhlschläger also notes that confusion about the object of the gaze of St George is compounded by the different editions of *Schwindel. Gefühle*. and *Vertigo*, which variously place the images of the eyes of St George and the princess above each other and on following pages. Compare, for example, *Schwindel. Gefühle*. (Frankfurt: Fischer Taschenbuchverlag, 2002), p. 87, where both pairs of eyes appear on the same page, with *Vertigo* (London: Harvill, 1999), pp. 75–76, where St George's feminized eyes first appear alone. This renders initial gendering of the eyes problematic, as the princess's eyes are only reproduced over the next page.

32. Ahmed, *Queer Phenomenology*, p. 66.

33. Jacques Derrida, *Specters of Marx: The State of the Debt, the Work of Mourning and the New International*, trans. by Peggy Kamuf (New York and London: Routledge, 2006), p. 22.

34. Webber, *The Doppelgänger*, p. 10.

35. Freud, *Schreber*, p. 39.

36. Webber, *The Doppelgänger*, p. 49.

37. Ibid., p. 46.

38. Ibid., p. 44.

39. Ibid.

40. Webber argues that, if the doppelganger is a figure of displacement, appearing out of place in order to displace its host, Italy is recurrently the site of displacement for the German doppelganger. The doppelganger's function of displacement extends to the sexual agency of the self: 'it recurrently introduces voyeurism and innuendo into the subject's pursuit of a visual and discursive sense of self' (Webber, *The Doppelgänger*, pp. 3–4).

41. Martin Klebes, 'Infinite Journey: From Kafka to Sebald', in *W. G. Sebald: A Critical Companion*, ed. by J. Long and Anne Whitehead (Edinburgh: Edinburgh University Press, 2004), pp. 123–39 (p. 131).

42. E. T. A. Hoffmann, *Der Sandmann* (Stuttgart: Reclam, 1996), p. 39.

43. Prager, 'Sebald's Kafka', p. 119.

44. Webber, *The Doppelgänger*, p. 49.

45. Deleuze and Guattari, *Anti-Oedipus*, p. 15.

46. Deleuze and Guattari, *Kafka*, p. 69.
47. Ibid., p. 68.
48. 'Kafka im Kino', in *Campo Santo*, pp. 193–209.
49. Sebald, 'Tiere, Menschen, Maschinen: Zu Kafkas Evolutionsgeschichten', *Literatur und Kritik*, 21 (1986), 194–201 (p. 201).
50. See Donna Haraway, *Simians, Cyborgs and Women: The Reinvention of Nature* (New York; Routledge, 1991), pp. 149–81.
51. Deleuze and Guattari, *Kafka*, p. 69.
52. Ibid., p. 57.
53. See here, for example, Gabriella Rovagnati's 'Canetti, Sebald und die Quellen des Feuers: Zum apokalyptischen Schluß von W. G. Sebalds Erzählung "Il ritorno in patria"', in *Sebald: Lektüren*, pp. 116–21.
54. See Susanne Schedel, *'Wer weiß, wie es vor Zeiten gewesen ist?' Textbeziehungen als Mittel der Geschichtsdarstellung bei W. G. Sebald* (Würzburg: Königshausen and Neumann, 2004), pp. 155–57, for a list of allusions to the year 1913 and number 13 in the text, including references to the intertext of Leonardo Sciascia, *1912 + 1*, trans. by Sacha Rabinovitch (Manchester: Carcanet, 1989).
55. Jaggi, 'Recovered Memories'.
56. Freud, *Schreber*, p. 59.
57. Deleuze and Guattari, *Kafka*, p. 68.
58. Ibid., p. 69.
59. Long, *Image, Archive, Modernity*, p. 73.
60. Santner, *On Creaturely Life*, p. 15.
61. Rovagnati, 'Das unrettbare Venedig des W. G. Sebald', p. 152.
62. Deleuze and Guattari, *Kafka*, p. 51.
63. Walter Benjamin, *Sprache und Geschichte* (Stuttgart: Reclam, 2003), p. 142.
64. *Campo Santo*, pp. 39–51 (p. 46).
65. See Gustave Flaubert, 'The Legend of Saint Julian the Hospitaler', trans. by Michel Grimaud, in *Saint/Oedipus: Psychocritical Approaches to Flaubert's Art*, ed. by William J. Berg, Michel Grimaud, and George Moskos (Ithaca: Cornell University Press, 1982), pp. 231–55 (p. 255): 'Julian took off his clothes; then, naked as on the day he was born, again took his place in the bed; and he could feel against his thigh the Leper's skin, colder than a snake and rough as a file'.
66. Johann Wolfgang von Goethe, *Sämtliche Werke nach Epochen seines Schaffens* (Münchner Ausgabe), ed. by Karl Richter with the co-operation of Herbert G. Göpfert and others, 33 vols (Munich: Hanser, 1991), XVII: *Wilhelm Meisters Wanderjahre: Maximen und Reflexionen*, ed. by Gonthier-Louis Fink and others, p. 687.
67. Hartmut Böhme, *Natur und Subjekt* (Frankfurt a. M.: Suhrkamp, 1988), p. 158.
68. The importance of the gaze, and its relation to the uncanny, in Sebald has been extensively discussed: see particularly Jan Ceuppens, 'Seeing Things: Spectres and Angels in W. G. Sebald's Prose Fiction', in *W. G. Sebald: A Critical Companion*, ed. by J. J. Long and Anne Whitehead (Edinburgh: Edinburgh University Press, 2004), pp. 190–202, as well as the extensive list of publications that deal with the gaze of the camera in Sebald's work.
69. Eric Santner, 'My Own Private Germany: Daniel Paul Schreber's Secret History of Modernity', in *Modernity, Culture and 'the Jew'*, ed. by B. Cheyette, L. Marcus, H. Bhabha, and P. Gilroy (Stanford: Stanford University Press, 1998), pp. 40–62 (p. 43).
70. *Campo Santo*, pp. 179–83; *Campo Santo*, trans. by Hulse, pp. 140–45.
71. Franz Kafka, *Tagebücher 1910–1923*, ed. by Max Brod (Frankfurt a. M.: Fischer, 1973), p. 384.
72. Deleuze and Guattari, *Kafka*, p. 65.
73. Ibid., p. 65.
74. Kafka, *Briefe an Felice*, pp. 456ff.
75. Deleuze and Guattari, *Anti-Oedipus*, p. 46.
76. Ibid., p. 9.
77. Martin Klebes, 'If You Come to a Spa', p. 133.
78. Prager, 'Sebald's Kafka', p. 119.
79. Duttlinger '"A Wrong Turn of the Wheel": Sebald's Journeys of (In)Attention', p. 99.

80. Franz Kafka, 'Beschreibung eines Kampfes' (Fassung A), in Franz Kafka, *Beschreibung eines Kampfes und andere Schriften aus dem Nachlaß* (Frankfurt a. M.: Fischer, 1994), pp. 47–98 (p. 60); Franz Kafka, 'Description of a Struggle', trans. by Tania Stern and James Stern, in Franz Kafka, *The Complete Short Stories*, ed. by Nahum L. Glatzer (London: Minerva, 1992), pp. 9–51 (p. 15).

81. Long, in his discussion of Sebald's relation to Foucault, discusses the function of the confessional in Sebald's work. For him, sexuality is peripheral to Sebald's work, whereas confessional is central to his motivation to write. Jonathan J. Long, 'Disziplin und Geständnis', in *W. G. Sebald: Politische Archäologie und melancholische Bastelei*, ed. by Michael Niehaus and Claudia Öhlschläger (Berlin: Schmidt, 2006), pp. 219–40 (p. 233).

82. Kafka, 'Beschreibung eines Kampfes', p. 60; 'Description of a Struggle', p. 50.

83. *Unheimliche Heimat*, pp. 87–103 (p. 91).

84. Sebald sets out his understanding of messianism in *Döblin*. See particularly pages 59–61, where he describes the influence of Scholem's thinking on Döblin and the Expressionist movement in general after the First World War.

85. Sebald, 'Tiere, Menschen, Maschinen', p. 200.

86. 'As Möbus and others have noted, however, Kafka ultimately saw the voyage as an opportunity to separate himself physically and psychologically from Felice, whom he did not wish to marry' (Prager, 'Sebald's Kafka', p. 117).

87. Medin, *Three Sons*, p. 145.

88. Ibid., p. 13.

89. Sebald, 'Tiere, Menschen, Maschinen', p. 194.

CONCLUSION

Return to Oedipus?

Has Sebald's queer Eros, then, triumphed over Oedipal Thanatos? As we see in Dr
Selwyn's suicide, homosexual love and queer desire are subject to the same negative
forces of destruction that sweep through all of Sebald's work. Even though 'All'estero'
is structured as a Deleuzian 'series', and resists narrative coherence, the entire text
of *Schwindel. Gefühle.* is not a fully realized revolutionary literary machine in the
sense that it could become 'the relay for a revolutionary machine to come', nor does
it complete the project of collective, minor enunciation that Deleuze and Guattari
claim for Kafka.[1] Instead, the queer lines of flight here become baffled, both by
Oedipal structures — the narrator ends up, in 'Il ritorno in patria', returning to his
fatherland of W. — and by the Thanatic logic of history. 'Il ritorno in patria' serves
as a model for the dismal returns to repetitive history, and to German history in
particular, throughout Sebald's texts. Twice, the narrator of *Schwindel. Gefühle.* is
driven back across the Alps into the land of his fathers, his *patria* of W. This is a
most uncanny homeland, governed by the twin laws of patriarchy and history. The
return to W. is loaded with ominous signs that the line of escape is being closed off:
the narrator is repulsed by the Tyrolean newspaper he reads on the way, he visits the
Krummenbach chapel where he is terrified both by pictures depicting the cruelty of
the Stations of the Cross and by his memories of the terror as a child, and, crucially,
the last stretch of the journey takes the narrator past a memorial commemorating
a 'last skirmish' of the war in April 1945. The return to the homeland is a return
to the German language, more specifically, to the narrator's hated home dialect,
to the Christian *via dolorosa* and to the historical legacy of Nazi perpetration. The
unfriendliness of W. and its coldness to outsiders is confirmed, in some accounts,
by Sebald's own experience of Wertach im Allgäu.[2] The Sebaldian narrator's ill-
omened journey passes through a bleak rain-swept landscape, whose miserable spell
is finally broken when the sun comes out and shows him the valley like a revelation
(SG, 192; *V*, 175).

The narrative of 'Il ritorno in patria' is henceforth constructed by this dialectical
movement between idyll and hellhole, between the Odyssean return to Ithaca and
a nightmarish katabasis, suggesting both a yearning for the traditions of *Heimat*
and a revulsion from its patriarchal order. Continuing home, the narrator finds
the lodgings where he spent his earliest childhood, but they are changed beyond
recognition, altered by the prosperity of the post-war years. Here, the levelling of
post-war consumer society has erased, simultaneously, the traces of his childhood
and of Germany's history prior to 1945. The narrator's home becomes transformed
by his parents' move upwards into the officially classless post-war German society
that supposedly followed on the bourgeois age. Although, in the course of his stay,

the narrator remembers the return of the lost son from the Bohemian woods in a local production of *Die Räuber* and tacitly identifies with Schiller's tragic hero, the return of neither Odysseus nor the lost son Karl Moor is appropriate to his situation. W. is neither Ithaca, nor poetic Bohemian wood, nor unalienated *Heimat*, but, instead, is the place of origin of the horrors of German history, and the primary locus of the repression of that history. It is ruled by the stern patriarchal law of castration. Thus, the Sebaldian narrator remembers a postcard of the smoking cone of Vesuvius that had somehow found its way into his parents' photo album, which in turn had mysteriously come into his own possession. The smoking volcano of sexuality is restrained within the bourgeois confines of the photo album, and the man who owned the postcard collection whence the picture of Vesuvius came bears the mark of breaking the paternal proscriptions on sexuality.

> Es hieß, er liege in dem an das Zimmer der Rosina anschließenden Raum und er habe an der Hüfte eine große Wunde, die nicht mehr verheilen wolle. Er habe, so hieß es, in seiner Jugend eine Zigarre, die er verbotenerweise geraucht hat, vor seinem Vater verbergen wollen und in den Hosensack gesteckt. Die Brandwunde, die er sich dabei zugezogen habe, sei zwar bald besser geworden, sie sei aber später, als der Engelwirt gegen fünfzig ging, immer wieder aufgegangen und schließe sich nun überhaupt nicht mehr, ja, sie würde größer von Jahr zu Jahr, und es könne, so wurde gesagt, darum wohl sein, daß er bald am Brand sterben müsse. Diese mir unverständliche Äußerung empfand ich al seine Art Urteilsspruch.
>
> [People said that he lay in the room adjoining Rosina's and had a large wound in his hip which would not heal. They said that as a youngster he had tried to hide a cigar, which had been secretly smoking, from his father, and had put it in his trouser pocket. The burn he had sustained had soon mended, but later, when he was nearly fifty, it opened up again and now refused to close at all, indeed it became larger every year, and he might well, so they said, end up dying of gangrene. I considered this statement, which I could not understand, to be some sort of judgement.] (*SG*, 215; *V*, 198)

Sometimes, it seems, a cigar is very much not just a cigar. The dolorous wound of the Engelwirt signifies the patriarchal law, with its associated threat of castration, which hangs about W. As we have seen from the Legend of St Julian, and from Gracchus the huntsman, a queer touch can heal such wounds and deflect judgements, but not in the patriarchy of W. Equally, W. is the site of the narrator's primal heterosexual scene, when as a child he spies the hunter Schlag — an aspect of Gracchus — having sex with Romana, another of *Schwindel. Gefühle.*'s alluring barmaids. As at the scene at Covehithe in *Die Ringe des Saturn*, the sight of heterosexual copulation is connected to horror and death: Romana's open eyes as she copulates are compared to the lifeless, wide-open eyes of the dead Dr Rambousek (*SG*, 261; *V*, 238). The narrator then fantasizes about stepping into the ice store with Romana and freezing to death with her as they hold each other tight (*SG*, 262; *V*, 239). Further, once the narrator has witnessed this primal scene, he becomes overwhelmed by a fear of castration, being afraid of the barber's razor, fantasizing about Salome bearing the severed head of John the Baptist, and finally having a delirious dream where he is horrified by the feeling of eyes — a clear link to Hoffman's *Der Sandmann*.[3] Schlag, in his turn, dies. As these anxiety-ridden heterosexual scenarios show, in W., desire is re-Oedipalized and becomes Thanatic. The apocalyptic ending to 'Il ritorno in patria' thus becomes ambivalent; it either signifies a return to the catastrophic course of history, indicated by the history of devastating fires in W., or a return to Schreberian paranoia as the only possible line of flight left to the narrator.

The third triptych of *Nach der Natur* manifests another re-Oedipalization of the lyrical self. 'Die dunckle Nacht fährt aus' returns to the site of W. and to the narrator's genealogy. Here, the Sebaldian narrator mythologizes his conception and birth in extravagant terms, designating the place of his conception as a *locus amoenus*:

> ein Schwan und sein Spiegel-
> bild auf der schwarzen Fläche des Wassers,
> ein völliges Gleichnis des Friedens.
>
> [a swan and its reflection
> on the water's black surface,
> a perfect emblem of peace.] (*NdN*, 72; *AN*, 83)

Most significantly, perhaps, 'das Ganze macht zunächst einen | irgendwie undeutschen Eindruck' [the whole leaves an impression | that is somehow un-German] (*NdN*, 72; *AN*, 83). The Sebaldian self displaces (or disorients) his origins to a 'non-German' space, one that appears innocent of historical guilt. However, the poem dialectically reverses this impression a few lines later, by linking his conception to the bombing of Nuremberg, comparing the spectacle of the city in flames to Altdorfer's 1537 painting of *Lot and his Daughters*:

> Am Horizont
> lodert ein furchtbares Feuer,
> das eine große Stadt verdirbt [...]
> Im Mittelgrund ist ein Stück
> grüne idyllische Landschaft,
> und dem Beschauer zunächst
> wird das neue Geschlecht
> der Moabiter gezeugt.
>
> [On the horizon
> a terrible conflagration blazes,
> devouring a large city [...]
> In the middle ground there is a strip
> of idyllic green landscape,
> and closest to the beholder's eye
> the new generation of
> Moabites is conceived.] (*NdN*, 74; *AN*, 85)

The idyllic space where the Sebaldian narrator is conceived, then, is not a utopia beyond history, but a guilty paradise won at the expense of those whom the lovers have destroyed and burned. The history of the new race of the Moabites is built on the ruins of Sodom and Gomorrah, an image that burns out all traces of queer desire in favour of the sterner law of paternal succession. Woven into this image is an intertextual moment of incest: the Moabites are conceived in incest.

> 'Come, let us make our father drink wine,' says Lot's eldest daughter, 'and we
> will lie with him, that we may preserve seed of our father.' And they made
> their father drink wine that night: and the firstborn went in, and lay with her
> father; and he perceived not when she lay down, nor when she arose. (Gen. 19:
> 32–33)

The poetic narrator's return to his origins reveals neither pre-Oedipal bliss nor
an authentic origin. Instead, it is linked to destruction, deviation from the Judaic
line of Abraham, and an Oedipal incest. Unlike schizo-incest, which, as we have
seen, enables the line of flight, Oedipal incest 'is connected to photos, to portraits,
to childhood memories, to a false childhood that never existed but that catches
desire in the trap of representation'.[4] Oedipal incest binds the Sebaldian self back
into the logic of melancholy, mourning, and memory, just as Oedipal structures in
'Il Ritorno in Patria' bind the narrator back into the patriarchal order of German
history.

Yet my study of the Sebaldian queer has itself followed a very queer order.
Darting to and fro in Sebald's oeuvre, it has proceeded backwards to *Schwindel.
Gefühle.* and ended at the beginning, *Nach der Natur*, Sebald's first major literary
publication of 1988. While both of these texts return to the patriarchal order and
are re-Oedipalized, *Il Ritorno in Patria* retains its associative structure to the end.
Its narrative coherence is greater than 'All'estero', but nonetheless its kaleidoscope
images of childhood memories, local myths, and avenging gods and angels are
far from the linear narrative of the *Odyssey*. The text, then, strains against full
re-Oedipalization, with its paranoid and apocalyptic ending. However, 'Il Ritorno
in Patria' is not the last literary text published by Sebald in his lifetime; that was
Austerlitz, published in 2001. Of all Sebald's texts, *Austerlitz* is the one that conforms
most nearly to a novelistic structure. While *Austerlitz* deploys such classically
Sebaldian techniques as *bricolage*, *mémoire involuntaire*, digression, intertextuality, and
intermediality to disrupt the linearity of the text, it still follows the recognizable
structure of a biographical novel. Jacques Austerlitz, the central character, tells
the Sebaldian narrator a linear life story that starts with early memories, moves
into his middle years, is disrupted by the return of repressed childhood memories
from Prague, and is then concerned with the retrieval of those memories. While
it would be going too far to call this the *Bildungsroman* or even anti-*Bildungsroman*
that 'Beyle oder das merckwürdige Faktum der Liebe' rejects, it is certainly a novel
that conforms more closely to inherited structures of the bourgeois capitalist model
that the young Sebald condemned. Further, while, as we have seen, it contains a
queer moment of escape between Austerlitz and Gerard, it remains firmly tied to an
Oedipal narrative of inheritance. Indeed, the crises of the novel occur at moments
with a direct connection to major European literatures. Austerlitz's first moment
of *mémoire involuntaire* — his first adult memory of his Czech childhood — comes
when he is in the shop of a woman named Penelope Peaceful (*A*, 207; *Ae*, 200).
This Odyssean reference sends Austerlitz on his own *ritorno in patria*, which turns
out to be an Oedipal fantasy.

On his return to Prague, Austerlitz discovers his origins at the heart of the
scrupulously bohemian and Francophile Austerlitz-Aychenwald family. His parents,

Agáta Austerlitzova and Max Aychenwald, display the *Bildungsbürgertum* attributes that the narrator's family conspicuously lacks in 'Die dunckle Nacht fahrt aus', 'Il Ritorno in Patria', or 'Ambros Adelwarth'. Their well-loved volumes of French bourgeois novels, for instance, contrast with the narrator's family's ostentatiously bound sets of Shakespeare, Schiller, Hebbel and Sudermann in *Schwindel. Gefühle.* These books have never been opened by the narrator's family, and were only bought in a passing moment of *Kulturbewusstsein* [cultural consciousness] from a travelling salesman (*SG*, 212; *V*, 194). By locating Austerlitz's origins in the Czech Jewish bourgeoisie, Sebald allows the text of *Austerlitz* to express nostalgia for the aesthetic and political integrity of a *Bildungsbürgertum* family structure, while it directs moral outrage at the destructive progress of history in the bourgeois age. As we have seen, Sebald views German bourgeois culture as irremediably tainted by Nazism, a taint that extends to German-Jewish culture. Writing about the half-Jewish writer Peter Weiss, he concurs with Weiss that merely having Jewish parentage does not cleanse one of guilt.

> Die allzu leichtfertige Exoneration verschlägt nicht; ganz im Gegenteil, es spricht aus ihr das Bewußtsein, daß er [...] eben doch zu den Deutschen gehört, zumindest insofern, als auch im Haus seiner Eltern die sogenannte deutsche Gesittung herrschte. (*CS*, 143)
>
> [This facile exoneration does not fail to make its point; on the contrary, it shows his awareness that he [...] is also a German, at least in so far as German ideas of morality prevailed in his parental home.][5]

Here again, the German taint is predominantly a family affair. Indeed, Austerlitz's father himself supports the thesis that the culture of the German family was inextricably complicit in Nazism. In *Austerlitz*, Sebald exempts Czech Jewish bourgeois culture from his general condemnations of the 'bourgeois age'. Although the novel elegiacally details the dark side of almost all bourgeois cultural institutions, from the spa town to the library to the university, Austerlitz is portrayed as the heir of an idyllic family with classic *Bildungsbürger* credentials. Aychenwald is a classic radical intellectual bourgeois, who dreams of making Czechoslovakia an island of freedom amid the fascist flood swamping Europe. By including a speculation that Maximilian may have tried to cross the Pyrenees on foot and have got lost there, Sebald encourages the identification of Austerlitz's father with the biography of Walter Benjamin. He thereby links paternal virtue to mourning, confirming the link between Oedipal and Thanatic structures. Austerlitz is last seen setting off across the Pyrenees in search of his father's traces, a Telemachus repeating the paternal lines of pain in history.

The Oedipal drama of *Austerlitz* deepens in his relationship to his mother. Although Austerlitz recovers some of his father's history prior to setting forth in search of him, his maternal inheritance has an erotic significance lacking in his relationship to his Welsh father or to Aychenwald. Although he senses his father's presence in the Gare d'Austerlitz, he inherits both his first and last name from his mother. If Austerlitz's Czech father is a portrait of the masculine civic virtues, Agáta, his mother represents the aesthetic institution of the theatre, and her vision of a better world comes from Jacques Offenbach. Agáta's stage career is described without the knowing irony and mockery with which Henri Beyle remembers the tawdry danger of theatre ladies. Rather, Agáta's stage appearances elevate her even further above the material into a magical, spectral being. The figure of Agáta combines the erotic, the theatrical, and the maternal, as is evident in Austerlitz's description of her unrobing after a performance:

> Sie trägt ein vorne geschnürtes, aschgraues Seidenmieder, aber ihr Gesicht kann ich nicht erkennen, sondern nur einen irisierenden, niedrig über der Haut schwebenden Schleier von weißlich getrübter Milchfarbe, und dann sehe ich, sagte Austerlitz, wie ihr der Schal von der rechten Schulter gleitet, als sie mir mit der Hand über die Stirne streicht.

> [I see her wearing an ashen-grey silk bodice laced up in front, but I cannot make out her face, only an iridescent veil of pale, cloudy milkiness wafting close to her skin, and then, said Austerlitz, I see the scarf slip from her right shoulder as she lays her hand on my forehead.] (*A*, 237; *Ae*, 229)

In this passage, we are once again returned to the motif of incest, but here, this is an Oedipal incest, like that at the end of 'Die dunckle Nacht fahrt aus', rather than a schizo-incest 'in which memory-less childhood blocks introduce themselves in full vitality into the present to activate it, to precipitate it, to multiply its connections'.[6] Agáta is a figure of the recovery of memory, not of liberation from it, and Jacques Austerlitz's breakdown subsequent to the recovery of his childhood memories does not constitute a schizo-liberation, but is rather an after-effect of trauma that emphasizes the devastations of history. Indeed, it is he, more than the queer bachelor Adelwarth, who seems to suffer from a version of Korsakoff's syndrome.

We are thus dealing here with a re-Oedipalized text, one which moves from the systems of desiring-production in *Schwindel. Gefühle.* to a system of melancholic reductions:

> reduction of desiring production to a system of representation called unconscious, ... reduction of the factories of the un-conscious to a theater stage, Oedipus, Hamlet; reduction of social investments of the libido to familial investments, onto familial coordinates, Oedipus again.[7]

Austerlitz circles around the refusal of immanence, due to the traumas of the past, and around the recovery of memory. The apparent double perfection of Austerlitz's mother and of his infant memory is shown when the adult Austerlitz returns to the empty theatre in which Agáta performed in Offenbach's *Contes d'Hoffmann*. On arrival, he cannot read the scene at all, and the proscenium appears to him like a blind eye (*A*, 235; *Ae*, 227). However, by a mystical alchemy, he sees the stage curtain sway, the orchestra begins to play, and he catches a glimpse of Agáta in stage costume:

> [ich] glaubte auf einmal, zwischen dem Kopf eines der Musikanten und dem Hals einer Baßgeige hindurch, in dem hellen Lichtstreif zwischen dem Bretterboden und dem Saum des Vorhangs einen himmelblauen, mit Silberflitter bestickten Schuh zu erblicken.

> [I thought that in between one of the musicians' heads and the neck of a double bass, in the bright strip of light between the wooden floorboards and the hem of

the curtain, I caught sight of a sky-blue shoe embroidered with silver sequins.] (*A*, 236; *Ae*, 228)

This passage with the sky-blue shoe appears to be a moment of kitsch, where irony is absent and a yearning for the identity of real and ideal is expressed in a somewhat twee picture. Iris Radisch also levelled the accusation of kitsch at *Austerlitz* in a review in *Die Zeit*. Discussing the scene where Austerlitz lists the contents of an antique shop window in Theresienstadt, a scene that is essential to the Benjaminian poetics of *bricolage* that underlie memory in *Austerlitz*, she comments that this belief in the affinity and timelessness of things that lie apart from each other is 'black kitsch'.[8] The twinkling sky-blue shoe, magically transported to the present, is the fetishistic symbol of a hope for the reconciliation of the real and the ideal, for the perfect recovery of memory. In his essay on Stifter and Handke, Sebald himself condemned kitsch as the illegitimate attempt to create a bourgeois heaven on earth, noting that:

> die von der bürgerlichen Phantasie betriebene Säkularisierung der Utopie, der Versuch, sich einen Himmel auf Erden zu schaffen, leicht ins Kitschige hinüberschwingt und also in einen Bereich, in welchem die Legitimation des Erzählers in seinem Werk nicht mehr zu bewerkstelligen ist. (*BU*, 176)

> [the secularization of utopia conducted by the bourgeois imagination, the attempt to create a heaven on earth, easily sways into the realm of kitsch, and thus into an area in which the legitimation of the narrator can no longer be accomplished in his works.]

Yet despite the kitschily restorative function of the sky-blue shoe in the context of *Austerlitz*'s narrative, the shoe is also ironized through its status as an intertextual quote, which comes from the very beginning of Hofmannsthal's *Andreas*.[9] When Andreas enters the town of Venice, he recalls the forbidden visits that he made in childhood to the theatre in Vienna. As they are for the infant Austerlitz, these visits are a trip into a fantastic land; in the adult Andreas's memory, between the neck of a double bass and the head of a musician, the sky-blue shoe appears more appealing than either the actress or the play to him. Although both princess and music are beautiful,

> es war nicht das zweischneidige Schwert von zartester Wollust und unsäglicher Sehnsucht, das durch die Seele ging, bis zu Weinen, Bangen und Beglückung, wenn der blaue Schuh allein unter dem Vorhang da war.[10]

> [it was not the two-edged sword which had pierced his soul, from the tenderest delight and unutterable longing to tears, awe, and ecstasy, when the blue shoe lay alone beneath the curtain.[11]]

Glossing this passage towards the end of 'Venezianisches Kryptogramm: Hofmannsthals *Andreas*', Sebald claims that this passage is about the 'unexpected epiphany of images' that nurtures the creative imagination. He argues:

> Es ist der fetischistischen Neigung, die die Libido genau dort verbirgt, wo niemand sie vermuten möchte, zutiefst adäquat. In solchen Bildern allein restituiert sich — aufs schmerzlichste — das Glück jener besseren Zeit, aus der wir vermeinen gefallen zu sein. (*BU*, 77)

[It is the fetishistic tendency that appropriately hides the libido precisely where no-one would suspect it. Only in such images can — most painfully — the happiness of that better time, out of which we believe ourselves to have fallen, be restored.]

Sebald considers *Andreas* to be an abandoned *Bildungsroman*, as we know, subject to illicit and repressed drives, among which he counts not merely the erotic drives but also the lust for art, and it is with this libidinous but irenic vision of art that the essay ends. The kitschy retrieval, intertextual allusions, and bourgeois family structures of *Austerlitz*, then, return us to Sebald's well-known position in 'Ein Versuch der Restitution', that only in art — literature in particular — is restitution possible, and that, *pace* Benjamin, and also Derrida, such restitution is the task owed by the living to the dead.[12] The lines of flight opened up by Sebald's earlier work, Gerald's dream of flight, and the possibilities for queer resistance and disorientation appear to be subjected to this overriding melancholy-moral requirement of literature, which finds its final, most polemic expression in *Luftkrieg und Literatur*. It is to be noted that this text, too, after its broad survey of German literature and the bombing raids, compulsively returns not only to Sebald's home town of Sonthofen, but also to Sebald's parents' marital bed, a picture of which is even reproduced in the text.[13] Thanatic re-Oedipalization would appear to have won a victory over queer Eros.

Is, then, the Sebaldian queer nothing but a distraction from the more weighty, more morally urgent question of uncovering the past and granting a history to the dead in his overall poetic project? Naegeli's bones tell us otherwise. As I showed in the Introduction, queer *Wahlverwandtschaften* with the dead as well as with the living can be a way to perform such restitution, to restore neighbourliness in the place of creaturely subjection. But the forms and structures of queer desire and queer textuality in Sebald's work are too unruly, too camp, playful, ethically contaminated, disorienting — too *queer* — to be easily assimilated to an overriding narrative of mourning and restitution. The brotherly homoerotics between Kobal and his Slovenian waiter, Edward FitzGerald's feather boa, Cosmo and Adelwarth's idyll in Greece, the ghostly image of a queer Kafka in a station toilet mirror — these textual elements are not merely incorporated into the melancholy body of the Sebaldian opus, providing yet another opportunity for stiffness and pain.[14] Rather, they leave open lines of flight from historical domination in his texts, lines with a powerful political potential; they allow for the possibility of encounters with the other, and for escape from the realm of subjection and returns of history. If at times the Sebaldian queer itself borders on kitsch, dallies with Orientalism, and avails itself of a range of creakily outmoded theories of homosexuality, it nonetheless represents a real attempt to resist the oppressive orders of history in a way not solely conditioned by melancholia, Thanatos, and mourning. Sebald's idiosyncratic portrayal of queer desire is located right at the fault lines of history, memory, identity, theory, and narrative, and as such represents a significant contribution to queer letters. If, as has so often been claimed, Sebald's work represents a profoundly important intervention in European literature and politics, some of its most radical, joyful, and political potential is queer.

Notes to the Conclusion

1. Deleuze and Guattari, *Kafka*, p. 17.
2. See Patricia Hellweg, 'Lokaltermin Wertach: Noch ein eigenartiger Novembergast', in *Mitteilung über Max: Marginalien zu W. G. Sebald*, ed. by Gerhard Köpf (Oberhausen: Karl Maria Laufen, 1998), pp. 21–31 (p. 24).
3. Zilcosky, 'Sebald's Uncanny Travels', p. 108.
4. Deleuze and Guattari, *Kafka*, p. 67.
5. Sebald, *On the Natural History of Destruction: With Essays on Alfred Andersch, Jean Améry and Peter Weiss*, trans. by Anthea Bell (London: Hamish Hamilton, 2003), p. 191.
6. Deleuze and Guattari, *Kafka*, p. 67.
7. Deleuze and Guattari, 'Sur Capitalisme et Schizophrénie', *L'Arc*, 49 (1972), 50, cited in Charles J. Stivale, 'Gilles Deleuze & Félix Guattari: Schizoanalysis & Literary Discourse', *SubStance*, 9 (1980), 46–57 (p. 47).
8. Iris Radisch, 'Der Waschbär der falschen Welt', *Die Zeit*, 5 April 2001, Literatur section, pp. 55–56 (p. 56).
9. Hofmannsthal abandoned work on the text in August 1913, a historical moment laden with Sebaldian significance.
10. Hugo von Hofmannsthal, *Andreas*, ed. by Mathias Mayer (Stuttgart: Reclam, 2000), p. 17.
11. Hugo von Hofmannsthal, *Andreas*, trans. by Marie D. Hottinger (London: Pushkin Press, 1998), p. 21.
12. *Campo Santo*, pp. 240–48 [206–15].
13. Sebald, *Luftkrieg und Literatur: Mit einem Essay zu Alfred Andersch* (Frankfurt a. M.: Fischer, 2001), p. 79; *On the Natural History of Destruction*, p. 73.
14. Santner, *On Creaturely Life*, p. 172.

BIBLIOGRAPHY

Literature by W. G. Sebald, in Chronological Order

Carl Sternheim: Kritiker und Opfer der Wilhelminischen Ära (Stuttgart: Kohlhammer, 1969)

'Mord an den Vätern: Bemerkungen zu einigen Dramen der spätbürgerlichen Zeit', *Neophilologus*, 60 (1976), 432–41

Der Mythus der Zerstörung im Werk Döblins (Stuttgart: Klett, 1980)

'Die Mädchen aus der Feenwelt — Bemerkungen zu Liebe und Prostitution mit Bezügen zu Raimund, Schnitzler und Horvath', *Neophilologus*, 67 (1983), 109–17

Die Beschreibung des Unglücks: Zur österreichischen Literatur von Stifter bis Handke (Salzburg: Residenz Verlag, 1985)

'Tiere, Menschen, Maschinen: Zu Kakfas Evolutionsgeschichten', *Literatur und Kritik*, 21 (1986), 194–201

(edited) *A Radical Stage: Theatre in Germany in the 1970s and 1980s* (Oxford: Berg, 1988)

Nach der Natur: Ein Elementargedicht (Frankfurt a. M.: Fischer, 1989)

'Damals vor Graz — Randbemerkungen zum Thema Literatur und Heimat', in *Heimat im Wort: Die Problematik eines Begriffes im 19. und 20. Jahrhundert*, ed. by Rüdiger Görner (Munich: iudicium, 1992), pp. 131–39

Schwindel.Gefühle. (Frankfurt a. M.: Fischer, 1994)

Unheimliche Heimat: Essays zur österreichischen Literatur (Frankfurt a. M.: Fischer, 1994)

Vertigo, trans. by Michel Hulse (London: Harvill, 1999)

The Emigrants, trans. by Michael Hulse (London: Harvill, 1996)

Die Ringe des Saturn. Eine englische Wallfahrt (Frankfurt a. M.: Fischer, 1997)

The Rings of Saturn, trans. by Michael Hulse (London: Harvill, 1998)

Logis in einem Landhaus (Frankfurt a. M.: Fischer, 2000)

Austerlitz, trans. by Anthea Bell (London: Penguin, 2002)

Luftkrieg und Literatur: Mit einem Essay zu Alfred Andersch (Frankfurt a. M.: Fischer, 2001)

After Nature, trans. by Michael Hamburger (London: Penguin, 2003)

Die Ausgewanderten: Vier lange Erzählungen (Frankfurt a. M.: Fischer, 2002)

Austerlitz (Frankfurt a. M.: Fischer, 2003)

On the Natural History of Destruction: With essays on Alfred Andersch, Jean Améry and Peter Weiss, trans. by Anthea Bell (London: Hamish Hamilton, 2003)

Campo Santo, ed. by Sven Meyer (Munich: Hanser, 2003)

Campo Santo, ed. by Sven Meyer, trans. by Anthea Bell (London: Penguin, 2006)

The Emergence of Memory: Conversations with W. G. Sebald, ed. Lynne Sharon Schwartz (New York: Seven Stories, 2007)

'Aufzeichnungen aus Korsika: Zur Natur- & Menschenkunde', Zweite Fassung, *Wandernde Schatten: W. G. Sebalds Unterwelt*, ed. by Ulrich von Bülow, Heike Gfrereis, and Ellen Strittmatter (Deutsche Schillergesellschaft: Marbach am Neckar, 2008), pp. 159–211

Interviews with Sebald

'Wie kriegen die Deutschen das auf die Reihe? Ein Gespräch mit W. G. Sebald', interview with Marco Poltronieri, in *W. G. Sebald* (Porträt 7), ed. by Franz Loquai (Eggingen: Isele, 1997), pp. 138–44

'Ich fürchte das Melodramatische', interview with Martin Doerry and Volker Hage, *Der Spiegel* (Hamburg), 11, 12 March 2001, pp. 228, 230, and 232–34

'Who is W. G. Sebald? Interview', Sebald in conversation with Carole Angier, in *The Emergence of Memory: Conversations with W. G. Sebald*, ed. by Lynne Sharon Schwartz (New York: Seven Stories, 2007), pp. 63–75

Secondary Literature

ADORNO, THEODOR W., *Minima Moralia: Reflections on a Damaged Life*, trans. by E. F. N. Jephcott (London: Verso, 2005)

AHMED, SARAH, *Queer Phenomenology: Orientations, Objects, Others* (Durham, NC and London: Duke University Press, 2006)

ALBES, CLAUDIA, 'Porträt ohne Modell: Bildbeschreibung und autobiographische Reflexion in W. G. Sebalds "Elementargedicht" *Nach der Natur*', in *W. G. Sebald: Politische Archäologie und melancholische Bastelei*, ed. by Michael Niehaus and Claudia Öhlschläger (Berlin: Schmidt, 2006), pp. 47–75

ANDERMATT CONLEY, VERENA, 'Thirty-six Thousand Forms of Love: The Queering of Deleuze and Guattari', in *Deleuze and Queer Theory*, ed. by Chrysanthi Nigianni and Merl Storr (Edinburgh: Edinburgh University Press, 2009), pp. 24–36

ANDERSON, MARK M., 'Fathers and Son: W. G. Sebald', *Bookforum* (Jan./Feb. 2007), <http://www.bookforum.com/>, accessed 16 December 2012

——'A Childhood in the Allgäu: Wertach, 1944–1952', in *Saturn's Moons: A W. G. Sebald Handbook*, ed. by Jo Catling and Richard Hibbitt (Oxford: Legenda, 2011), pp. 16–41

ATZE, MARCEL, and SVEN MEYER, '"Unsere Korrespondenz": Zum Briefwechsel zwischen W. G. Sebald und Theodor W. Adorno', *Sebald: Lektüren*, ed. by Marcel Atze and Franz Loquai (Eggingen: Edition Isele, 2005), pp. 17–38

BAKHTIN, MIKHAIL, 'The Bildungsroman and its Significance in the History of Realism (Towards a Historical Typology of the Novel)', in *Speech Genres and Other Late Essays*, trans. by Vern W. McGee, ed. by Caryl Emerson and Michael Holquist (Austin: University of Texas Press, 1986), pp. 10–59

BARZILAI, MAYA, 'Facing the Past and the Female Spectre in W. G. Sebald's *The Emigrants*', in *W. G. Sebald: A Critical Companion*, ed. by J. Long and Anne Whitehead (Edinburgh: Edinburgh University Press, 2004), pp. 203–16

BECK, JOHN, 'Reading Room: Erosion and Sedimentation in Sebald's Suffolk', in *W. G. Sebald: A Critical Companion*, ed. by J. J. Long and Anne Whitehead (Edinburgh: Edinburgh University Press, 2004), pp. 75–88

BENJAMIN, *Gesammelte Schriften*, ed. by Rolf Tiedemann, Hermann Schweppenhäuser, with the contribution of Theodor W. Adorno and Gerschom Scholem, 7 vols (Frankfurt a. M.: Suhrkamp, 1972–91), I: *Abhandlungen*, ed. by Rolf Tiedemann and Hermann Schweppenhäuser (1974)

——*Sprache und Geschichte* (Stuttgart: Reclam, 2003)

BOEHRER, BRUCE THOMAS, 'Early Modern Syphilis', *Journal of the History of Sexuality*, 1 (1990), 197–214

BÖHME, HARTMUT, *Natur und Subjekt* (Frankfurt: Suhrkamp, 1988)

BOONE, JOSEPH A., 'Vacation Cruises; or, the Homoerotics of Orientalism', *PMLA*, 110 (1995), 89–107

BORGES, JORGE LUIS, 'Tlön, Uqbar, Orbis Tertius', in *Collected Fictions*, trans. by Andrew Hurley (New York: Penguin Putnam, 1988), pp. 68–69

BOYARIN, DANIEL, 'Freud's Baby, Fliess's Maybe: Homophobia, Anti-Semitism, and the Invention of Oedipus', *GLQ*, 2 (1995), 115–47

BOYCE, DAVID GEORGE and ALAN O'DAY, eds, *The Making of Modern Irish History: Revisionism and the Revisionist Controversy* (London: Routledge, 1996)

BRUZELIUS, MARGARET, 'Adventure, Imprisonment, and Melancholy: *Heart of Darkness* and *Die Ringe des Saturn/The Rings of Saturn*', in *The Undiscover'd Country: W. G. Sebald and the Poetics of Travel*, ed. by Markus Zisselsberger (Rochester, NY: Camden House, 2010), pp. 247–73

BUDE, HEINZ, *Bilanz der Nachfolge: Die Bundesrepublik und der Nationalsozialismus* (Frankfurt a. M.: Suhrkamp, 1992)

BUNZL, MATTI, 'Jews, Queers, and Other Symptoms: Recent Work in Jewish Cultural Studies', *GLQ*, 6 (2000), 321–41

——*Symptoms of Modernity: Jews and Queers in Late-Twentieth-Century Vienna* (Berkeley: University of California Press, 2004)

BUTLER, JUDITH, *Gender Trouble* (New York and London: Routledge, 1990)

CEUPPENS, JAN, 'Seeing Things: Spectres and Angels in W. G. Sebald's Prose Fiction', in *W. G. Sebald: A Critical Companion*, ed. by J. J. Long and Anne Whitehead (Edinburgh: Edinburgh University Press, 2004), pp. 190–202

CHRYSANTHI, NIGIANNI, and MERL STORR, 'Introduction', in *Deleuze and Queer Theory*, ed. by Chrysanthi Nigianni and Merl Storr (Edinburgh: Edinburgh University Press, 2009), pp. 1–10

CORKHILL, ALAN, 'Angles of Vision in Sebald's *After Nature* and *Unrecounted*', in *W. G. Sebald: Schreiben ex patria/Expatriate Writing*, ed. by Gerhard Fischer (Amsterdam: Rodopi, 2009), pp. 347–68

COSGROVE, MARY, 'Sebald for Our Time: The Politics of Melancholy and the Critique of Capitalism in his Work', in *W. G. Sebald and the Writing of History*, ed. by Anne Fuchs and J. J. Long (Würzburg: Königshausen & Neumann, 2007), pp. 91–110

——'Austerlitz', in *The German-Language Novel since 1990*, ed. by Stuart Taberner (Cambridge: Cambridge University Press, 2011), pp. 195–210

DAUB, ADRIAN, 'Donner à Voir: The Logics of the Caption in W. G. Sebald's *Rings of Saturn* and Alexander Kluge's *Devil's Blind Spot*', in *Searching for Sebald: Photography after W. G. Sebald*, ed. by Lise Patt with Christel Dillbohner (Los Angeles: Institute of Cultural Inquiry, 2007), pp. 306–29

DELEUZE, GILLES and GUATTARI, FÉLIX, 'Sur Capitalisme et Schizophrénie', *L'Arc*, 49 (1972), 50, cited in Charles J. Stivale, 'Gilles Deleuze & Félix Guattari: Schizoanalysis & Literary Discourse', *SubStance*, 9 (1980), 46–57 (p. 47)

——*Kafka: Toward a Minor Literature*, trans. by Dana Polan (Minneapolis and London: University of Minnesota Press, 1986)

——*Anti-Oedipus: Capitalism and Schizophrenia*, trans. by Robert Hurley, Mark Seem, and Helen R. Lane (London: Continuum, 2004)

DELLAMORA, RICHARD, *Masculine Desire: The Sexual Politics of Victorian Aestheticism* (Chapel Hill: University of North Carolina Press, 1990)

DENNELER, IRIS, *Von Namen und Dingen: Erkundungen zur Rolle des Ich in der Literatur am Beispiel von Ingeborg Bachmann, Peter Bichsel, Max Frisch, Gottfried Keller, Heinrich von Kleist, Arthur Schnitzler, Franz Wedekind, Vladimir Nabokov und W. G. Sebald* (Würzburg: Königshausen & Neumann, 2001)

DERRIDA, *Specters of Marx: The State of the Debt, the Work of Mourning and the New International*, trans. by Peggy Kamuf (New York and London: Routledge, 1994)

DIEDRICH, LISA, 'Gathering Evidence of Ghosts: W. G. Sebald's Practices of Witnessing', in *Searching for Sebald: Photography after W. G. Sebald*, ed. by Lisa Patt with Christel Dillbohner (Los Angeles: Institute of Cultural Inquiry, 2007), pp. 256–79

DUTTLINGER, CAROL, '"A Wrong Turn of the Wheel": Sebald's Journeys of (In)Attention', in *The Undiscover'd Country: W. G. Sebald and the Poetics of Travel*, ed. by Markus Zisselsberger (Rochester, NY: Camden, 2010), pp. 92–122

ECKART, GABRIELE, 'Against "Cartesian Rigidity": W. G. Sebald's Reception of Borges', in *W. G. Sebald: Schreiben ex patria/Expatriate Writing*, ed. by Gerhard Fischer (Amsterdam: Rodopi, 2009), pp. 509–21

EDELMAN, LEE, *No Future: Queer Theory and the Death Drive* (Durham, NC and London: Duke University Press, 1994)

ELLMANN, RICHARD, *Oscar Wilde* (London: Penguin, 1988)

ESHEL, AMIR, 'Against the Power of Time: The Poetics of Suspension in W. G. Sebald's *Austerlitz*', *New German Critique*, 88 (2003), 71–96

FINCH, HELEN, 'Die irdische Erfüllung: Peter Handke's Poetic Landscapes and W. G. Sebald's Metaphysics of History', in *W. G. Sebald and the Writing of History*, ed. by Anne Fuchs and J. J. Long (Würzburg: Königshausen & Neumann, 2007), pp. 179–97

FIPPINGER, ANDREW, 'Intimations and Imitations of Immortality: Swinburne's "By the North Sea" and "Poeta Loquitur"', *Victorian Poetry*, 47 (2009), 675–90

FLAUBERT, GUSTAVE, 'The Legend of Saint Julian the Hospitaler', trans. by Michel Grimaud, in *Saint/Oedipus: Psychocritical Approaches to Flaubert's Art*, ed. by William J. Berg, Michel Grimaud, and George Moskos (Ithaca: Cornell University Press, 1982), pp. 231–55

FOUCAULT, MICHEL, *Wahnsinn und Gesellschaft: Eine Geschichte des Wahns im Zeitalter der Vernunft*, trans. by Ulrich Köppen (Frankfurt a. M.: Suhrkamp, 1972)

——'Of Other Spaces (1967), Heterotopias', trans. by Jay Miskowiec, <http://www.foucault.info/documents/heteroTopia/foucault.heteroTopia.en.htm> (accessed 15 December 2012)

——*Madness and Civilization: A History of Insanity in the Age of Reason*, trans. by Richard Howard, with an introduction by David Cooper (London: Routledge, 2001)

FREUD, SIGMUND, 'Massenpsychologie und Ich-Analyse', in *Kulturtheoretische Schriften*, ed. by Alexander Mitscherlich, Angela Richards, and James Strachey (Frankfurt a. M.: Fischer, 1974), pp. 61–134

——*The Schreber Case*, trans. by Andrew Webber (London: Penguin, 2002)

FUCHS, ANNE, *Die Schmerzzensspuren der Geschichte: Zur Poetik der Erinnerung in W. G. Sebalds Prosa* (Cologne: Böhlau, 2004)

————, MARY COSGROVE, and GEORGE GROTE, eds, *German Memory Contests: The Quest for Identity in Literature, Film and Discourse* (Rochester, NY: Camden House, 2006)

GARLOFF, KATJA, 'Kafka's Crypt: W. G. Sebald and the Melancholy of Modern German Jewish Culture', *The Germanic Review*, 82.2 (2007), 123–40

GOETHE, JOHANN WOLFGANG VON, *Sämtliche Werke nach Epochen seines Schaffens* (Münchner Ausgabe), ed. by Karl Richter with the co-operation of Herbert G. Göpfert and others, 33 vols; XVII: *Wilhelm Meisters Wanderjahre: Maximen und Reflexionen*, ed. by Gonthier-Louis Fink and others (Munich: Hanser, 1991)

HALBERSTAM, JUDITH, *In a Queer Time and Place: Transgender Bodies, Subcultural Lives* (New York: New York University Press, 2005)

HALPERIN, DAVID M., *One Hundred Years of Homosexuality: And Other Essays on Greek Love. The New Ancient World* (New York: Routledge, 1990)

HANDKE, PETER, *Die Wiederholung* (Frankfurt a. M.: Suhrkamp, 1986)

HARAWAY, DONNA, *Simians, Cyborgs and Women: The Reinvention of Nature* (New York; Routledge, 1991)

HAVELOCK ELLIS, HENRY, *Studies in the Psychology of Sex*, II (1927), available in e-book form at http://www.gutenberg.org/files/13611/13611-h/13611-h.htm (accessed 15 December 2012)

HELLWEG, 'Lokaltermin Wertach — Noch ein eigenartiger Novembergast', in *Mitteilung über Max: Marginalien zu W. G. Sebald*, ed. by Gerhard Köpf (Oberhausen: Karl Maria Laufen, 1998), pp. 21–31

HERMANN, ANNE, *Queering the Moderns: Poses, Portraits, Performances* (New York: Palgrave, 2000)

HETHERINGTON, KEVIN, *The Badlands of Modernity: Heterotopia And Social Ordering* (London: Routledge, 1997)

HOFFMANN, E. T. A., *Der Sandmann* (Stuttgart: Reclam, 1996)

HOFMANNSTHAL, HUGO VON, *Andreas*, trans. by Marie D. Hottinger (London: Pushkin Press, 1998)

——*Andreas*, ed. by Mathias Mayer (Stuttgart: Reclam, 2000)

HULSE, MICHAEL, 'Englishing Max', in *Saturn's Moons: A W. G. Sebald Handbook*, ed. by Jo Catling and Richard Hibbitt (Oxford: Legenda, 2011), pp. 192–205

HUTCHINSON, BEN, 'Bausteine 3: Sprachen', in *Wandernde Schatten: W. G. Sebalds Unterwelt*, marbacherkatalog 62, ed. by Ulrich von Bülow, Heike Gfrereis, and Ellen Strittmatter (Marbach am Neckar: Deutsche Schillergesellschaft, 2008), pp. 115–27

——*W. G. Sebald: Die dialektische Imagination* (Berlin: De Gruyter, 2009)

JACKMAN, GRAHAM, '"Gebranntes Kind"? W. G. Sebalds "Metaphysik der Geschichte"', *German Life and Letters*, 57 (2004), 456–71

JACOBS, JÜRGEN, *Wilhelm Meister und seine Brüder* (Munich: Wilhelm Fink, 1972)

JÄGER, LORENZ, *Adorno: A Political Biography*, trans. by Stewart Spencer (New Haven: Yale University Press, 2004)

JAGGI, MAYA, 'Recovered Memories. The Guardian Profile: W. G. Sebald', *The Guardian*, 22 September 2001

JEFFRIES, STUART, 'Atlas of the Soul', *The Guardian*, 18 December 1999

KAFKA, FRANZ, *Briefe an Felice und andere Korrespondenz aus der Verlobungszeit*, ed. by Erich Heller and Jürgen Born (Frankfurt: Fischer, 1976)

——*Tagebücher 1910–1923*, ed. by Max Brod (Frankfurt a. M.: Fischer, 1973)

——'Description of a Struggle', trans. by Tania Stern and James Stern, in Franz Kafka, *The Complete Short Stories*, ed. by Nahum L. Glatzer (London: Minerva, 1992), pp. 9–51

——'Beschreibung eines Kampfes' (Fassung A), in Franz Kafka, *Beschreibung eines Kampfes und andere Schriften aus dem Nachlaß* (Frankfurt a. M.: Fischer, 1994), pp. 47–98

KAUFMANN, DAVID, 'Angels Visit the Scene of Disgrace: Melancholy and Trauma from Sebald to Benjamin and Back', *Cultural Critique*, 70 (2008), 94–119

KILBOURN, R. J. A. 'Kafka, Nabokov ... Sebald: Intertextuality and Narratives of Redemption in *Vertigo* and *The Emigrants*', in *W. G. Sebald: History — Memory — Trauma*, ed. by Scott Denham and Mark McCulloh (Berlin: De Gruyter, 2006), pp. 33–63

KLEBES, MARTIN, 'Infinite Journey: From Kafka to Sebald', in *W. G. Sebald: A Critical Companion*, ed. by J. J. Long and Anne Whitehead (Edinburgh: Edinburgh University Press, 2004), pp. 123–39

——'If You Come to a Spa: Displacing the Cure in *Schwindel. Gefühle*. and *Austerlitz*', in *The Undiscover'd Country: W. G. Sebald and the Poetics of Travel*, ed. by Markus Zisselsberger (Rochester, NY: Camden House, 2010), pp. 123–41

KONTJE, TODD, *German Orientalism* (Ann Arbor: University of Michigan Press, 2004)

LAMOS, COLLEEN, *Devant Modernism: Sexual and Textual Errancy in T. S. Eliot, James Joyce, and Marcel Proust* (Cambridge: Cambridge University Press, 1998)

LEWIS, BRIAN, 'The Queer Life and Afterlife of Roger Casement', *Journal of the History of Sexuality*, 14 (2005), 363–82

LÖFFLER, '"Wildes Denken". Gespräch mit W. G. Sebald', in *W. G. Sebald* (Porträt 7), 135–37

LONG, J. J., 'History, Narrative, and Photography in W. G. Sebald's *Die Ausgewanderten*', *The Modern Language Review*, 98 (2003), 117–37

——'Disziplin und Geständnis', in *W. G. Sebald: Politische Archäologie und melancholische Bastelei*, ed. by Michael Niehaus and Claudia Öhlschläger (Berlin: Schmidt, 2006), pp. 219–40

——*W. G. Sebald: Image, Archive, Modernity* (Edinburgh: Edinburgh University Press, 2007)

——and ANNE WHITEHEAD, eds, *W. G. Sebald: A Critical Companion* (Edinburgh: Edinburgh University Press, 2004)

LOVE, HEATHER, *Feeling Backward: Loss and the Politics of Queer History* (Cambridge, Mass.: Harvard University Press, 2007)

MANN, THOMAS, *Death in Venice*, trans. by Michael Henry Heim (New York: HarperCollins, 2004)

MATZ, JESSE, 'Masculinity Amalgamated: Colonialism, Homosexuality, and Forster's Kipling', *Journal of Modern Literature*, 30 (2007), 31–51

MCCREA, BARRY, *The Company of Strangers: Family and Narrative in Dickens, Conan Doyle, Joyce, and Proust* (New York: Columbia University Press, 2011)

MEDIN, DANIEL, *Three Sons: Franz Kafka and the Fiction of J. M. Coetzee, Philip Roth and W. G. Sebald* (Evanston, IL: Northwestern University Press, 2010)

MERIVALE, PATRICIA and SUSAN ELIZABETH SWEENEY, 'The Game's Afoot: On the Trail of the Metaphysical Detective Story', in *Detecting Texts: The Metaphysical Detective Story from Poe to Postmodernism*, ed. by Patricia Merivale (Philadelphia: University of Pennsylvania Press, 1999), pp. 1–26

MORGAN, PETER, 'The Sign of Saturn: Melancholy, Homelessness and Apocalypse in W. G. Sebald's Prose Narratives', *German Life and Letters*, 58.1 (2005), 75–92

MORGAN, THAÏS E., 'Reimagining Masculinity in Victorian Criticism: Swinburne and Pater', *Victorian Studies*, 36 (1993), 315–32

MOSER, 'Peripatetic Liminality: Sebald and the Tradition of the Literary Walk', in *The Undiscover'd Country: W. G. Sebald and the Poetics of Travel*, ed. by Markus Zisselsberger (Rochester, NY: Camden House, 2010), pp. 37–62

MOSSE, GEORGE, *The Image of Man* (Oxford: Oxford University Press, 1996)

ÖHLSCHLÄGER, CLAUDIA, *Beschädigtes Leben, erzählte Risse: W. G. Sebalds poetische Ordnung des Unglücks* (Freiburg i. Br., Berlin, and Vienna: Rombach, 2006)

OSBORNE, 'Topographical Anxiety and Dysfunctional Systems: *Die Ausgewanderten* and Freud's *Little Hans*', in *The Undiscover'd Country: W. G. Sebald and the Poetics of Travel*, ed. by Markus Zisselsberger (Rochester, NY: Camden House, 2010), pp. 299–321

PATT, LISE, 'Searching for Sebald: What I Know for Sure' (Introduction), in *Searching for Sebald: Photography after W. G. Sebald*, ed. by Lise Patt with Christel Dillbohner (Los Angeles: Institute of Cultural Inquiry, 2007), pp. 16–97

PENNY, LAURA, 'Parables and Politics: How Benjamin and Deleuze & Guattari Read Kafka', *Theory & Event*, 12 (2009), <http://muse.jhu.edu/journals/theory_and_event/vo12/12.3.penny.html> [accessed 16 December 2012]

POLNAY, PETER DE, *Into an Old Room: The Paradox of Edward Fitzgerald* (London: Secker & Warburg 1950)

PRAGER, BRAD, 'Sebald's Kafka', in *W. G. Sebald: History — Memory — Trauma*, ed. by Scott Denham and Mark McCulloh (Berlin: De Gruyter, 2006), pp. 105–25

RADISCH, IRIS, 'Der Waschbär der falschen Welt', *Die Zeit*, 5 April 2001, Literatur section, pp. 55–56

ROHDE, ACHIM, 'Der Innere Orient: Orientalismus, Antisemitismus und Geschlecht im Deutschland des 18. bis 20. Jahrhunderts', *Die Welt des Islams*, 45 (2005), 370–411

ROTHSCHILD, BRUCE M., 'History of Syphilis', *Clinical Infectious Diseases*, 40 (2005), 1454–63

ROVAGNATI, GABRIELLA, 'Canetti, Sebald und die Quellen des Feuers: Zum apokalyptischen Schluß von W. G. Sebalds Erzählung "Il ritorno in patria"', in *Sebald: Lektüren*, ed. by Marcel Atze and Franz Loquai (Eggingen: Edition Isele, 2005), pp. 116–21

——'Das unrettbare Venedig des W. G. Sebald', in *Sebald: Lektüren*, ed. by Marcel Atze and Franz Loquai (Eggingen: Edition Isele, 2005), pp. 143–56

RYAN, JUDITH, '"Lines of Flight": History and Territory in *The Rings of Saturn*', in *W. G. Sebald: Schreiben ex patria/Expatriate Writing*, ed. by Gerhard Fischer (Amsterdam: Rodopi, 2009), pp. 45–60

SANTNER, ERIC, 'My Own Private Germany: Daniel Paul Schreber's Secret History of Modernity', in *Modernity, Culture and 'the Jew'*, ed. by B. Cheyette, L. Marcus, H. Bhabha, and P. Gilroy (Stanford: Stanford University Press, 1998), pp. 40–62

—— *On Creaturely Life: Rilke, Benjamin, Sebald* (Chicago: University of Chicago Press, 2006)

SCHEDEL, SUSANNE, '*Wer weiß, wie es vor Zeiten gewesen ist?' Textbeziehungen als Mittel der Geschichtsdarstellung bei W. G. Sebald* (Würzburg: Königshausen and Neumann, 2004)

SCHMIDT, GARY, 'Sublime Melancholy: The Function of the Homoerotic in Sebald's *Die Ausgewanderten*', in *Über Gegenwartsliteratur: Interpretationen und Interventionen. Festschrift für Paul Michael Lützeler zum 65. Geburtstag von ehemaligen StudentInnen*, ed. by Mark W. Rectanus (Bielefeld: Aisthesis, 2008), pp. 297–313

SEDGWICK, EVE KOSOFSKY, *Between Men: English Literature and Male Homosocial Desire* (New York: Columbia University Press, 1985)

—— *Tendencies* (Durham, NC and London: Duke University Press, 1993)

SHEPPARD, RICHARD, 'Dexter–Sinister: Some Observations On Decrypting the Mors Code in the Work of W. G. Sebald', *Journal of European Studies*, 35 (2005), 419–63

——'The Sternheim Years: W. G. Sebald's *Lehrjahre* and *Theatralische Sendung* 1963–75', in *Saturn's Moons: A W. G. Sebald Handbook*, ed. by Jo Catling and Richard Hibbitt (Oxford: Legenda, 2011), pp. 42–80

SIEG, KATRIN, *Ethnic Drag: Performing Race, Nation, Sexuality in West Germany* (Ann Arbor: University of Michigan Press, 2002)

SNEDICKER, MICHAEL, 'Queer Optimism', in *Postmodern Culture: An Electronic Journal of Interdisciplinary Criticism*, 16 (2006)

—— *Queer Optimism: Lyric Personhood and Other Felicitous Persuasions* (Minneapolis: University of Minnesota Press, 2009)

TABERNER, STUART, 'German Nostalgia? Remembering German-Jewish Life in W. G. Sebald's *Die Ausgewanderten* and *Austerlitz*', *Germanic Review*, 79 (2004), 181–202

TÓIBÍN, COLM, 'The Tragedy of Roger Casement', *The New York Review of Books*, 51 (27 May 2004) <http://www.nybooks.com/articles/17136>, accessed 17 December 2012

VARGAS LLOSA, MARIO, *The Dream of the Celt*, trans. by Edith Grossmann (London: Faber and Faber, 2012)

WEBBER, ANDREW J., *The Doppelgänger: Double Visions in German Literature* (Oxford: Clarendon, 1996)

WEIGEL, SIGRID, 'Téléscopage im Unbewussten: Zum Verhältnis von Trauma, Geschichtsbegriff und Literatur', in *Trauma: Zwischen Psychoanalyse und kulturellem Deutungsmuster*, ed. by Elisabeth Bronfen, Birgit R. Erdle, and Sigrid Weigel (Cologne: Böhlau, 1999), pp. 51–76

——'"Generation" as a Symbolic Form: On the Genealogical Discourse of Memory since 1945', *The Germanic Review*, 77 (2002), 264–77

YOUNG, ROBERT, *Colonial Desire: Hybridity in Theory, Culture, and Race* (London: Routledge, 1995)

ZILCOSKY, JOHN, 'Sebald's Uncanny Travels: The Impossibility of Getting Lost', in *W. G. Sebald: A Critical Companion* ed. by J. J. Long and Anne Whitehead (Edinburgh: Edinburgh University Press, 2004), pp. 102–20

INDEX